D1504884

Hello Swift!

iOS App Programming for Kids and Other Beginners

Tanmay Bakshi

MANNING
SHELTER ISLAND

For online information and ordering of this and other Manning books, please visit www.manning.com. The publisher offers discounts on this book when ordered in quantity. For more information, please contact:

Special Sales Department
Manning Publications Co.
20 Baldwin Road
PO Box 761
Shelter Island, NY 11964
Email: orders@manning.com

Manning Publications Co.
20 Baldwin Road
PO Box 761
Shelter Island, NY 11964

Acquisitions editor: Mike Stephens
Development editor: Helen Stergius
Technical development editor: Francesco Bianchi
Review editor: Aleks Dragosavljević
Production editor: Anthony Calcara
Copyeditor: Kathy Simpson
Proofreader: Michelle Melani
Technical proofreader: Doug Warren
Typesetter: Marija Tudor
Cover designer: Leslie Haimes

ISBN: 9781617292620

Printed in the United States of America
1 2 3 4 5 6 7 8 9 10 – SP – 24 23 22 21 20 19

Brief contents

Contents

Preface

Writing a book is a journey that, unless you have passion and love for, I'd say is difficult and unreasonable. My passion and drive were to create a book for those who don't know anything, or little, about computers and programming so that they can understand programming, create meaningful apps, and take off to higher levels. I want the book to be a kick-starter for those who want to start writing apps but face roadblocks when they pick up a book or another resource to start learning. Moreover, the useful knowledge about programming with Swift is scattered in pieces across the internet, and I wanted it to be accessible as a unified package, in sequence. This was my motive to write the book, and to the best of my abilities, I'll support it through the liveBook Discussion Forum by answering your questions and solving the problems that you'll encounter in your journey of learning.

Objective-C was the first language that took me ahead a great deal. I started learning it at the age of 8, and I had my first app, tTables (times-tables practice app), accepted in the App Store when I was 9. The app helped me in my studies, so I wanted to share it. I also have a goal of reaching out to and helping at least 100,000 beginners to help them learn how to code, so I started writing a book on Objective-C as one way to achieve this goal. The moment that Apple released Swift, a new programming language that lets people write apps for its devices, I immediately got to it. I found that Swift was easier and faster to learn than Objective-C, and it had Apple's full support, so it was a much better choice for the new learner. Soon, Apple open sourced Swift, making it even more popular. Apple provided library support for graphics, animations, games, and even CoreML to support developing artificial-intelligence-based apps, too. Today, Swift is one of the top choices for learners and professionals alike. After you learn it, you're all set to create apps for devices such as the iPhone, iPad, macOS, Apple TV, and Apple Watch. Because Swift is open source, you can create apps for Linux, Windows, or Android as well.

Learning Swift to create apps for your ideas is easy. You *can* do it!

Acknowledgments

I sincerely thank the entire team at Manning Publications who were involved in the creation of this book, including (but surely not limited to) Michael Stephens, Helen Stergius, Doug Warren, Francesco Bianchi, and Christopher Kaufmann. Special thanks to Michael for giving me a great start and to Helen for a great relationship as my development editor; I really learned a lot from you. More special thanks to all the reviewers who gave their valuable time, intellect, and feedback to remove errors from the manuscript and for their suggestions for improvement.

I also convey my thanks to family members, friends, and well-wishers who supported me to create this book so that it can reach those who need it to learn coding and creating apps.

I dedicate this book to the readers who use this book to learn the basics of programming and iOS app development.

Finally, I would like to thank my reviewers, whose feedback and help improving this book were deeply appreciated, including Ahmed Chicktay, Becky Huett, Christopher and Sydney Haupt, David Barkol, Diego Acuña Rozas, Eric Giannini, Essa Hashmi, Georgerobert Freeman, Harald Kisch, Itai Platnik, Jason Pike, Matt Deimel, Matt Lemke, Maxim Kisch, Michael Anderson, Mike Jensen, Patrick Tien Lu, Robert Walsh, Rodney J. Woodruff, Roy Legaard Jr., Tahir Akhtar, Terry Rickman, and Tidjani Belmansour.

About this book

I always wanted to reach out to 100,000 beginners so that they can learn programming and take their first few steps into the world of coding computers so that they can give shape to their ideas. I found that whereas more and more people want to learn programming, there aren't enough resources available for them to fulfil their needs, and providing them with the right kind of resource, a stepping stone, was my intention in creating this book.

Audience

This book is for beginners of any age who want to start learning programming to create apps and to give shape to their own ideas. You may want to create apps for your children, grandchildren, yourself, your parents, or for the App Store. You should be able to create something yourself to make the life of someone around you easier, better, and more productive.

Road map

Thank you for being with me on this journey of learning Swift and iOS app programming! You'll complete this journey through 14 milestones (chapters). I start by making you ready for this journey, helping you set up your hardware, software, and developer account. You find out how to create an app for your Apple Watch and even how to take off from there in terms of resources, references, learning by participating in online forums, and being future-ready. Before you proceed on this journey, however, I'd like to let you know where you're heading.

You'll be learning the Swift programming language and using it to create apps. You may be hoping to be able to design and code an amazing game like Temple Run when you're done with this book. I hate to be the one to break the news to you, but you'll have more to learn when you finish. In this book, you learn fundamental Swift and iOS concepts and some simple graphics manipulation—a necessary first step, but a first step. So much information about programming and games is available that it's probably hard to figure out where to start. So I've created a list of things you can learn after this book so that you'll have all the skills you need to write high-quality games that you could add to the App Store.

I've put these things in the order in which I think it makes the most logical sense to learn them, first to last. If I wrote a book that had everything in it you needed to know, I'd choose this order of chapters. I didn't list the topics from easiest to hardest, or most in demand by employers first (are you thinking of that already!?)—only what I think will work best. You may already know which of these skills you need most for the type of games you want to develop. If you do, focus on those skills, and move on to your game development journey!

1	Using Xcode's debugger: solving exceptions and other bugs by using Xcode's built-in debugger
2	REST APIs and networking: communicating with different services on the internet to get more information and to interact with websites and other users
3	Asynchronous events: allowing long-running operations to run in the background using the Grand Central Dispatch (GCD) so that the UI isn't stuck while things happen in the background
4	Audio: playing the right sounds at the right time
5	Gyroscope, accelerometer, GPS, camera, and Bluetooth: meshing the real world with your iOS games
6	Spatial sense: understanding the 3D world and being able to program graphics that represent it
7	3D geometry: understanding the geometry and dimensions of a 3D world (latitude, longitude, altitude) and (x, y, z) coordinates
8	Physics of motion, dynamics, and gravity: understanding how things interact with other things in 2D and 3D environments

9	Animation: understanding how objects move and transition when a user interacts with them
10	SpriteKit: using Apple's SpriteKit library to develop 2D games easily
11	SceneKit: using Apple's SceneKit library to develop 3D games easily
12	ARKit: using Apple's ARKit library to develop augmented-reality apps easily

I recommend that you thoroughly study the first ten chapters. Study the material in chapters 11 to 13 depending on your needs, and read the appendices only after you've gone through all the chapters. Be patient, learn step by step, and learn well.

You start by getting ready to build apps with Swift in chapter 1. I'm sure that you know what apps are and how useful they are. You've probably come across well-designed apps and the apps you don't like much, but you, as a user, can tell the difference. I briefly go through the design elements that make a good app your favorite app and why you don't like some other apps. I also tell you what goes into making an app work and how you can go about creating your own apps. I introduce you to the programming language. Also I let you know what hardware and software you need and how to set up your device to start your journey of learning Swift and creating apps.

In chapter 2, you get a feel for developing a real app, albeit a basic one. This chapter familiarizes you with the screens, commands, and options you'll be using often to build even complex apps. One of your favorite topics probably is going to be building an app with segues—that is, an app with multiple screens.

In chapter 3, you start to know the concepts of programming real apps by learning about variables: how to create them, their types, and their use in apps. This chapter takes you to a level where you'll be able to start understanding data. You start manipulating data contained in the variables you create. You also do some basic math that not only helps you create meaningful apps, but also makes you better at math itself.

In chapter 4, you learn how your app will interact with its users: by prompting users and getting their responses in the form of text, numbers, and taps. You also learn how to use text fields, buttons, and labels on your device's screen in an app.

In chapter 5, you learn how your apps can make decisions depending on your actions rather than running on a preset path. Your apps do this by evaluating conditions and give you responses based on the outcome of those conditions. I walk you through a few types of checking the conditions to solve problems through programming, using example apps. All programming languages provide the constructs for condition checking, which makes a programmer's work much easier.

Loops are an equally important set of constructs. Loops let you perform a certain task over and over, depending on the outcome of a certain condition. You learn about loops in chapter 6. I introduce three types of loops and how loops are used with the help of example apps.

In chapter 7, you revisit variables. I teach you how to bunch variables together in arrays and to manipulate a lot of them easily by using arrays. This chapter also introduces you to dictionaries. Again with the help of example apps, you learn the concept and application of arrays and dictionaries, as well as how to add, modify, and delete data.

In programming, you often face situations in which you have to run a set of instructions at numerous places in an app. You do this by using functions, which you learn about in chapter 8. Using functions makes your programs and apps compact, easy to maintain, and easy to understand how your apps work, for you and other programmers.

Chapter 9 makes you feel like a mature programmer by teaching you the concept of classes. You create apps by using classes and learn how to create object-oriented code that you can maintain and reuse.

Chapter 10 teaches you how to make your apps read, modify, and write (create) files on your device so that you can access your stored information at any time in the future.

Chapter 11 is about frameworks, which are sets of code that can be compiled to be reused in other apps.

You understand and use SpriteKit in Chapter 12. SpriteKit is a framework built and provided by Apple that lets you animate objects onscreen without having to worry too much about all the graphics, physics, and other concepts involved.

Chapter 13 helps you understand WatchKit, which helps you create applications for the Apple Watch.

Finally, chapter 14 helps you smoothly take off to higher levels in the field of your choice.

During this journey, if you feel uncomfortable or lose direction, I'll be glad to help you out through this book's liveBook Discussion Forum. Here's the link: https://livebook.manning.com/#!/book/hello-swift/discussion.

Keep your focus, and get going, I wish you a happy journey of learning!

Source-code downloads

At any point, if you don't feel like typing code but still want to see the example apps in this book running, you'll be able to download the code. Here's the link: https://github.com/tanmayb123/Hello-Swift-Code/archive/master.zip. I discourage this practice, though. Coding is better learned by typing, which gives you time to look at what you're typing, understand why you're typing it, sometimes make mistakes, find those mistakes, and make corrections.

liveBook discussion forum

Purchase of *Hello Swift! iOS App Programming for Kids and Other Beginners* includes free access to a private web forum run by Manning Publications where you can make comments about the book, ask technical questions, and receive help from the author and from other users. To access the forum, go to https://livebook.manning.com/#!/book/hello-swift/discussion. You can also learn more about Manning's forums and the rules of conduct at https://livebook.manning.com/#!/discussion.

Manning's commitment to our readers is to provide a venue where a meaningful dialogue between individual readers and between readers and the author can take place. It is not a commitment to any specific amount of participation on the part of the author, whose contribution to the forum remains voluntary (and unpaid). We suggest you try asking the author some challenging questions lest his interest stray! The forum and the archives of previous discussions will be accessible from the publisher's website as long as the book is in print.

Software and hardware requirements

To learn programming and iOS app development, you need some software and hardware or access to them. For the hardware, you should have any Mac with macOS Mojave 10.14 running on it. The Mac should have at least 15 GB of free space so that you can store and retrieve your projects quickly. You also have to download free software called Xcode (version 10), which helps you create, debug, and run your apps. Xcode has software built into it that allows you to simulate iDevices so that you can test and run your apps even if you don't have access to an actual iDevice. You also need iOS 12. If you want to run apps on an Apple Watch, you also need an Apple Watch with watchOS 5 on it. I used these versions of software in the book, but if newer versions of any software become available, use the latest versions, because Apple doesn't support downgrading iOS or watchOS to older versions.

Online and other resources

Every one of us needs help at some point. Often, the solution is right there, but you don't see it. At these times, online resources are great. You can get help, learn from these resources, and also provide help to others. Here are a few resources that I recommend:

- Stack Overflow: https://stackoverflow.com
- GitHub: https://github.com
- Hello Swift! liveBook Discussion Forum: https://livebook.manning.com/#!/book/hello-swift/discussion
- YouTube channels such as https://www.youtube.com/c/tanmaybakshiteaches

You can get deeper by learning from a book called *iOS Development with Swift*, by Craig Grummit.

If you want to know more about online and other resources, and how to take your next step, read chapter 14 of this book.

About the author

Tanmay Bakshi is an AI and Machine Learning Systems Architect. He supports and contributes extensively to the open source community and is known for his passion to share what he learns through his YouTube channel, blogs, and speeches. He is a TED speaker and has keynoted at numerous conferences around the world for the United Nations, IBM, Apple, KPMG, SAP, NASSCOM, The Linux Foundation, and Walmart, just to name a few. His first major keynote address was at IBM Interconnect 2016, where he presented his algorithm "AskTanmay," which is the world's first web-based natural language question answering system to be powered by IBM Watson.

His passion lies in developing machine learning and AI-based systems, mainly in the fields of healthcare and education, where he believes that this next generation technology can make the biggest impact.

He has addressed computer science and technology students globally, doing countless workshops in universities, colleges, and schools, and has held seminars for institutions such as Apple Education, HSBC, Citigroup, and Credit Suisse. His YouTube channel, Tanmay Teaches, is where he shares his research and knowledge with audiences of all ages. He loves to interact with, respond to, and help people with their queries and hence, he has had the honor of being the recipient of the Twilio Doer Award, Knowledge Ambassador Award, Global Goodwill Ambassador at LinkedIn, and is an IBM Champion for Cloud.

Bakshi, as a kid, considered computers, laptops, modems, networking, cables, and electronics as his toys for years. This kid coder's journey began at the early age of five, when he developed with DOS batch files, C, FoxPro, and Visual Basic and then created iOS apps. When he was nine, his first app, tTables, was published to the iOS App Store. This news inspired many kids who always wanted to code but never knew how to take the first step.

Hello Swift! is the outcome of his goal of reaching out to at least 100,000 coders and beginners in their journey of learning how to program. Since Tanmay himself is a 15-year-old coder, he wanted to create a resource for kids and beginners from around the globe, who aspire to learn programming and have waited for someone to communicate with them in their language.

He is a homeschooled tenth grader in Canada, where he lives with his older sister and parents. He likes biking and playing table tennis with his friends. Tanmay also contributes his time being a Computational Thinking Coach at the 4th Industrial Revolution Organization, and an advisor and lead faculty at Grad Valley Data Science.

1

Get ready to build apps with Swift!

Do you want to build an app but don't know where to start?

This chapter covers

- *What is an app?*
- *What is Swift?*
- *What do you need to use this book?*
- *How do you install Xcode?*
- *What is the playground?*

Every single day, you use computers. From doing homework to chatting with friends online, listening to music, and playing games, you spend lots of your time on computers and mobile devices.

So why can't you create programs that people will want to use? The only thing stopping you is taking the time to learn how. Ready to get started? Let's go!

Your "I can do it!" journey begins

When I was nine years old, I phoned my dad while he was at work. I had to tell him my news. I was screaming with joy because my app, tTables (figure 1.1), an app that helps you learn your multiplication tables, made it to the App Store!

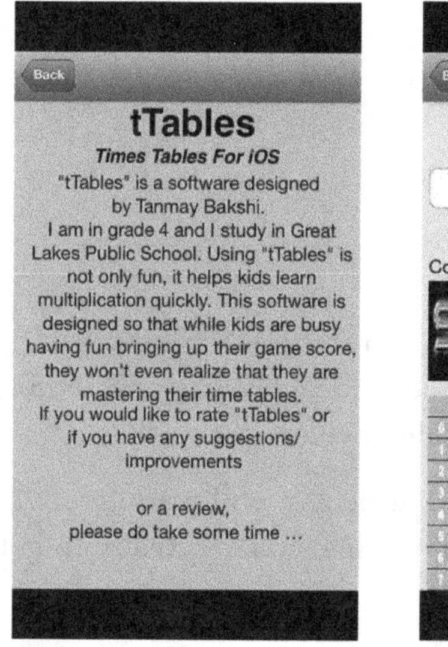

Figure 1.1 Screenshots from my first app in the App Store

This book is about how you can experience this joy yourself. In these pages, you'll be going on a journey to the land of app development. When you start reading this book, as you travel through Xcode tools, the Swift language, and the iOS platform, you too will want to shout "Yes, I can do it!"

The journey ahead—and beyond

As I mentioned in the "About the book" section, together, we'll complete this journey in 14 milestones and learn a lot about app development. But don't worry—you don't have to wait that long. You'll start building your own meaningful and productive apps soon after you begin. You may be hoping to be able to design and code an amazing game like Temple Run after you're done with this book. I hate to be the one to break this news to you, but you'll have more to learn.

In this book, you'll learn fundamental Swift and iOS concepts, as well as some simple graphics manipulation—a necessary first step, but only a first step. So much information about programming and games is available, it's probably hard to figure out where to start. So I've created a list of things you can learn after this book so that you'll have all the skills you need to write high-quality games that you could add to the App Store.

I've put these skills in the order in which I think it makes the most logical sense to learn them, first to last. If I wrote a book that had everything in it you needed to know, I'd choose this order for chapters. I don't list the skills from easiest to hardest or put the ones that are most in demand by employers first (are you thinking of that already!?)—only what I think works best. You may already know which of these skills you need most for the type of games you want to develop. If you do, focus on them, and move on in your game development journey!

1	Using Xcode's debugger: solving exceptions and other bugs by using Xcode's built-in debugger.
2	REST APIs and networking: communicating with different services on the internet to get more information and to interact with websites and with other users.
3	Asynchronous events: allowing long-running operations to run in the background, using Grand Central Dispatch (GCD), so that the UI isn't stuck while things happen in the background.
4	Audio: playing the right sounds at the right time.
5	Gyroscope, accelerometer, GPS, camera, and Bluetooth: meshing the real world with your iOS games.

6	Spatial sense: understanding the 3D world and being able to program graphics that represent it.
7	3D geometry: understanding the geometry and dimensions of a 3D world (latitude, longitude, altitude; x, y, z coordinates).
8	Physics of motion, dynamics, and gravity: understanding how things interact with other things in 2D and 3D environments.
9	Animation: understanding how objects move and transition when a user interacts with them.
10	SpriteKit: using Apple's SpriteKit library to easily develop 2D games.
11	SceneKit: using Apple's SceneKit library to easily develop 3D games.
12	ARKit: using Apple's ARKit library to easily develop augmented-reality apps.

You'll see this map for each milestone on your journey. The first one is *Get ready to build apps with Swift!* You'll learn what an app is, what it means to program and write code, and just a little bit about the Swift programming language. After that, you'll install the software you need and write your very first line of code!.

What is an app, anyway?

The word *app* is short for *application*. An app is a program that a developer writes for a purpose. Apps are created to do lots of things, such as entertain, educate, inform, or anything else that the developers want them to do.

Think of ideas! Apps are for everyone!

When people talk about apps, they often mean programs that run on mobile devices.

What do you mean by *mobile devices*?

Many people use their phones mainly for apps, and one reason is that they're mobile. iPhones, iPads, and iPods (and all other tablets, phablets, and phones) can be used anywhere on the go. If you're walking to the mall or eating at a café, or if you're in a classroom, you can use a mobile device. You can't use a desktop or laptop computer with that level of ease (figure 1.2)—and you might drop it!

Figure 1.2 Walking with a mobile device and walking with a laptop

The pieces of a good app

There's more to understanding what apps are than knowing that they run on mobile devices. The best apps need to meet some basic requirements that make people want to use them.

Take a look at the pieces that make an app good (figure 1.3). While you look through these features, think about your favorite apps and about how they have all these elements:

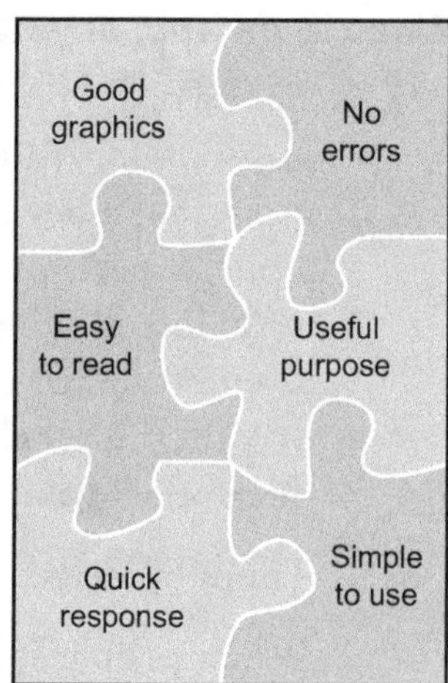

Figure 1.3 All these app pieces are necessary!

- *Good graphics*—Good graphics are one of the prime requirements for an app to become someone's favorite. Users are more attracted to memorable, colorful graphics than black-and-white graphics (depending on the situation).
- *No errors*—Your app should have no mistakes or errors, and it should perform correctly what it promises.
- *Easy to read*—Always try to present your text in an easy-to-read, legible font. Also, make sure that your font color contrasts with whatever is behind the text of your message so that it's more readable.
- *Useful purpose*—The app should have a purpose. It could entertain you, teach you something, keep you updated, or solve some specific problem.
- *Quick response*—Try not to make one button do too much work; the app can slow down. Users don't like to wait for responses from apps.
- *Simple to use*—The app should be simple and easy to use, with a clean, uncluttered design. At the same time, the screen shouldn't be too blank unless it has to be blank for some purpose.

What is programming?

Before you start making apps, you need to understand a little about programming. When you *program*, you write a set of instructions on a computer that tells the computer to do a particular task. These written instructions are called *code*.

When you program, you start by writing a bunch of instructions, like these:

```
instruction 1
instruction 2
instruction 3
instruction 4
instruction 5
...
...
```

To get a computer to do tasks, you need to tell (instruct) it exactly what you want it to do. Giving a computer step-by-step instructions in its own language is programming (figure 1.4).

These instructions are similar to the ones you might give your younger sibling for washing the car (1. Get the soapy water in a bucket, 2. Soak the sponge in soapy water, and gently rub the outside of the car. 3. Turn on the hose and rinse the car clean with the jet of water. 4. Take a dry cloth. . .)

Computers are extremely good at doing calculations. They have the ability to calculate huge numbers that you throw at them. They can figure out 29174 × 28039 in a tiny fraction of a second!

Computers are also great at doing repetitive work that a human would quickly get sick and tired of doing. So we can make programs and give these tasks to our devices to free ourselves to do things we like more.

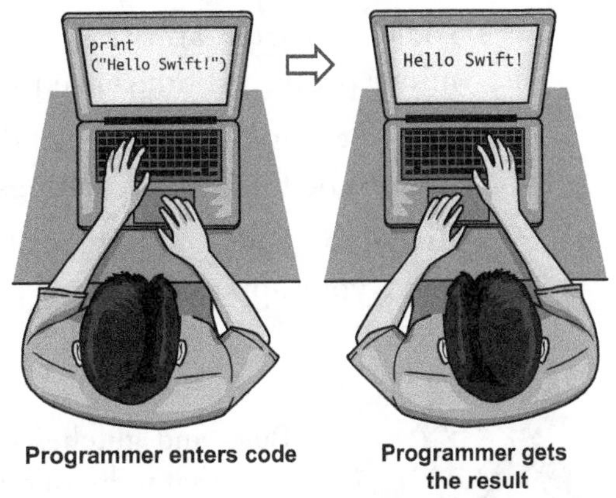
print
("Hello Swift!")
Hello Swift!
Programmer enters code
Programmer gets the result

Figure 1.4 The programming process

From idea to app

The journey from idea to an app that gets into the App Store has many steps. Here's a mental map that shows you these steps (figure 1.5):

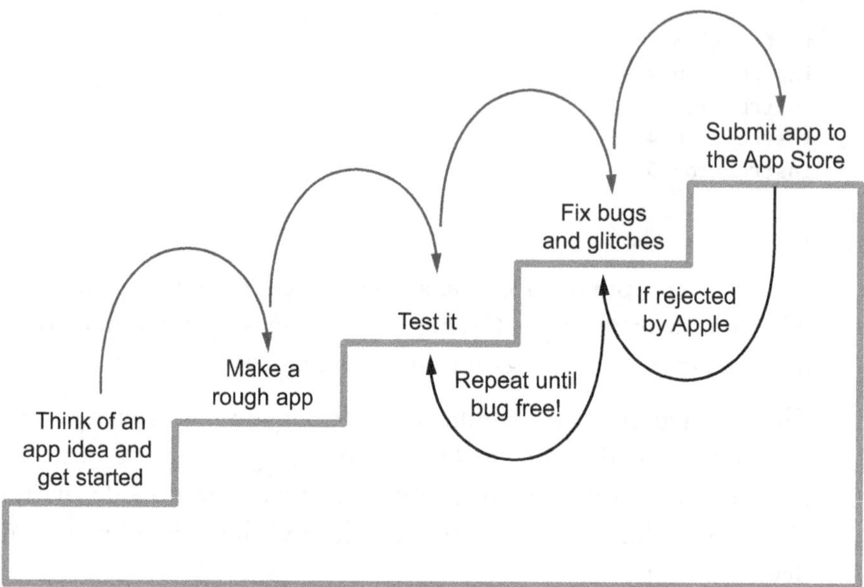

Figure 1.5 The steps in creating an app

1. You have an idea for an app in your head. It's time to get started!
2. Make a starter app that does what you want. It may have a few minor problems, but those problems can be fixed later.
3. Test the app. Try it out, and write down whatever you think may need to be fixed (such as bugs and glitches).
4. Fix all the bugs and glitches that you encounter. Also use this step to make your app look nicer.

Bugs and glitches are problems that interfere with your app such that it doesn't work the way it's supposed to.

5 Repeat steps 3 and 4 until you find no more bugs or glitches while testing your creation.
6 Submit your app to the iOS App Store.
7 If Apple rejects the app, repeat steps 3 and 4 while taking into account the feedback from Apple.
8 Keep repeating steps 3 and 4, submitting the app until Apple accepts it. PERSEVERE!

You've told us about the pieces of a good app. When do we work on those?

It's important to think about those pieces even while you're on step 1. Try to use good design when you build the app in step 2. And each time you test and fix the app (steps 3 and 4), you can continue to improve its look and feel so that your users find it fun and easy to use.

At this point, you may already have completed step 1: having an idea. But to get to step 2, you need to start learning Swift. Let's go.

What is Swift?

Swift is Apple's new programming language for iOS, watchOS, tvOS, and macOS. Before Swift, Apple developers wrote programs in Objective-C, which Apple didn't create. Apple knew that it needed to create a new, more efficient, more modern language, so it secretly began creating Swift in 2010. Swift was announced on June 2, 2014.

We'll be learning Swift and will start creating apps using Swift soon.

iOS is the software that runs on all iDevices (such as the iPhone and iPad). iOS is an operating system, much like Windows or macOS.

What's so special about Swift?

In this book, you'll learn how to create your own iOS apps by using the Swift programming language. Here are some things that I learned through my own experience as a Swift programmer and how I felt when I started working with Swift:

1. Programs tend to be short, which means less typing, less code, and less chance for bugs and glitches.
2. The program grammar is extremely Englishlike and easy to understand, which means less memorizing for you.
3. Apple is the maker of the Swift language, so Apple has complete control of it. Also, the language is now *open source*, which means that programmers themselves can contribute to Swift to make it a better language. If lots of programmers have trouble with some syntax (programming grammar), the open-source community or Apple can modify Swift to make it better.
4. A new feature of Swift is called *playgrounds*. Playgrounds are great because they allow you to test your code in real time. You can test, play around with, and learn from a lot of code before you include it in your app, which makes code testing easy for you.

While I was learning this language and working to make apps in Swift, I found hardly any resources to help me keep going ahead. This is one of the reasons why I decided to write this book.

When you write programs in Swift, you use the playground, but the word playground doesn't mean that Swift isn't a professional language. Both beginners and professional programmers test their code in the playground.

Swift can't do everything

Swift is great, but like any programming language, it can't do everything. Advanced programmers often use features of other languages in their Swift programs. Later in your programming journey, you may have to use a little bit of Objective-C (figure 1.6) and cocoa.

Objective-C was the language for building apps before Swift was released. Objective-C has been in use for around three decades now.

Cocoa is a set of frameworks (lots of code that Apple writes for your convenience, to make things like playing music in programming much simpler) for heavy and complex tasks such as audio and video, graphics and animation, user applications, data management, and networking and internet.

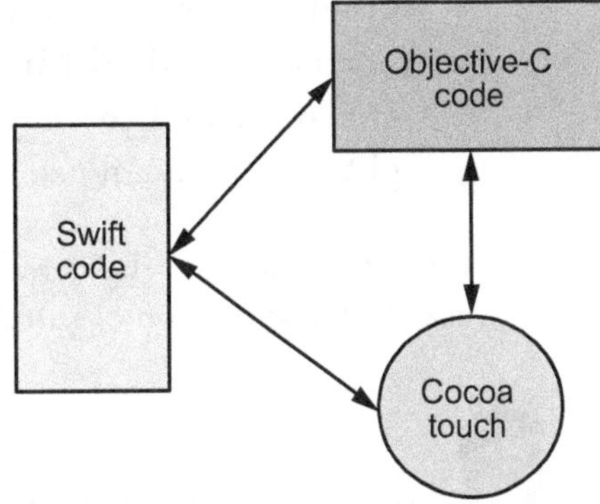

Figure 1.6 You'll work mostly with Swift, but you'll need a little Objective-C and Cocoa to make your apps better.

Prepping your app toolbox

The time has come to make a checklist and gather the hardware and software you need to start creating apps. In this section, you learn exactly what hardware you need, how to install the software, and what accounts you may want to create with Apple.

Gather hardware

You need to have the following hardware (computer equipment) to install Xcode 10 and develop your apps in Swift 5 (the screenshots in this book use Xcode 9, so while your screens may look a little bit different, you should still be able to follow along):

- A Mac with at least macOS Mojave (10.14) and at least 6 GB of free hard disk space; any Mac desktop or laptop that meets these requirements will do. You must have access to a Mac to make Swift apps.

- (Optional) An iPhone (5c or newer), iPod touch (6 or newer), iPad (5 or newer), iPad Mini (2, 3, 4, or newer), iPad Air (any generation), or iPad Pro (any generation). If you don't have an iDevice right now, you can use the free simulator that's included with Xcode.

TIP Regardless of the version of hardware and software mentioned, always use the latest version of software available for your hardware.

A *simulator* is a lookalike of a real iDevice that can run on your Mac. You can use it to do basic app testing. A simulator is included with Xcode.

Because the iPhone and iPod touch are fairly small, it's easier to learn coding by creating iPhone or iPod apps rather than iPad apps. iPad apps are harder to design and work with because the iPad's screen is bigger than the screen of the Xcode display; you have to keep scrolling the iPad's view up and down to view other parts of the screen (figure 1.7). The Xcode window doesn't allow you to see the whole iPad screen without zooming out.

Figure 1.7 The MacBook Air and Mac mini are a couple of options for developing your apps (left); the iPad, iPhone, and iPod touch are testing options (right).

Install Xcode

Before you begin, you need two things:

- You need the admin username and password for your Mac and your Apple ID (or get the help of someone who has this information).
- You also need to know that Xcode 10 works only in macOS Mojave (10.14) or later.

In addition to the hardware, to create apps with Swift 4, you need a free program called Xcode. To get Xcode, search the Mac App Store for the app Xcode and then install it. The steps are in table 1.1.

Table 1.1 Get and install Xcode

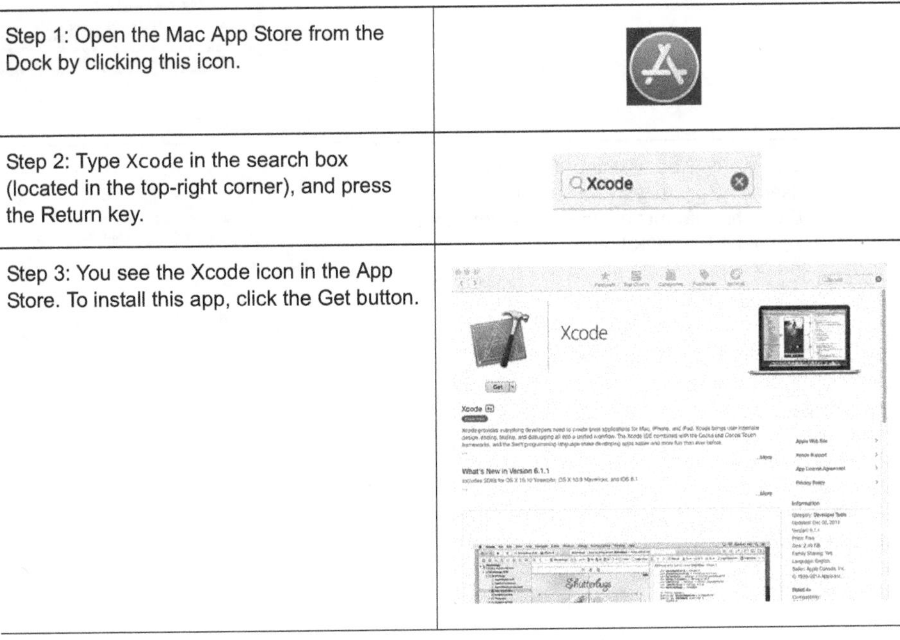

Step 1: Open the Mac App Store from the Dock by clicking this icon.	
Step 2: Type `Xcode` in the search box (located in the top-right corner), and press the Return key.	Xcode
Step 3: You see the Xcode icon in the App Store. To install this app, click the Get button.	Xcode

Table 1.1 Get and install Xcode *(continued)*

Step 4: You'll be asked to sign in with your Apple ID. The Sign In button becomes blue (enabled). Click it to proceed. With a 20 Mbps internet connection, you'll have to wait about half an hour for Xcode to download, but the timing depends on your internet speed; the download may take more or less time.	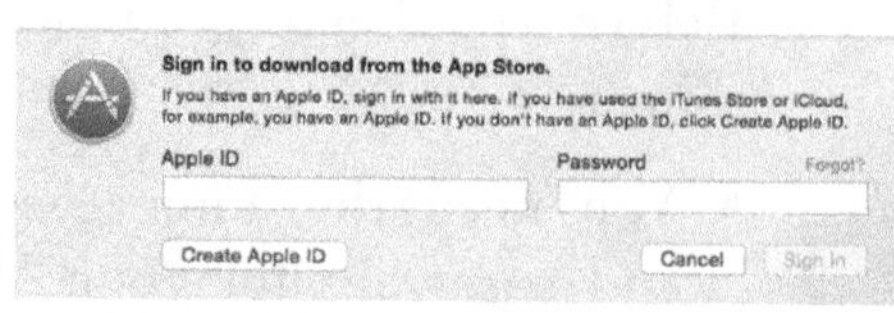
Step 5: When the app is done downloading, you'll see a sparkling Xcode icon in Launchpad. Open Launchpad by clicking the silver rocket icon on the Dock.	 
Step 6: Read, and then click Agree to accept the license agreement (if you agree with it).	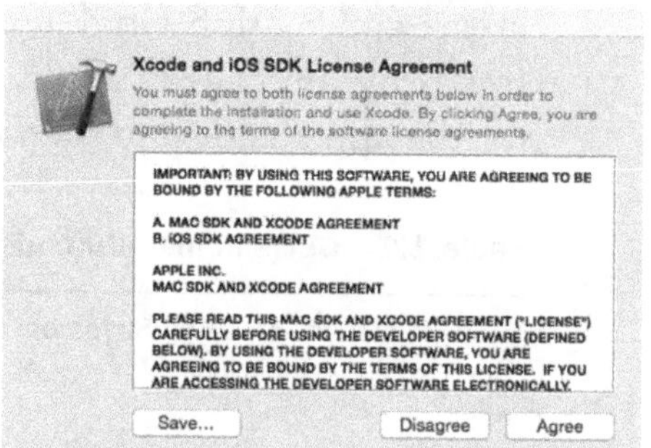
Step 7: You'll be asked for the administrator username and password for your computer. Enter this information; then press the Return key or click the OK button.	

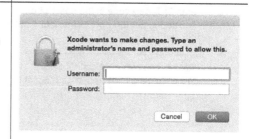

Table 1.1 Get and install Xcode *(continued)*

Step 8: Wait a minute while your computer installs a few more parts of Xcode. When it's finished, you'll see the Welcome to Xcode screen. That's it! You're done downloading and installing the software you need to use Swift to create your own apps.	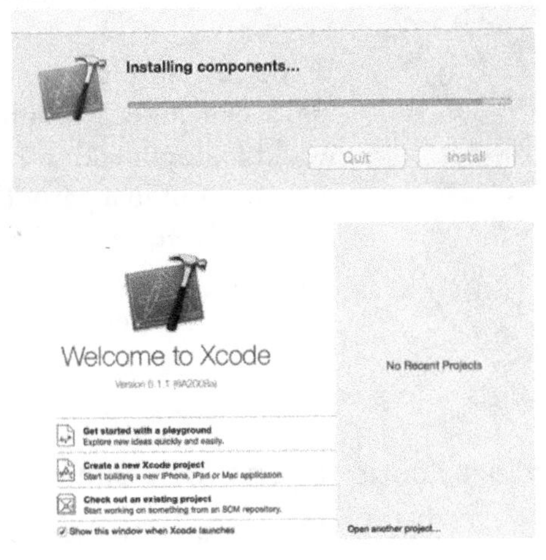

Set up an optional developer account

Apart from the equipment (Mac) and software (Xcode), you may want to purchase a developer account. A developer account is optional, but there's an important limitation if you don't purchase a developer account: you can't upload your app to the iOS App Store! Don't worry, though; you can always get your apps ready, buy an account, and then submit your app to the App Store.

A developer account costs $99 per year. I can't afford to pay that right now. What should I do?

If you're creating apps only so you can learn, I don't recommend buying a developer account. If you want to submit apps for the whole world to download for money (or for free), you must buy the $99-per-year account in a parent's name (unless you're older than 18). I recommend that you do this only after you gain experience building apps. This fee, by the way, includes an iOS, macOS, watchOS, and tvOS developer subscription.

Start Xcode for the first time

The first time you run Xcode, you need to follow the special steps listed in table 1.2. You have to perform them only once, though.

Table 1.2 The first time you run Xcode, to work with playgrounds . . .

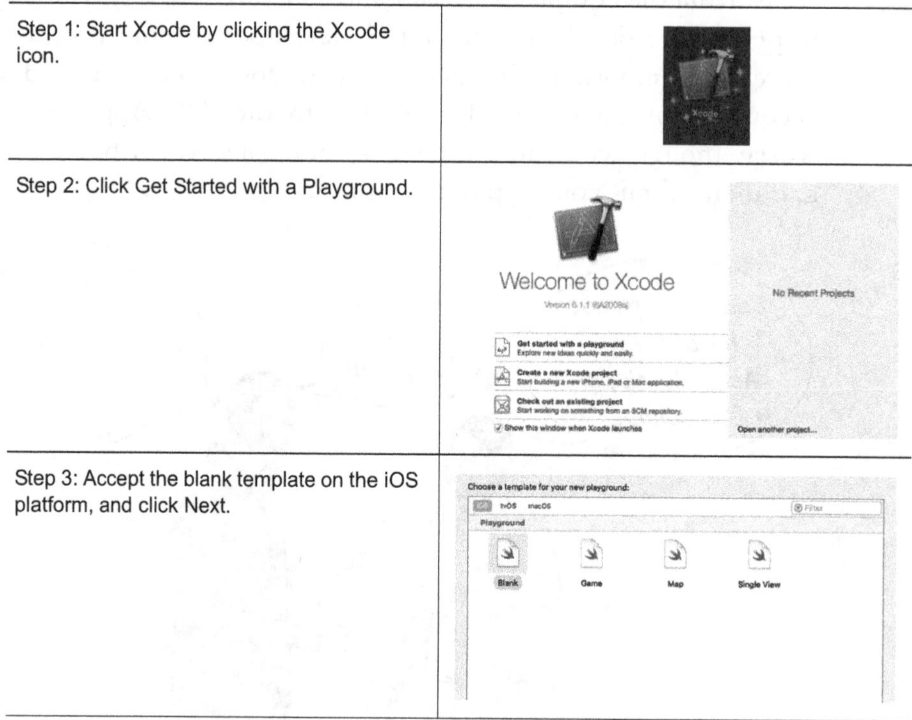

Step 1: Start Xcode by clicking the Xcode icon.	
Step 2: Click Get Started with a Playground.	
Step 3: Accept the blank template on the iOS platform, and click Next.	

Table 1.2 The first time you run Xcode, to work with playgrounds . . . *(continued)*

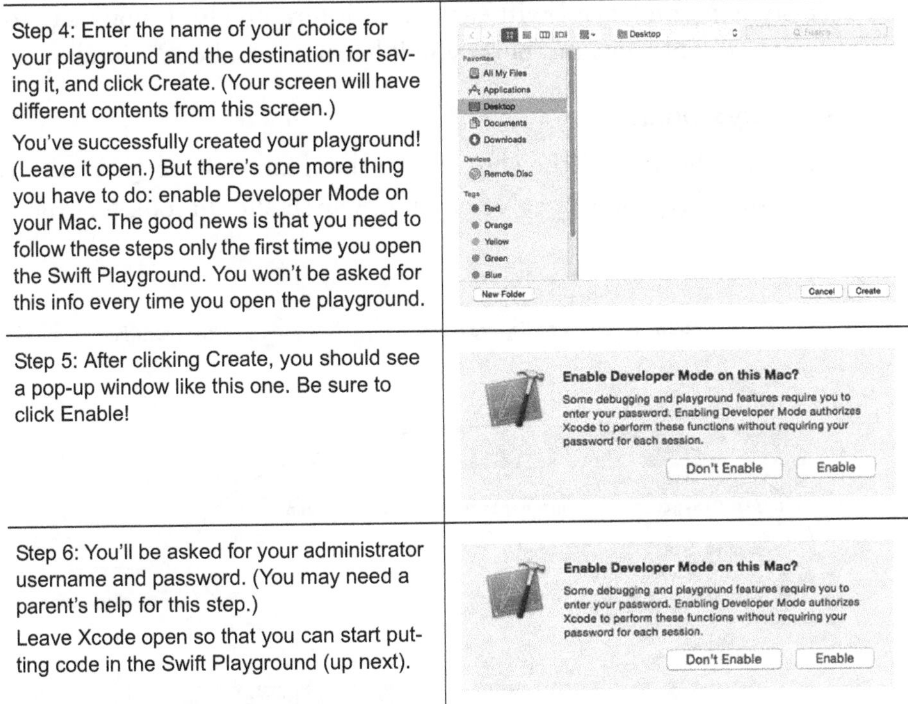
Desktop
Favorites
All My Files
Applications
Desktop
Documents
Downloads
Devices
Remote Disc
Tags
Red
Orange
Yellow
Green
Blue
New Folder
Cancel
Create
Enable Developer Mode on this Mac?
Some debugging and playground features require you to enter your password. Enabling Developer Mode authorizes Xcode to perform these functions without requiring your password for each session.
Don't Enable
Enable

Step 4: Enter the name of your choice for your playground and the destination for saving it, and click Create. (Your screen will have different contents from this screen.) You've successfully created your playground! (Leave it open.) But there's one more thing you have to do: enable Developer Mode on your Mac. The good news is that you need to follow these steps only the first time you open the Swift Playground. You won't be asked for this info every time you open the playground.	
Step 5: After clicking Create, you should see a pop-up window like this one. Be sure to click Enable!	
Step 6: You'll be asked for your administrator username and password. (You may need a parent's help for this step.) Leave Xcode open so that you can start putting code in the Swift Playground (up next).	

Now that you've installed Xcode and run it for the first time, you're ready to start playing with code in the Swift Playground.

Write code and see it work in the Swift Playground

In this section, you get to know your environment so you can use it easily in the chapters to come. You also have your first hands-on experience in writing and running a line of Swift code, using the playground feature of Xcode.

What is the playground?

The Xcode playground is . . . well, a playground where you, as an iOS developer, can interactively play around with your Swift code. The playground lets you type code and get results as your code runs in real time, line by line.

Playgrounds help you test your code to make sure that it works; they also help you learn Swift easily and interactively. I won't say too much about the playground here; you'll learn more about it in chapter 3.

Create a playground

If you followed all the steps up to this point correctly, you're ready to use the playground you've created, which should look like figure 1.8.

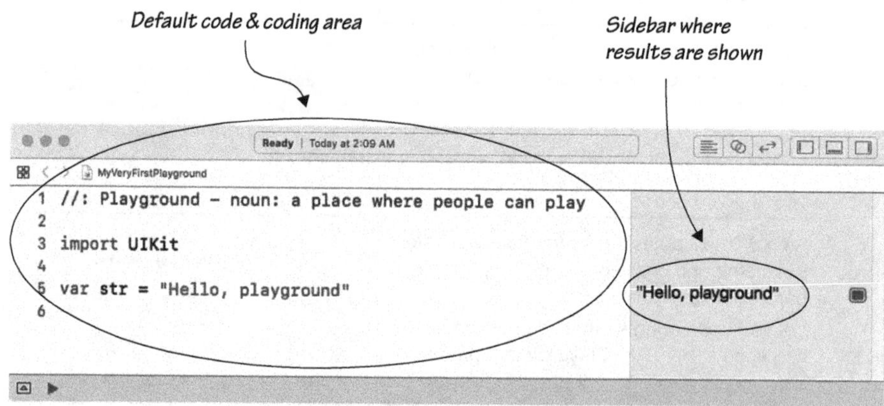

Figure 1.8 The default playground

Play with code in the playground

You're about to write and execute your first lines of Swift code! The first thing you do is print a message to the screen that says `Hello Swift Apps`. You also get to know the Swift Playground a little bit.

First, erase everything in the coding area you see onscreen. You should have a blank screen.

Next, type `print("Hello Swift Apps")`, as shown in figure 1.9.

I'll explain more soon, but `print` makes Swift print what you want on your screen.

On the right side of the screen, you should see the text `Hello Swift Apps`, which is the result of the first line of code you wrote.

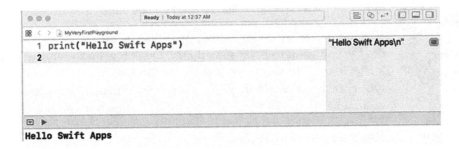

Figure 1.9 After you've typed your first line of code, the screen looks like this.

EXERCISE

Try typing other things inside the quotes, such as this:

```
print("How are you, Frank?")
```

You should see whatever you typed in the sidebar, as shown in figure 1.10.

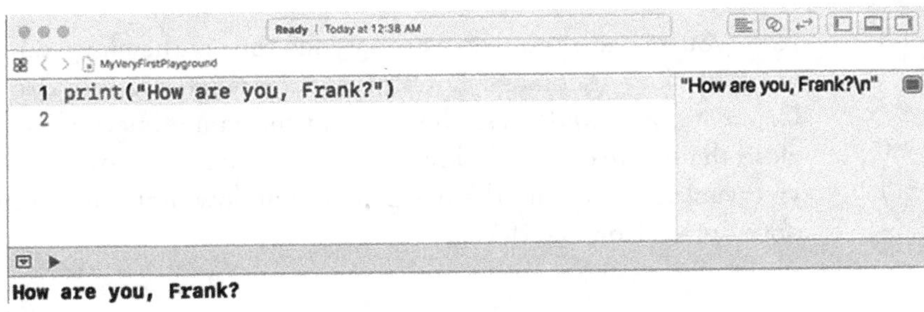

Figure 1.10 See how the text changed in the sidebar?

Congratulations! You wrote and executed your first line of Swift code! In chapter 2, you learn to create a real iOS app. You also learn quite a bit about running apps and a little bit about something called a user interface, which sounds scarier than it is.

You've completed your journey to the first milestone!

Why can't we type only `"Hello Swift Apps"` and not the rest?

If you type `"Hello Swift Apps"`, Swift has no idea what you want it to do. Do you want to print something? Do you want to send an email to a friend? Or do you want some calculations to be done? When you type `print`, you're telling Swift that you want to print something on the bottom bar (console log); the result is also shown in the sidebar.

What does `print` mean?

`print` is known as a function. (You'll learn more about functions later, so don't worry.) A function tells Swift to do something and how to do it. In everyday English, *function* means to perform a task.

The `print()` function is built into Swift, which means that Apple wrote that function for you. So the `print` function tells the Swift compiler to print whatever you write in its parentheses, and the Swift compiler does it. You'll be using this feature a lot to test your code, so get ready!

How do I close the playground?

After you've had enough fun trying your code in the playground, you'll want to close it. Here's how: press Command-Q. (Hold down the Command key, and press the q key at the same time.) This way, you close the playground window. All other Xcode windows close too. If you want to close only the playground window, not other Xcode windows, press Command-W.

Check your app knowledge

Try the following:

1 What would you type to display `"Good morning Swift"` in the playground?
2 What is displayed if you type `print("5+4")`?
3 What is displayed if you type `print(5+4)`? Guess and check by running this command in playground.
4 What qualities should your app have to be a good app, and why?

2

Create your first app

Are you ready to start building your first app? Before you start, make sure you've followed the instructions in chapter 1 to set up your programming environment!

This chapter covers

- *Creating a simple app*
- *Testing your app and seeing it run*
- *Knowing what a user interface is and why you should care about it*

You're now all set to cover your second milestone: create your first app. If you have your own iDevice, you'll be able to run your app on it. If you don't, you'll still be able to run it by using a simulator. Let's go ahead!

Hello apps!

You've reached the first stop on your journey. You've installed Xcode, the app-building software, and you're ready to go.

In this chapter, you travel to your next location and build your first simple app along the way. You learn how to create a simple app that can run on an iPhone or iPad. You learn how to try out the apps you create by using a special program called a simulator. And before you're done, you'll get some design tips for making apps that you and your users will like even more.

When I say *iDevice*, I mean an iPhone or an iPad. It's just a quick way to say "any Apple device that runs iOS apps."

Your first app: Hello World!

It's time for you to build your first app!

There's a tradition that the first program you learn to write in any programming language displays the words `Hello World!` on the screen. Your first app does the same thing, displaying `Hello World!` on the screen of an iDevice.

NOTE You can find the code for this application in the folder Chapter02_HelloWorld, inside the folder called Hello-Swift-Code-master that you downloaded from Github. If you haven't downloaded the code, go to: https://github.com/tanmayb123/Hello-Swift-Code/archive/master.zip. You should download the code only once for all chapters.

What does this app do?

Figure 2.1 shows what the Hello World app does when you run it on an iPhone.

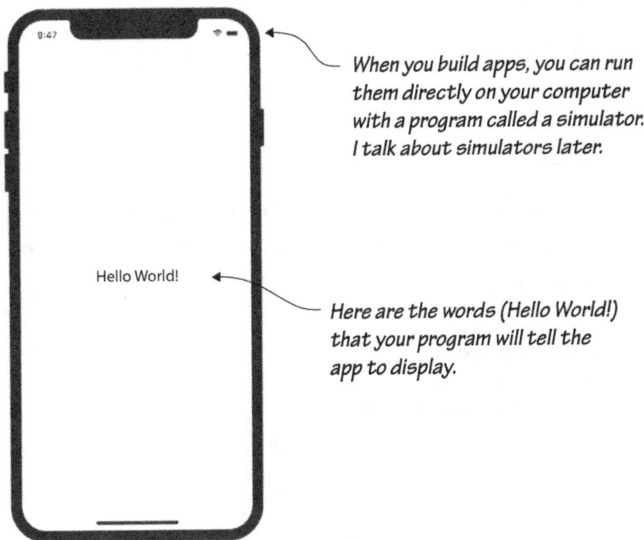

9:47
Hello World!
When you build apps, you can run them directly on your computer with a program called a simulator. I talk about simulators later.
Here are the words (Hello World!) that your program will tell the app to display.

Figure 2.1 Your first app displays the words `Hello World!` on a blank screen. You can test your app on a simulator if you don't have an iDevice.

Wait! Is that all my app does—displays some words on the screen? That's not very interesting. Why not do something more fun?

It's true that this app doesn't do much. But you have to learn to build simple things before you can create more complicated apps. You'll learn a lot about the basics of building apps as you build this one. And it's kind of cool to see words on the screen that you put there! Don't worry—I'll get to more interesting apps soon.

Set up the project

You have to do a few simple setup steps before you can create your app. These steps are kind of boring, but you have to do them only once for each app you create:

- Create a new project.
- Choose the project options.
- Save the project.

CREATE A NEW PROJECT

Follow the steps in table 2.1 to create a new project. You'll get some reminders in later chapters, but this table will be a good reference for you if you forget a step.

Table 2.1 Creating a new project

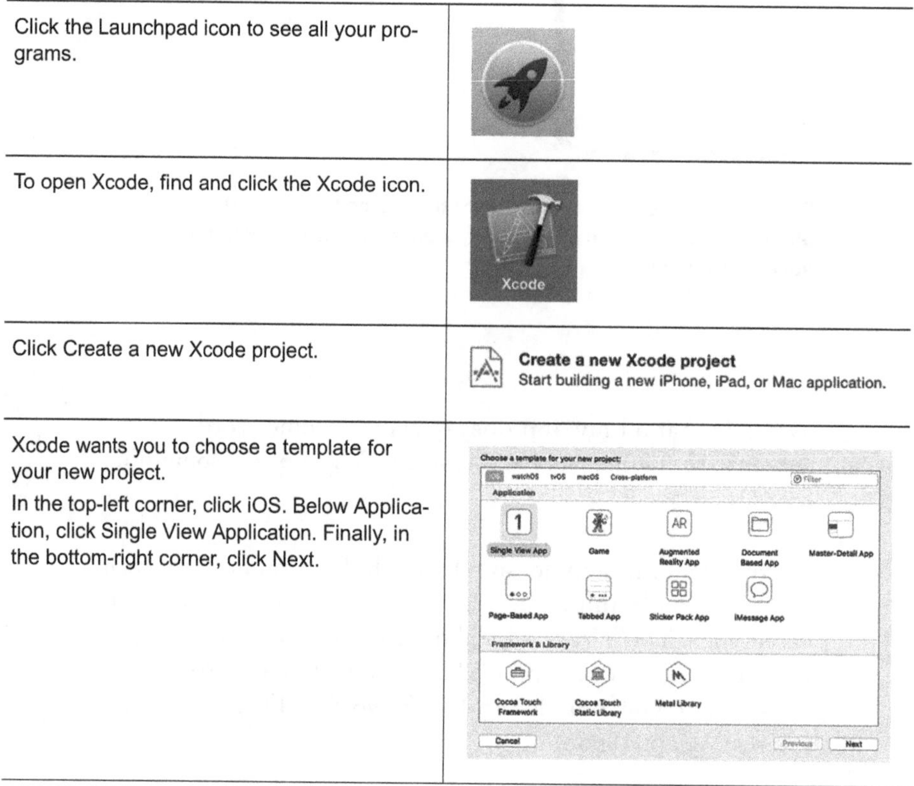

Click the Launchpad icon to see all your programs.	
To open Xcode, find and click the Xcode icon.	Xcode
Click Create a new Xcode project.	**Create a new Xcode project** Start building a new iPhone, iPad, or Mac application.
Xcode wants you to choose a template for your new project. In the top-left corner, click iOS. Below Application, click Single View Application. Finally, in the bottom-right corner, click Next.	

Table 2.1 Creating a new project *(continued)*

After you click Next, you'll fill out another form to choose project options. This is the form; don't close it!

Choose options for your new project:

Product Name: Hello World
Team: Puneet Bakshi
Organization Name: Tanmay Bakshi
Organization Identifier: TB
Bundle Identifier: TB.Hello-World
Language: Swift
Use Core Data
Include Unit Tests
Include UI Tests

Cancel Previous Next

All the details you need are in table 2.2 later in this chapter.

Keep going; you're almost done!

NOTE Make Xcode easier to open. You'll be using Xcode all through this book, so you'll want to be able to open it quickly. After you open Xcode this time, right click its icon in the Dock. Then choose Options > Keep in Dock. Now the icon will always show up in your Dock so that you can find and open it faster next time.

What's a view? And why did I pick Single View Application?

Think of a *view* as the screen people see when they use your app. Your app will have only one view: the one with the words `Hello World!` on it. Later in this chapter, you'll build an app with two views.

CHOOSE THE PROJECT OPTIONS

You have two more setup screens to get through. First, you need to tell Xcode what to call your app and where to save it on your computer—that is, choose the project options.

Table 2.2 Choosing the project options

This form is the one you're filling out. It should already be open if you completed the steps in table 2.1. Complete the form with the following details:	
Product Name	The name of your app. Call this one Hello World.
Team	The name associated with your Apple ID or developer account. The name you see in the screenshot, Puneet Bakshi, is the one linked with my developer account.
Organization Name	The name of your company. You can use your name if you don't have a company.
Organization Identifier	The initials of your company. You can use your initials if you don't have a company.
Bundle Identifier	This identifier is created for you based on what you put in the other fields. Apple uses this identifier when you're finally ready to submit your app to the App Store. When you fill out the information, the identifier is created this way: OrganizationIdentifier.ProductName. Mine is TB.Hello-World.
Language	Choose whether you want to code your app in Objective-C or in Swift. Because this book teaches you the new language Swift, choose Swift from the menu.

Table 2.2 Choosing the project options *(continued)*

After you fill out the form, click Next. This form appears so that you can save your project. Don't close it! Table 2.3 shows you how to use this form.	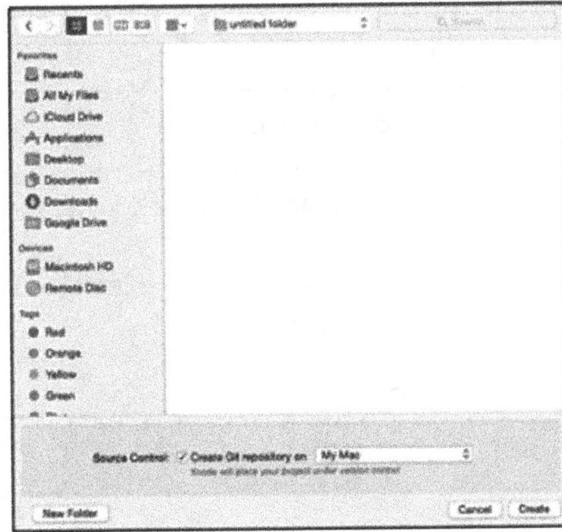

SAVE THE PROJECT

Finally, you have to tell Xcode where to save your app's files and settings.

You should see the screen in table 2.3, which asks you where to save your project. I created a folder called Apps inside my Documents folder, and I store all my apps in there. You can save yours wherever you like, but do make sure that you remember the name!

Table 2.3 Saving the project

This form should be on your screen if you finished the previous step successfully. Here, you tell Xcode where to save your project.	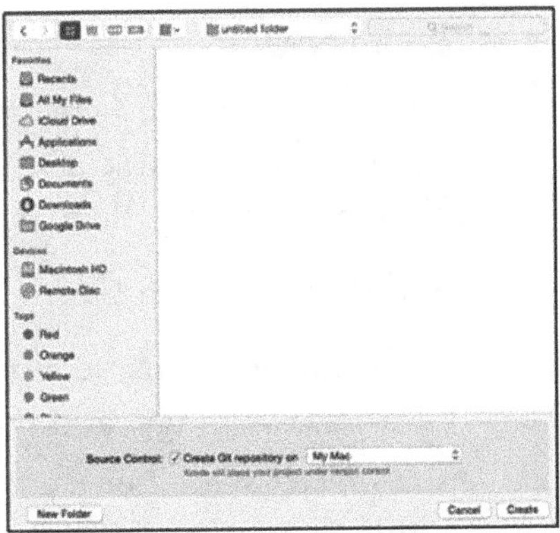
Navigate to the Documents folder by clicking it on the left side of the form.	

Table 2.3 Saving the project *(continued)*

Browse to wherever you'd like to store your apps.	I created a folder on my computer just for my apps. I called this folder Apps. :)
Click New Folder.	
Type the name of your new folder (such as Apps). Click Create on this form to create a new folder.	New Folder Name of new folder: Apps Cancel Create
You should see the form from the first step. Now click Create again to save your project. Yay—you're done!	

Well done! You've done the following things:

- Created a new project
- Chosen your project options
- Saved your project

The good news is that you have to do these steps only once for each app you create.

The Xcode interface

You're now on the General tab of your Xcode project (figure 2.2). It's important that you know the names of the parts of this screen, because I'll be mentioning them as you build your app.

Find these items in figure 2.2:

- *Navigator*—This section allows you to manage your project's files, errors, warnings, and many more things.
- *Inspectors*—When you select something on the main stage, you'll be able to manage the settings for it here.
- *Libraries*—If you want to add a common element (for example, some text or a button) to your app, you'll find it in a library.

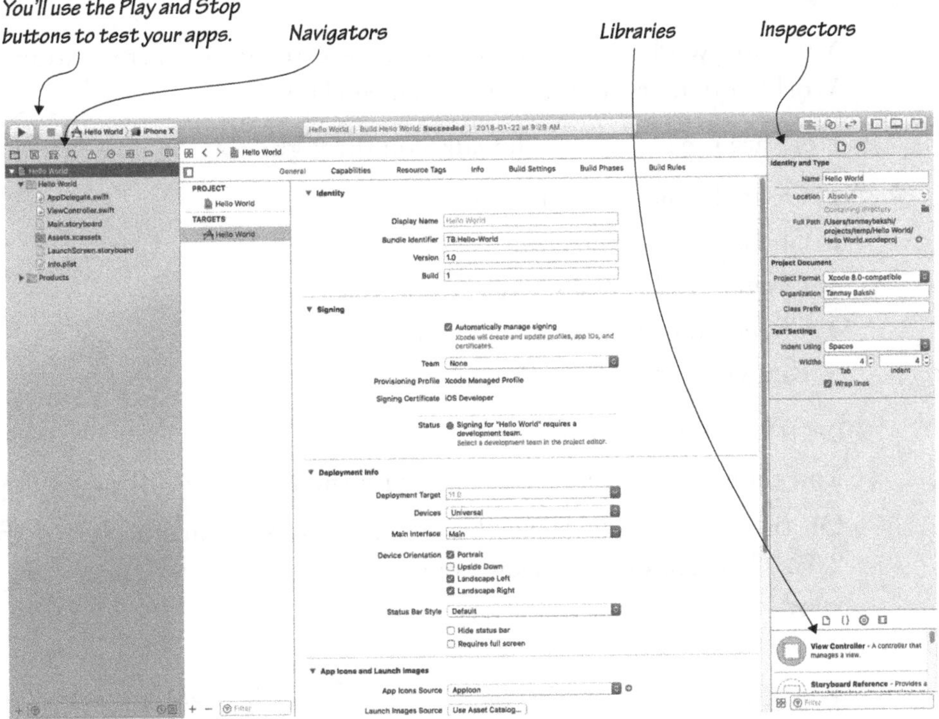
You'll use the Play and Stop buttons to test your apps.
Navigators
Libraries
Inspectors

Figure 2.2 The General tab of your Xcode project

- *Stage*—This middle section is where you'll build your app.
- *Toolbar*—You'll use the section at the top of Xcode to run and stop apps.

This screen looks super-complicated! Do I have to learn all these things?

Lots of things are going on here, and it's a lot to take in all at once. Don't worry about it right now. Later, you'll want to learn more parts of this screen. Right now, though, I'll talk only about the things you need to know to create your first app.

Create the UI

Your app workspace is set up, so you're ready to start creating Hello World! First, create the user interface (UI).

Here are the steps that I'll walk you through:

1 Open the main storyboard.
2 Change the screen size.
3 Drag a label to the view.
4 Change the label to say `Hello World!`
5 Run your app!

OPEN THE MAIN STORYBOARD

You should have Xcode running, with the Hello World! project open.

On the left side of the Xcode interface, click Main.storyboard (figure 2.3). This step opens a view controller, where you'll design your app's view.

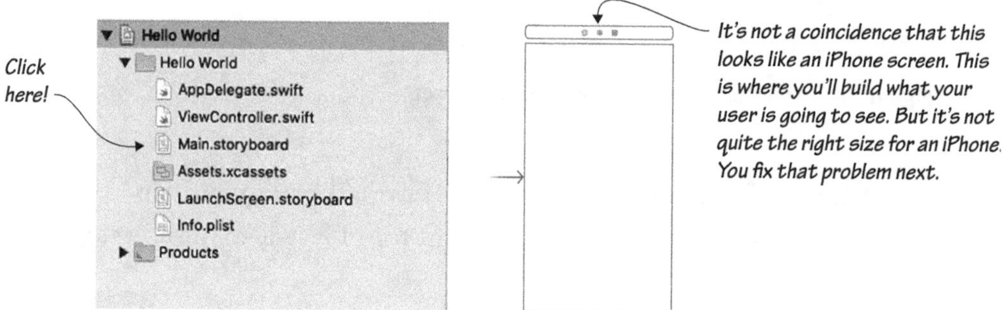
Click here!
Hello World
Hello World
AppDelegate.swift
ViewController.swift
Main.storyboard
Assets.xcassets
LaunchScreen.storyboard
Info.plist
Products
It's not a coincidence that this looks like an iPhone screen. This is where you'll build what your user is going to see. But it's not quite the right size for an iPhone. You fix that problem next.

Figure 2.3 The view controller in the main storyboard. The rectangle you see when you open the storyboard is called your ViewController, which allows you to control what you see onscreen.

A *storyboard* is an ordered set of drawings that are used to plan a movie or TV show. In this case, it's where you design the view that your users will see. You have only one view for this app, so your storyboard contains only one scene.

Figure 2.3 shows an iPhone 8 display size. For this book, however, I'm using an iPhone X display. You can keep the display size as iPhone 8 if you're using that phone. If you're using an iPhone X or any other compatible iPhone, please follow the next steps to change the size of the view in the ViewController.

You'll need to follow these quick steps for every app in this book.

SET THE SCREEN SIZE

To begin, look toward the bottom-left corner of the storyboard view. You should see a pane like the one shown in figure 2.4.

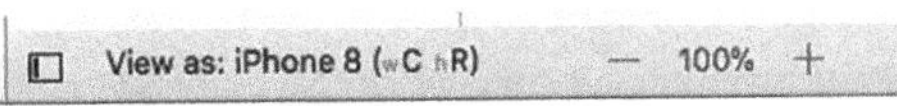

Figure 2.4 Click this pane to view different screen sizes.

When you've identified this area, click View as: iPhone 8. As you click it, you should see a few screen sizes, as shown in figure 2.5.

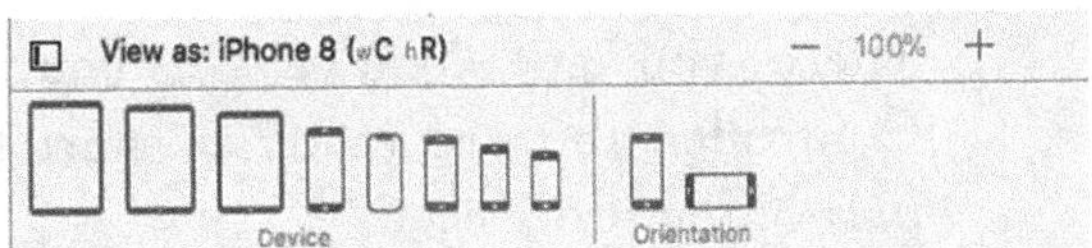

Figure 2.5 A selection of screen sizes

If you hover over the devices, you can see the device size that each one represents. A bit of added complexity is involved, however: if you have an iPhone 7, you need to choose the iPhone 8 size. You have to do this because the iPhone 6, 7, and 8 have the same size, but because the iPhone 8 is the latest model, Apple represents only that size in Xcode. Table 2.4 is a size chart that you can check for your device.

Table 2.4 Which device do you choose for your screen size?

If your device is an	Choose this device in Xcode
iPhone XS Max	iPhone XS Max
iPhone XR	iPhone XR
iPhone X, iPhone XS	iPhone XS
iPhone 6 Plus, 6S Plus, 7 Plus, or 8 Plus	iPhone 8 Plus
iPhone 6, 6S, 7, or 8	iPhone 8
iPhone 5S, iPhone SE	iPhone SE

Table 2.4 Which device do you choose for your screen size? *(continued)*

If your device is an	Choose this device in Xcode
3rd-Gen 12.9-inch iPad Pro	iPad Pro 12.9" (3rd Generation)
Any 11-inch iPad Pro	iPad Pro 11"
1st-Gen or 2nd-Gen 12.9-inch iPad Pro	iPad Pro 12.9"
Any 10.5-inch iPad	iPad Pro 10.5"
Any 9.7-inch iPad	iPad Pro 9.7"

When you know which device to choose, tap it, and the ViewController's size adjusts accordingly. Because I chose iPhone X, the ViewController also shows me the notch in the top-center of the iPhone X's screen (figure 2.6).

There you go! You've set your ViewController and are ready to start the fun part of the process.

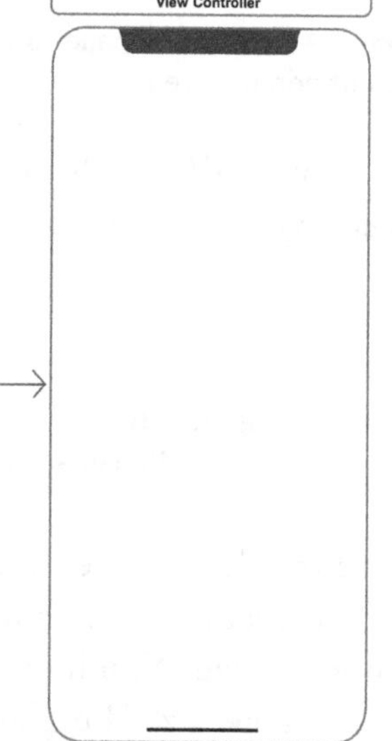

Figure 2.6 The iPhone X in the ViewController

DRAG A LABEL OBJECT TO THE VIEW

The Libraries panel is in the bottom-right corner of Xcode (figure 2.7). The Object Library is where you get objects and controls for your app. You use the Object Library to get your controls; specifically, you need the Label object so that you can show some text to the user.

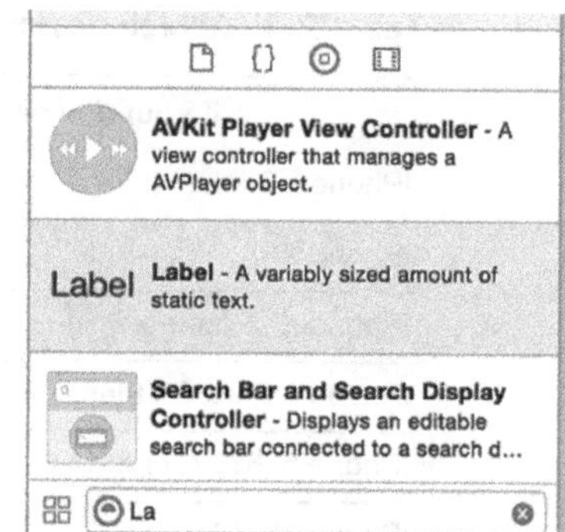

Figure 2.7 The Libraries panel stores objects and controls for your app.

Objects are things in your app that your user can see and interact with. The text label you're going to add to your app is an object.

A special type of object that users can interact with is called a *control*. Think of the apps you use. They have buttons, sliders, or text input boxes, all of which are controls.

To add your first object (a label) to the application, follow these steps:

1 Click the little circle with a square inside it to open the Object Library.
2 You need to find the Label object. You can scroll down in the panel or search for it. To search, start typing `Label` in the search box at the bottom of the panel. A box that has the word `Label` in it and a brief description of the object appears.
3 Drag the label to your view, as shown in figure 2.8.

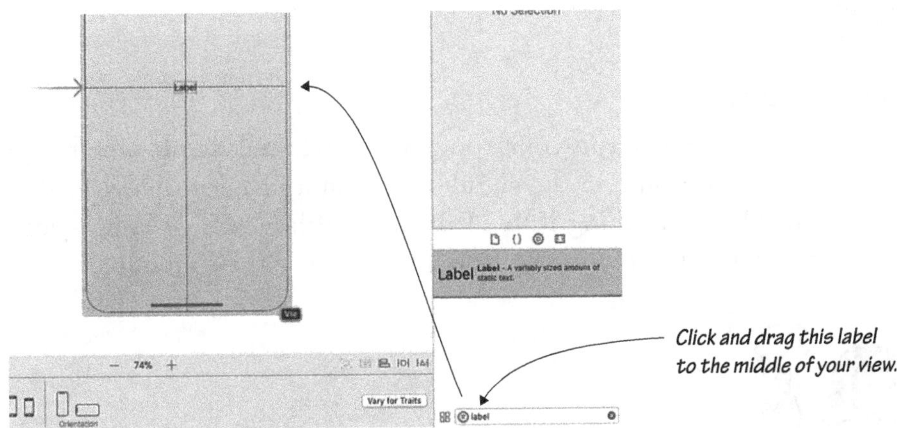
Click and drag this label to the middle of your view.
Label
Vary for Traits
74%
Orientation

Figure 2.8 Drag a label to your view.

TIP Your users interact with the app by using controls. They can gather input and give output.

4 Move the label to the center of the view until you see two dotted blue lines: one top to bottom and the other left to right. I call these lines *guide grids*. They help you align controls on the view so that you can

(for example) center a label onscreen without doing math. When these lines appear, you've centered the label control in the view.

5 Double-click the label, which is now in text-editing mode.
6 Delete the word `Label`, and type "`Hello World!`" (without the quotes) in its place.

Wait—do I have to type `Hello World!`? Can't I put something else there?

Sure, you can type whatever you want. Have fun!

Run your app

Before you can run your app, you have to tell Xcode whether you want to run your app in the simulator or on a physical iDevice. If you have an iDevice running iOS 11 or later (iPhone 5S or later), you can use your iDevice; otherwise, you'll have to use the simulator.

Do I have to run the app in a simulator? Can't I run it on my iPhone?

You can! But setting up your account is tricky; you'll find the steps in appendix F of this book.

What's this simulator thing, anyway?

A *simulator* is a computer program that lets you run your iOS apps on your Mac, as if you're running them on your iDevice so you can test them. But because your computer's screen isn't a touchscreen, you can't test touch actions (multigesture actions). You can use your computer's mouse to perform simple touch actions. Features that use iDevice hardware (such as the camera and the microphone) aren't available either.

Here are a few more things that you won't be able to test with the simulator:

- *Accelerometer*—Measuring acceleration or changes in speed.
- *Gyroscope*—Performing gyroscope functions, such as rotation. You see this feature in games such as Temple Run, in which you have to tilt the device to move the character to the left or right to collect coins or points.
- *Camera*—Taking a picture or making a video.
- *Microphone*—Recording sounds, such as someone's voice.
- *Proximity sensor*—Doing things like detecting whether you're close to the iPhone.
- *Fingerprint sensor*—Matching a fingerprint by tapping the Touch ID (home) button.

These limitations aren't going to be problems, as you learn in this book, but knowing about them will help you understand the simulator better.

RUN YOUR APP ON THE SIMULATOR

In this section, you try out your new app on the simulator.

The simulator lets you choose from a bunch of iDevices. You can choose one from the list to see what your app will look like when you run it on, say, an iPad versus an iPhone SE.

To run your app in the simulator, follow these steps:

1 You need to tell the simulator what kind of iDevice you want it to simulate, so find your project's name next to the big Play button in

the top-left corner of the screen. This area should look something like figure 2.9.

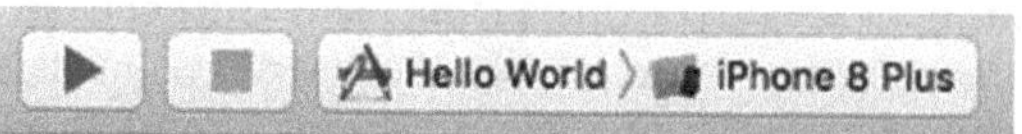

Figure 2.9 Click the Play button to run your app on the device you want to simulate.

I'm using the iPhone X, so I can't simulate with the iPhone 8 Plus! To change, I click iPhone 8 Plus; when the menu pops up, I choose iPhone X, as shown in figure 2.10.

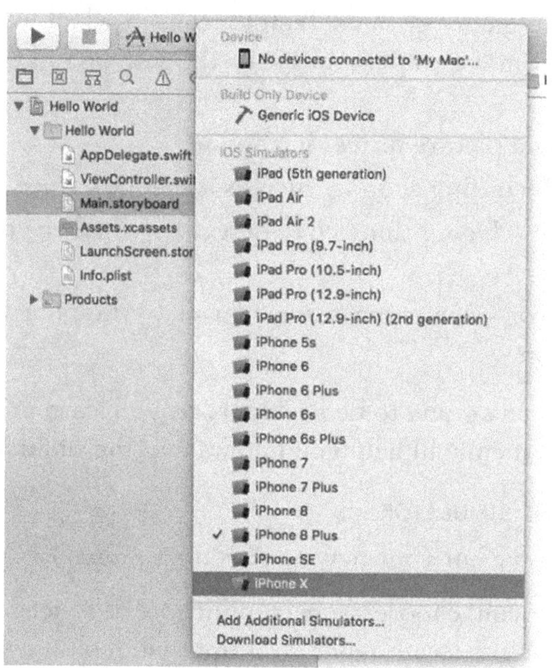

Figure 2.10 Choose the device you want to simulate from the pop-up menu.

2 Click the Play button near the top-left corner of the screen (figure 2.11). If you're asked for your admin password, enter it. (You have to enter your password only once: the first time you run your app.)

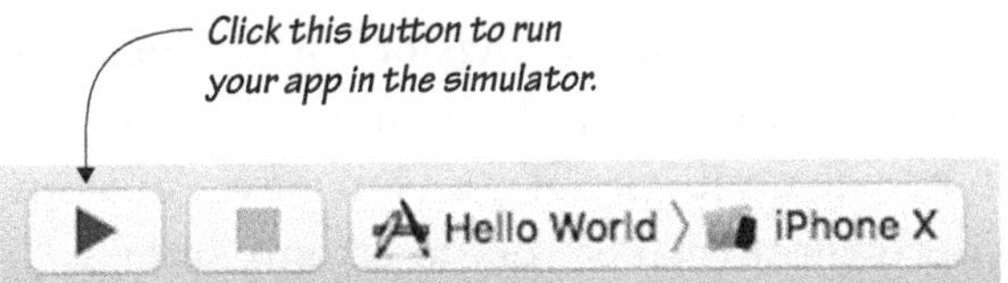
Click this button to run
your app in the simulator.
Hello World
iPhone X

Figure 2.11 Click the Play button to run the app in the simulator.

You see your app in the simulator (figure 2.12).

3 To stop your app running in the simulator, click the square Stop button in the top-left corner of Xcode, to the right of the Play button.

9:47
Hello World!

Figure 2.12 The simulator window opens with your app running in it.

(OPTIONAL) RUN YOUR APP ON YOUR IDEVICE

Setting up your account should be quick. If you're happy running your app in the simulator for now, however, skip these instructions, and come back later.

To run your app on a real iDevice, you have to follow a few more steps:

1 Check appendix F to make sure that you have your developer account set up correctly. (Apple explains the process well, so I provide links to Apple's instructions for you.)
2 Connect your iDevice to your Mac with a Lightning cable.
3 As you do when you run your app in a simulator, find your project name next to the big Play button in the top-left corner of the screen, and click the simulator name next to it. After you've opened the menu that allows you to choose a new simulator, choose the name of your device instead. The name will be near the top of the menu.

4 If you see a prompt mentioning provisioning profiles, click the Fix Issue button. Then select your Apple ID in the list and click Choose. This step adds a provisioning profile to your new developer account. (If you have to perform this step, you do so only once.)

You must be thinking, "I didn't create a developer account! What's happening?" Well, when you set up Xcode with your Apple ID, Xcode created a developer account for you, so it's adding a key that allows Xcode to install the app on your device and nobody else's.

5 If you see a prompt mentioning codesign and keychain, click the Always Allow button.

NOTE It's not *co-design*, but *code-sign*.

6 Click the Play button near the top-left corner of the screen. Your app runs on your iDevice.

Congrats! You've successfully run your first app on your iDevice.

Discover the user interface

The UI is how your user interacts with your app. And although there's more to an app, its UI is one of the most important parts. Let's take a closer look.

Believe it or not, you've already created a UI! When you dragged the label to the view in your Hello World! App, you created a user interface.

What is a UI?

The user interface is the way users interact with computers—or, in your case, with iDevices. By *interact with apps*, I mean that the user gets info from the app, and also gives responses and commands to the app. The words, pictures, graphics, buttons, sounds, vibrations, and everything else together on the screen is the UI (figure 2.13).

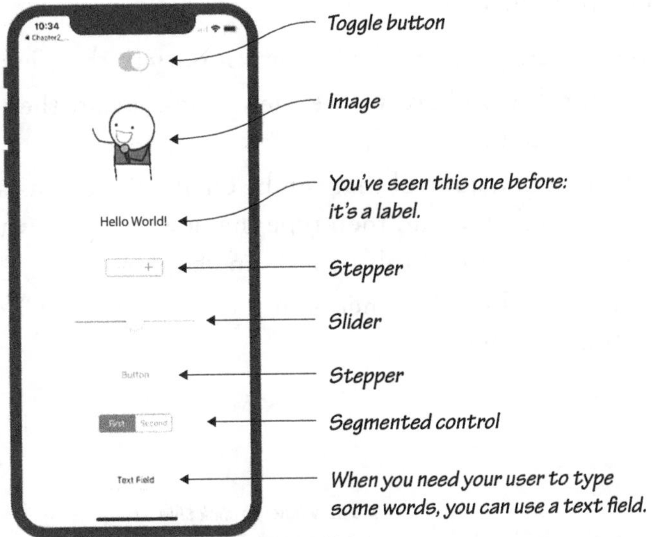

Figure 2.13 A UI is anything the user sees or can interact with. This figure is your app's UI, but I added a bunch of controls to the UI to make the app silly. These UI elements are only a few of the ones you could add.

The app you've created has a simple UI; the user sees the words "`Hello, World!`" onscreen. Most apps have lots more going on, however. Angry Birds, for example, has a much more complicated UI; the user sees birds, pigs, structures, and much more onscreen. Also, the user can touch the screen and make things happen.

Develop an app on your own

First, try to create an app with a button, a label, and a text field that looks like figure 2.14.

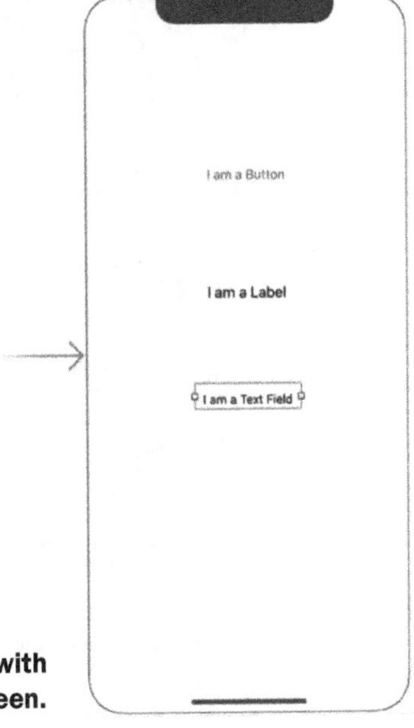

Figure 2.14 Try to make this app, with a button, a label, and a text field onscreen.

Here are some tips to help you:

- To add a control, drag it from the Object Library to the view.
- To move a control anywhere in the view, click it and then drag it where you want it to be.
- To change the text of a control that can be changed (such as a button or a label), double-click it and then type the new text you want in its place. You learn more about this process in chapter 4.
- You'll find many of the UI elements in the same place in Xcode: in the Object library (figure 2.15).

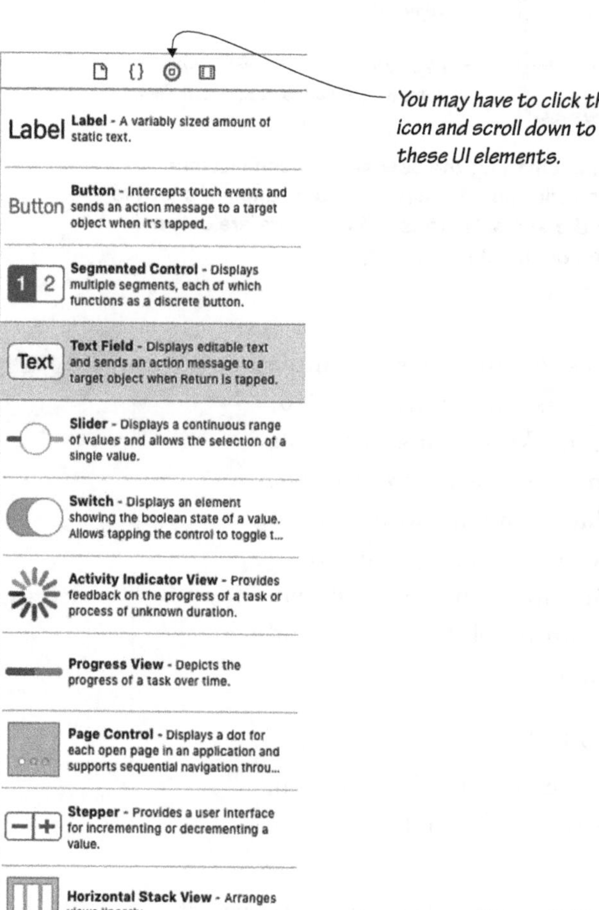

Label
Label - A variably sized amount of static text.
Button
Button - Intercepts touch events and sends an action message to a target object when it's tapped.
1 2
Segmented Control - Displays multiple segments, each of which functions as a discrete button.
Text
Text Field - Displays editable text and sends an action message to a target object when Return is tapped.
Slider - Displays a continuous range of values and allows the selection of a single value.
Switch - Displays an element showing the boolean state of a value. Allows tapping the control to toggle t...
Activity Indicator View - Provides feedback on the progress of a task or process of unknown duration.
Progress View - Depicts the progress of a task over time.
Page Control - Displays a dot for each open page in an application and supports sequential navigation throu...
Stepper - Provides a user interface for incrementing or decrementing a value.
Horizontal Stack View - Arranges views linearly.
You may have to click this icon and scroll down to find these UI elements.

Figure 2.15 Many UI interface elements are in the Object Library.

Okay, I'm done. Now can I make my UI a little more interesting?

Good job! Next, give your app some color. I'll show you how to change the colors of text and controls and the background color of the whole view. Again, I'm listing only a few examples, although sorting can be done in *many* more ways!

Change text colors

You can change the text colors of labels, buttons, text fields, and other UI controls that have text. Here's how:

1. Click a label, text field, button, or any other control that has text.
2. Click the Attributes Inspector button (on the right side of the Xcode interface).

   The Attributes inspector in figure 2.16 is a panel that lets you change all kinds of things about the interface elements in your app, including font size, color, and alignment.
3. Click the Color menu below the Label header to open the Colors palette.
4. Click the Colors palette and choose any color you want.

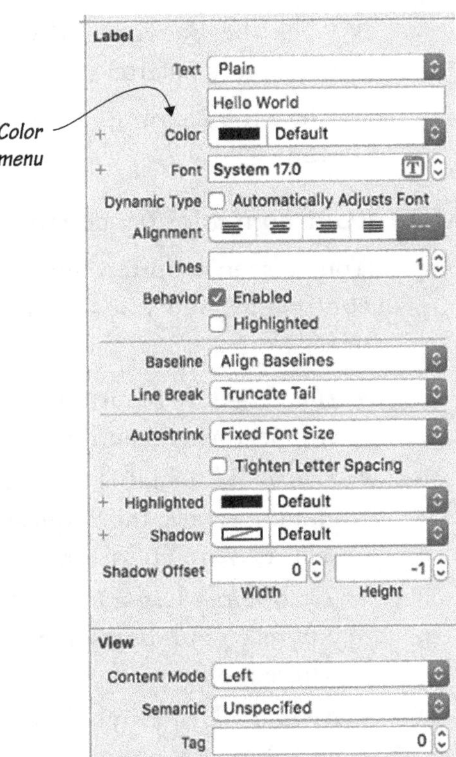

Figure 2.16 The attributes inspector

Change the background color of a control

You can change the background color of buttons or other controls that have background colors by following these steps:

1. Click a button, switch, or any other control that has a background.
2. Click the Attributes inspector button, if it's not already open.
3. Click the Background Color menu below the View header to open the Colors palette.
4. Click the Colors palette and choose any color you want.

Change the background color of a view

Changing the color of your entire view is easy, too. Follow these steps:

1. Click a part of your view that doesn't have any controls in it.
2. Click the Attributes inspector button, if it's not already open.
3. Click the Background Color menu below the View header to open the Colors palette.
4. Click the Colors palette and choose the new background color you want.

More about controls: Try these for a challenge

You've seen a button and a label, but you'll end up using a few other controls in your apps (figure 2.17). Take a look at the most common ones:

- *Button*—Use a button when you want the user to click it to make the app perform an action (such as ordering a pizza).
- *Label*—Use a label to display text onscreen to give users some information or ask them questions. For example, a label might display, `What is your first name?`
- *TextField*—Use a text field to let the user enter some information. If you ask your users for a first name, for example, the text field is where they type it.
- *Switch*—Use a switch to get an on/off or a true/false value from the user. You can use it, for example, to get a response to the question `Do you like pizza?`

- *TextView*—Use a text view to get a longer text answer from a user. Your app might prompt your user with, `Tell me about the last time you ate pizza`, for example.

Figure 2.17 Here are some things you can do with other controls in your app. Can you make these?

A few more things you can do with the Attributes inspector

You probably noticed lots of options in the Attribute inspector. Here are a few things you can change when you select a control:

- *Font*—You can change the font, font style (such as italic or bold), and font size.
- *Alignment*—You can align your text left, center, or right.
- *Shadow* and *Shadow Offset*—These options let you add a drop shadow or glow to your control or text label.

Try playing with these options. I talk about even more options later in the book.

Segues: Using controls to navigate screens

Let me introduce one essential feature of apps: navigation. Navigating is also called *segueing* through views.

You may be wondering what a segue is. (The word is pronounced like *segway*, by the way!) In the context of apps, a *segue* is a move without interruption between views. It's often used between songs when the first song ends and the second starts smoothly, without a break or gap and without a change in volume.

Here's an example that you may notice in an app (including tTables, a times-tables app developed by Tanmay Bakshi!) when you click a button to bring up a new screen or view. Clicking the Let's Start button in tTables, for example, brings up the main Quiz view. This switching of screens or views in which one screen disappears smoothly and the other shows up is called *segueing*.

To make a segue (which is surprisingly simple), follow these steps:

1. Put a button in the view you want to segue from.
2. If you don't have two views (one to segue from and a second one to segue to), search for View Controller in the Object Library, and drag the View Controller to the blank space (not to the existing view itself).
3. Right-click the button in the first view and drag it to the second view. Release the button when a blue line reaches the second view.

   There are many ways to do segueing, but I'm introducing the simplest of all segues: the modal.
4. Choose Modal from the dark menu that appears when you release the mouse button.

   Done! You have a segue! You can do the same thing with the button in the second view to go (segue) back to the first view.

Try an extra challenge

If you're up for a challenge, try your best to make the following screenshot into an app as you did in your Hello World! app. To get started, you need to design the UI, and to save you the trouble of doing that, I created it for you! All you need to do is duplicate the UI in figure 2.18 into your project.

TIP If you need to, you can scroll around and zoom in and out of the storyboard by using the multitouch gestures you already use to control apps such as Safari and Chrome.

Before I go further, here are some important features:

- The first (nicknamed the Question view) is where you ask the question and give possible answers for users to choose.
- The second view (nicknamed the Wrong Answer view) is where you tell users that they got the answer wrong.

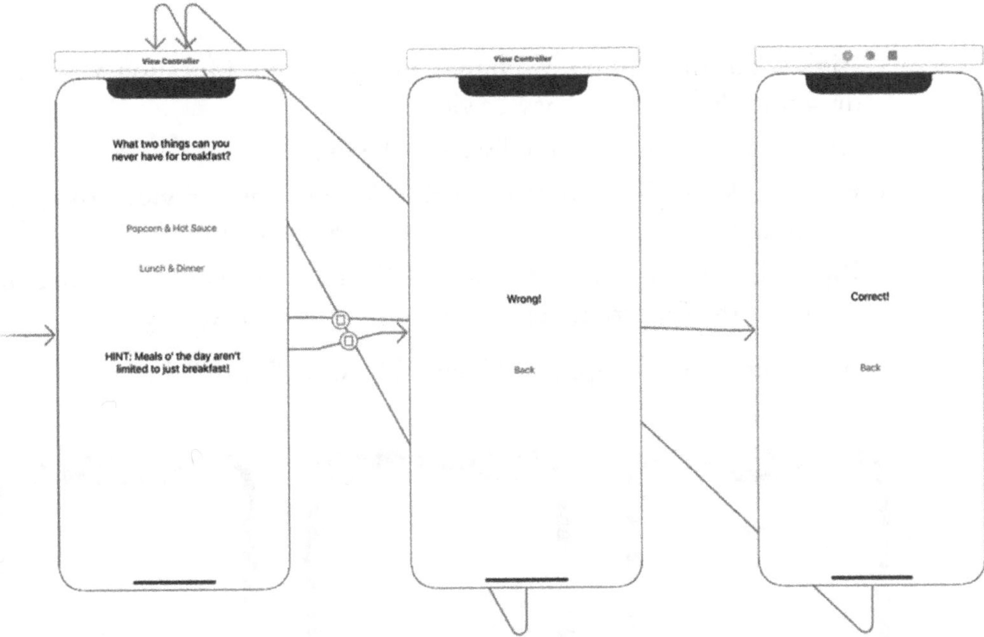

Figure 2.18 The UI with three screens for the Segues app

- The third view (nicknamed the Correct Answer view) is where you tell users that they got the answer correct.
- The two answers are represented as buttons, so they can be clicked. Lunch & Dinner is a button in the initial view, for example. There are also Back buttons in each of the result screens.
- The question in the initial view and the results in the result views (Wrong and Correct) are labels.

TIP Notice that every view has an arrow pointing to it on the left side. An arrow not coming from another view means that the view it's pointing to shows up first when the app is run. If the app has two or more views, then these arrows show some of the possible ways you can move from one view to another.

Now follow these steps to create the segue:

1 Right-click the Popcorn & Hot Sauce button in the Question view and drag it to the Wrong Answer view.
2 Select Present Modally from the gray list that pops up.

3. Right-click the Lunch & Dinner button in the Question view and drag it to the Correct Answer view.
4. Again, select Present Modally from the list.
5. Right-click the Back button in the Wrong Answer view, drag the button to the Question view, and select Present Modally.
6. Right-click the Back button in the Correct Answer view, drag the button to the Question view, and select Present Modally.

You're done! Run the app, and it should work (figure 2.19).

Figure 2.19 Segues application in action

Designing good UIs

Now that you know what a UI is, here's a list of best practices that will help you create apps with good UIs:

- Always use a legible font size for text on your labels, buttons, text fields, and other controls. Users need to be able to read them!
- To make sure that your controls are legible to users, always use system fonts unless you're required to use a different font for a special purpose.

- Stay consistent with color. Don't use a different color for each button, for example. The Notes app is an excellent example: it uses a consistent yellow color for all its buttons. Games sometimes ignore this rule, however, if many colors are more appealing to users (as in the Fruit Ninja game, for example).
- Take advantage of the whole screen! Don't cram everything into a little section of your app and leave a big empty area somewhere else. Because the latest iPhones have bigger screens, you could space your controls out more to give the user more space; you could even add more functionality to a single view. But this tip isn't a hard-and-fast rule. At times, it may make sense to let users focus on one thing. In a timer app, for example, you may want the time remaining to be large and in the center without much else in the view.
- Always pay attention to the needs of at least 80 percent of the users of your app. Don't implement a feature that only a few users will use or that a normal user would rarely use.

Some of these notes are from the iOS Human Interface Guidelines. To read more, download this document from iBooks on a Mac or iDevice.

These five main rules of UI design will help you create apps that your users will enjoy using.

Good job! With this section, you've completed the second milestone, and you're a mile closer to completing your journey. In chapter 3, you learn how to insert data into the computer's brain.

Try this app on your own

Create the app shown in figure 2.20, which has a button, a label, and a text field:

1 Add the label `My First App!` near the top-center of the screen.
2 Add the label `Play iSockey!` near the center of the screen.
3 Add the label `The mixed game of Hockey and Soccer!` below `Play iSockey!`

4 Add a black label stretching across the bottom with a white font that says `Swipe here to start!`

5 Add a white label with no text on the black label to make it look like a slider.

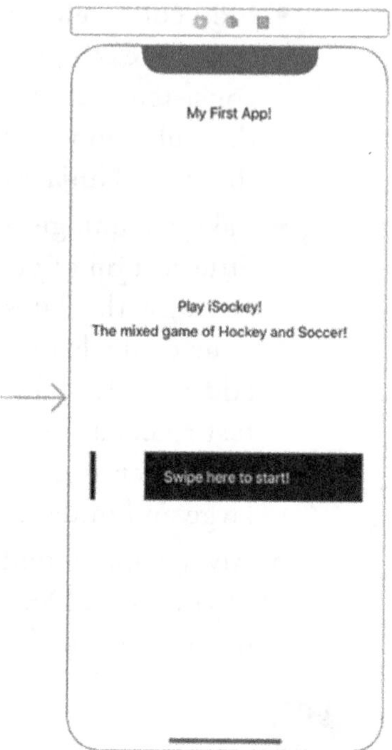

Figure 2.20 Try to create this app.

Test your app knowledge

In this section, I'm going to test your app knowledge to make sure you've been paying attention. :) Please answer the following questions (you may refer to the chapter to make sure you get them right):

- You create an app that uses the camera on an iPhone. Why can't you test the camera function with the simulator?
- What's the purpose of the iOS Human Interface Guidelines?
- Download the Bad App example from this book's website, and try your best to make it follow the rules of a good UI.

NOTE You can find the code for this application in the folder Chapter02_BadAppEg, inside the folder called Hello-Swift-Code-master that you downloaded from Github. If you haven't downloaded the code, go to: https://github.com/tanmayb123/Hello-Swift-Code/archive/master.zip. You should download the code only once for all chapters.

- What is a UI?
- Where is the Attributes inspector?

3

Your first real Swift code using variables

Next up: variables! You're about to take a close-up look at variables. You'll learn what they are, why you need them, and how to use them in your programs.

This chapter covers

- *How to make your program remember something*
- *What the different types of data are and why they're required*
- *How to convert one type of data to another*
- *How to do math in a program*

You're all set to cover your third milestone: writing your first real Swift code by using variables. By now, you may be thinking that this whole programming business is a breeze. You've used the Swift Playground, and you've used the `print()` function to output words on the screen. You've created a playground by adding a line or two of code. Things are about to get not so simple, but they'll be interesting and a lot of fun! In this chapter, you learn about using variables and doing math in your apps.

Apps store data in variables

In programming, you sometimes need to store data. Suppose that you need to save the names, email addresses, and phone numbers of 50 of your friends because you can't easily remember all of them. If you write an app that can store this information, you can use it to look up the information. You can even change this data if you need to (if someone gets a new phone number, for example).

What is a variable?

Look at this equation:

```
x = 4
```

If I asked you what x is, you would (I hope) say 4. Here, x is a variable, and its value at present is equal to 4.

Think of a variable as a name that's used to refer to a value that can change over time. But x isn't much of a name. You don't have any idea what x means, but you know that it equals 4.

In programming, you don't have to use a single letter like x as a variable name. You can use more descriptive variable names.

Now consider this code:

```
numberOfPlayers = 4
```

If I asked you how many players there are, I hope you'd say 4. But you'd also be able to guess that I'm keeping track of this number for a specific reason.

Why do apps need to store variables?

Think about this: when you're playing a game like Temple Run, your current score in the game is held in a variable so that the app can use it later and also display it to you. The score keeps increasing until your character dies.

Hands on!

In this section, you create and store a variable yourself.

NOTE You can find the code for this application in the Chapter03_Ex1.playground file inside the Hello-Swift-Code-master folder that you downloaded from GitHub. If you haven't downloaded the code, go to: https://github.com/tanmayb123/Hello-Swift-Code/archive/master.zip. You should download the code only once for all chapters.

Open a Playground, and type

```
var playerAge = 13
```

You've created a variable named `playerAge`, and you've stored a value of 13 in it.

Now suppose that you want to know, at any later time, what this variable contains. One way is to print the value inside the variable by using the `print()` function you learned in chapter 1.

Try typing this:

```
print(playerAge)
```

You see the output of this code on the right side of the Playground. It shows you what you saved in the `playerAge` variable.

You can use an even easier trick: type the variable name in the Playground, and Swift prints the value at the side of the Xcode window!

How does an app use and save variables?

When you create a variable in your code, you're telling your app that you need it to save a piece of information. The iDevice uses the variable name to create a place in its memory where it can store this important data. The reason you want to store data is that you need to use it again. As an example, take a look at figure 3.1.

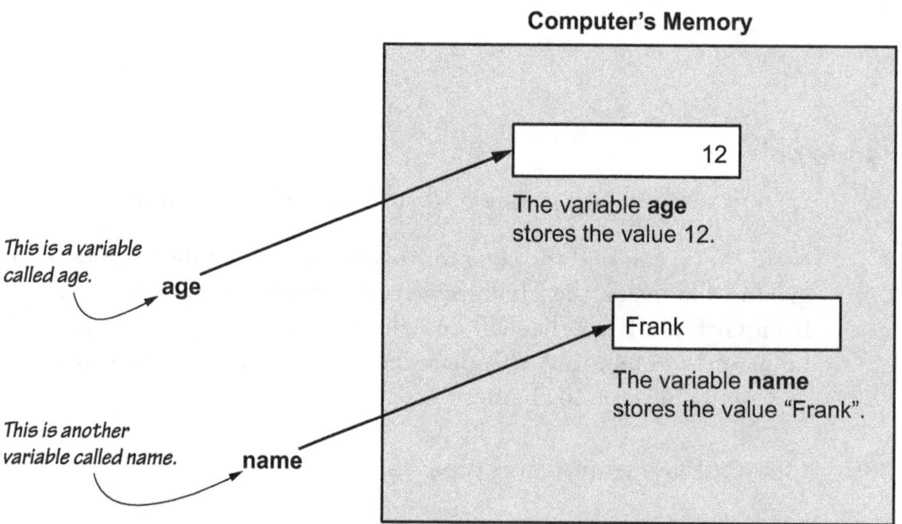
Computer's Memory
12
The variable **age** stores the value 12.
Frank
The variable **name** stores the value "Frank".
This is a variable called age.
age
This is another variable called name.
name

Figure 3.1 Two variables stored in the computer's memory. One variable is named `age`, with the value 12 stored in the computer's memory, and the other variable is called `name`, with the value `"Frank"` saved in the computer's memory.

Variables are useful. Think of a variable as being like a place in the computer's brain that can store data. This data can be anything, such as a name, an address, your grade, your age, or how much something costs. One reason why you need variables is because you may need to keep track of something that will change. Maybe the data you stored with the variable `age` is wrong now because you're a year older, for example. You can write a line of code that changes the data that the variable `age` points to in memory.

Wait a minute—I thought variables were just for storing numbers. How can I be using one to store a name?

You can create variables to store all kinds of information, including integers, text, and decimal values. In a few pages, you'll learn more about the types of data you can use with variables.

What types of variables are there?

You've seen that you can store more than just numbers in variables. You probably have many other types of data that you want to keep track of. In programming, you need to know what type (kind) of data you want to store.

If you wanted to store which grade a student is in, for example, you'd use a data type called an `Integer` to store it. Here, assume that somebody's grade will be 1, 2, 3, 4, 5, 6, 7, 8, 9, 10, 11, or 12. If you want to store a student's name, use something like a `String` (which you can think of as being like a string of characters). Use a `Double` to hold a decimal number, such as how much a pizza costs.

Table 3.1 shows the most common types that Swift uses and the ones you'll use most. You'll see many more variable types later in the book.

Table 3.1 Common types of variables in Swift

Type	Swift name	How it's used
Integer	`Int`	To store whole numbers and negative numbers, such as 12, 99, 200, 1000000, -32, 0
Double	`Double`	To store decimal values, such as 12.54, 8.23, -2.68, 89.99, 3.14159
Boolean	`Bool`	To store true/false values such as `true` and `false`
String	`String`	To store text, such as `"yellow"` and `"Today is Monday"`

> ### *Pop quiz*
>
> What variable types are these?
>
> **1** The number of kids playing a game
> **2** The height of a tree
> **3** Total bees in a beehive
> **4** Somebody's last name
>
> (Answers: 1. Int; 2. Double; 3. Int; 4. String)

You may wonder why you need to know what kind of data you have. You'll find out that there are lots of reasons, but here's one of the main ones: you can do math with numbers (Integers and Doubles) but not with text. You sometimes need to add, subtract, multiply, or perform some other math operation on a variable that contains a number. But if you have a variable that contains text, it doesn't make any sense to try to use math with it. To Swift, `"four"` and `4` aren't the same!

How to create variables

First, you have to come up with a variable name.

You've probably figured out that unlike in math, you usually don't use names like `x` or `y` for your variables unless you have a specific reason to do so. But although you can give your variables longer names, you still need to know some variable naming rules.

Swift provides a lot of features and a lot of flexibility in naming variables. But a variable name can start only with an alphabetical or underscore character, and it can't contain spaces or some special characters (%, $, &, *, ^).

Table 3.2 lists some examples of variable names you can use and some that you can't.

Table 3.2 Correct and incorrect examples of variable names

Correct	Incorrect	Why?
`ageOfUser`	`User'sAge`	Apostrophe is a special character.
`nameOfUser`	`User Name`	Name isn't a single word, and spaces can't be included.
`numberOfLikesOnPost`	`Number-Of-Likes-On-Post`	Dash is a special character.

Table 3.2 Correct and incorrect examples of variable names *(continued)*

Correct	Incorrect	Why?
`_fileName`	`Name of File`	Spaces can't be included.
`fifth_File`	`5thFile`	A variable can't start with a digit.
`_import`	`import`	"import" is a reserved word. It has a special meaning in the programming language (e.g. "import UIKit"). These reserved words can't be used as variable names because Swift doesn't know if you're referring to the special meaning, or your variable name.

In case you'd like to know more about reserved words in Swift, here's a partial list:

- class
- import
- struct
- func
- IBOutlet

Hands on!

Try creating variables for each of the different types in the playground and then use `print()` to see the data, as in this example:

```
var playerName = "Anne"
print(playerName)
```

When you create strings, you have to use quotes around them.

What's the big deal? What happens if I do break one of these rules?

Simple: your code won't work. But the good news is that if you accidentally (or purposely) break one of these rules, Xcode reports the error to you, and you can fix it. Xcode won't say that you have a bad variable name, but it shows you an error message—something like in figure 3.2.

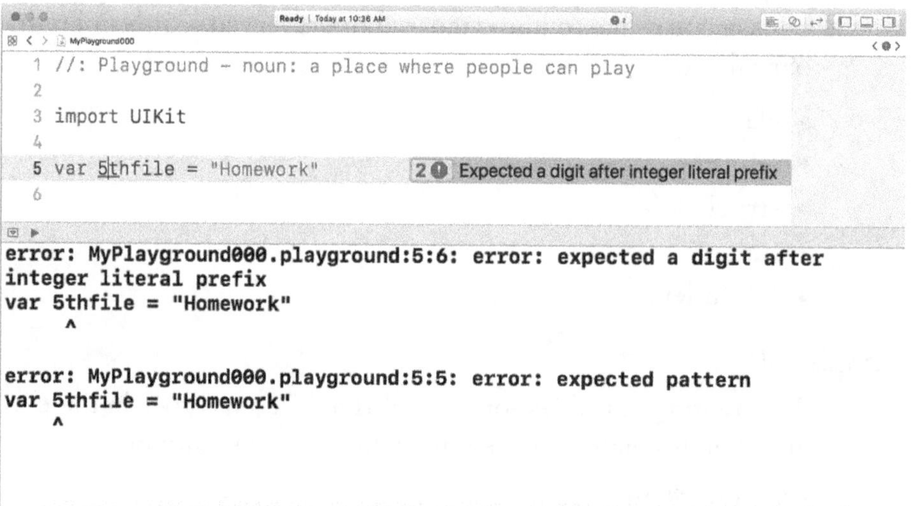

Figure 3.2 The Playground tells you that you broke a variable-naming rule.

Declaring variables and changing values

You tried creating some variables in the Playground earlier. In this section, you take a closer look at what it means when you create a variable. Then you see how to change the value that's stored in a variable after it's been created.

Declaring variables

In programming, creating a variable is called *declaring* a variable.

In Swift, if you were to declare (create) a variable named someonesAge that contains the value 23 (an integer), you'd do the following:

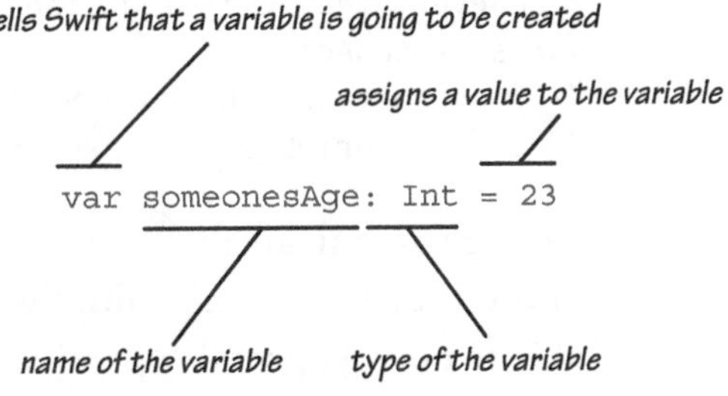


```
var someonesAge: Int = 23
// OR
var myAge = 11
```

To declare a variable of type String, you'd do the following:

```
var someonesName: String = "Johnny"
// OR
var name = "Julie"
```

What are those // marks?

Whenever you see // in the code, what follows it is a comment. You can write whatever you want after // on the same line; Swift ignores it and doesn't treat it like code. (Without the comment, the Swift compiler will give you an error.) If I type a comment in the code examples in this book, you don't need to write it in your code unless I tell you to (but you can if you want to). The comments here tell you what a particular line of code is doing or informs you of something.

The difference between the first and second variable declarations is that the first specifies that the variable should be an Int type with the number 23 stored in it. The second, however, leaves Swift to decide which type of variable it is; Swift correctly identifies it as an Int. Even though you don't have to, it's safer to tell Swift what kind of variable it is, and it's a good practice.

Sometimes, you need to create a variable, but you don't know the value of it yet. You may want to create a variable to hold the age of someone who uses your app, but before someone uses the app, there's no value available to store. What do you do? Well, in that case, you need to create a variable with no value. Here's how:

```
var someonesAge: Int!
//However, the following line will NOT work:
var someonesAge
//It doesn't work because Swift has no information to figure what
//kind of variable it's expected to create.
```

You must put an exclamation mark after the `Int` because Swift must know that you won't initially put anything in this variable. This variable is now a special type of variable called an `Optional`.

Pop quiz

See whether you can match each line of code with the text that describes it:

1 `var someonesAge: Int = 10`
2 `var someonesGrade: Int!`
3 `someonesAge = 11`
4 `someonesGrade = 6`

A A variable that didn't have a value now has one.
B A variable's value is being changed from one value to a different one.
C A variable is declared as an `Int` with a value in it.
D A variable is declared as an `Int` with nothing in it.

In this quiz, the age and grade are declared in different ways. If a variable already has something in it, it can still be changed; it can also be changed if it has nothing in it.

(Answers: 1. C; 2. D; 3. B; 4. A)

Changing variable's values

The important thing about using variables is that you can change the values they store. Suppose that you've created a game in which a player can go up in levels. When a player starts play, you might store his level as 1:

```
playerLevel = 1
```

When he goes up a level, you need to change his level to 2:

```
playerLevel = 2
```

In this section, you learn to store and update someone's age.

Hands on! Spying on data

NOTE You can find the code for this application in the Chapter03_Ex2.playground file inside the Hello-Swift-Code-master folder that you downloaded from GitHub. If you haven't downloaded the code from GitHub, go to: https://github.com/tanmayb123/Hello-Swift-Code/archive/master.zip. You should download the code only once for all chapters.

Let's display Amy's age and grade now, as well as one year later.

Spying on your data means viewing what's inside your variable while the app is running on an iDevice or simulator. (In this example, you're using a playground, not an app.)

You're not going to create an app yet, however. You start in the playground because you need to learn how to use it and create code in it before you create full apps.

Create a playground that displays the following:

```
Amy is 10 years old!
She is in grade 5!
1 year later...
Amy is now 11 years old!
She is in grade 6!
```

Type the code in listing 3.1 in the playground.

Listing 3.1 Spying on data

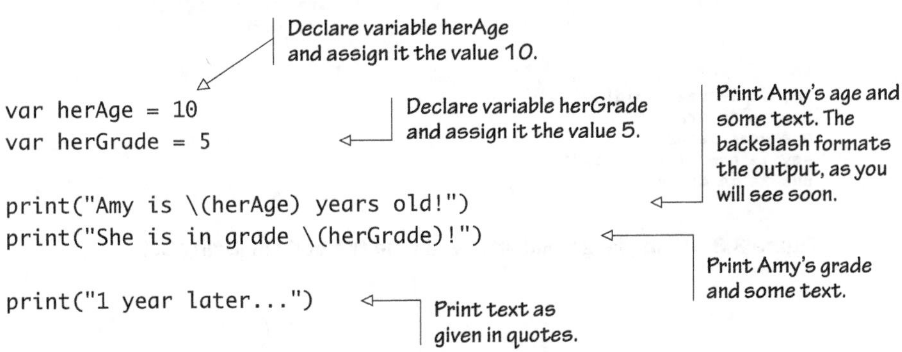


```
var herAge = 10
var herGrade = 5

print("Amy is \(herAge) years old!")
print("She is in grade \(herGrade)!")

print("1 year later...")
```

```
herAge = 11                                          ◁ Set value of variable herAge to 11.
herGrade = 6                                         ◁ Set value of variable herGrade to 6.
print("Amy is now \(herAge) years old!")             ◁ Print Amy's new age and some text.
print("She is in grade \(herGrade)!")                ◁ Print Amy's new grade and some text.
```

Your output will be kind of long, and not all of it may fit. If this situation happens to you, try this trick: hold down the Shift and Command keys at the same time, and then press the Y key. (Quick tip inside a tip: do the keys trick once more, and the bottom console log disappears!)

Your playground splits horizontally (left to right), and you should see the output at the bottom of the playground, as shown in figure 3.3.

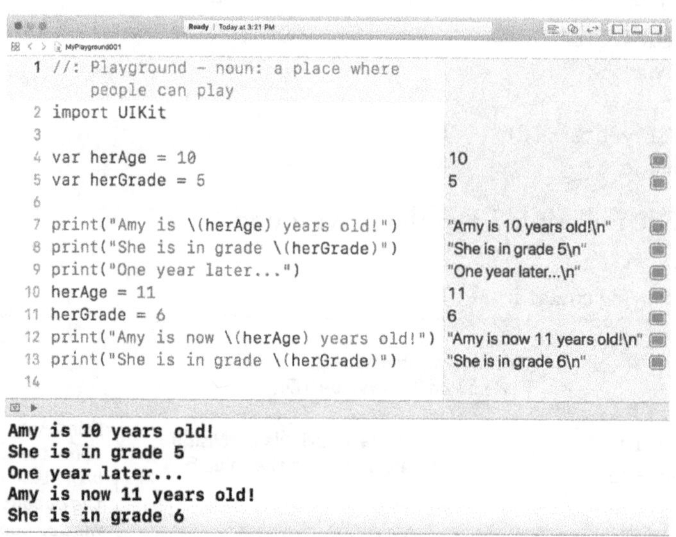

Figure 3.3 Your playground after you type the code in listing 3.1

Using \ and () to format text

In the code you typed in the Playground, I told you to use \, "", and () to format output. This code looks complicated, and you may wonder why you needed to type these things. Typing them allows you to put a variable's value in a `String`. If you typed `string1+string2` without "\()" covering it, Swift would print `string1+string2`. The same rule applies to the integers. Try entering the following code without "\()":

```
var string1 = "102"
var string2 = "3"
print("my output is 102+3=string1+string2")
```

Swift prints

```
my output is 102+3=string1+string2
```

This output isn't what you wanted to print, however. Now see what happens when you try enclosing `string1+string2` in "\()":

```
var string1 = "102"
var string2 = "3"
print("my output is 102+3=\(string1+string2)")
```

Swift prints

```
my output is 102+3=1023
```

Figure 3.4 shows you how all this code looks in the Playground.

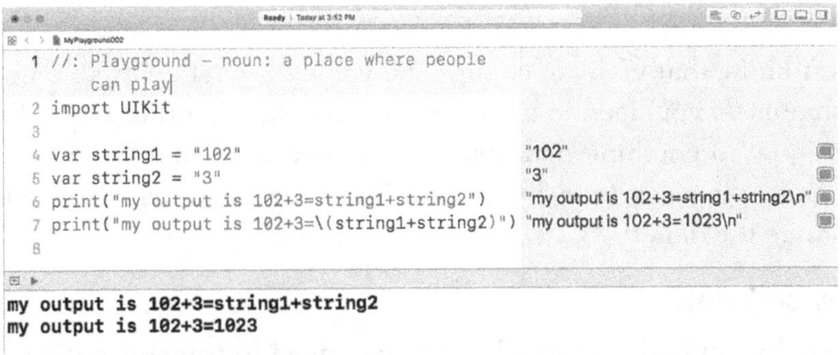

Figure 3.4 When you don't use \ and () to format your text output, Swift doesn't print the values of your variables.

That's it! You've learned to change variables after declaring them and print a variable's value with `print()` using `\()`. If you expected 105, you'll read next why you were surprised.

Pop quiz

Look at these variables:

- `var number1: Int = 1`
- `var number2: String = "1"`
- `var thing1: String = "Robot"`
- `var thing2: String = "Sponge"`

When you use these variables, what output do you get from each of these `print()` statements? Make your guess and then try them in the playground. (Hint: not all of them work.)

- `print(number1 + number1)`
- `print("\(thing1 + thing2)")`
- `print("\(thing1 + number1)")`
- `print(thing1 + number1)`
- `print(thing2 + thing1)`
- `print(thing2 + number1)`
- `print("(thing1 + number1)")`

What do you conclude from this pop quiz? Make a note of it.

Transforming your data

No, I don't mean the Robots in Disguise kind of Transformer. In this section, you learn some ways to transform your data and why you may need to.

You know that you can change the value of what a variable holds. But sometimes, you need to use or change the data in other ways. First, you see how to combine data with concatenation. Then you learn how to change the data type by converting your data, which is when you change the data type.

Concatenating data

To help you understand why you may need to transform your data, I'll tell you about concatenation. *Concatenating* is joining two or more strings of text by putting them one after another. If you add `"Spongebob"` and "Squarepants", for example, you get "SpongebobSquarepants". This format works when you're using string variables. But what do you think would happen if you had two string variables that contained numbers as their values?

You may have heard the joke 1 + 1 = 11. Well, in programming, this is sometimes true because strings store text, which can be any number of characters (any letter, symbol, or digit). If you add a string that stores "1" and another string that also stores "1", you get "11". Similarly, you add strings together by using a plus sign:

```
var first: String = "ro"
var second: String = "bot"

print(first + second)
```

You get the output

```
robot
```

Hands on!

Try concatenating data yourself. Go to the playground and type

```
var first: String = "home"
var second: String = "work"
print (first + second)
```

You should see the word homework.

Test these rules

Here are a few more things about concatenating strings to try. Using the playground code for concatenation as a model, change the strings and the operator in the print line to test these rules:

- You've seen that the + operator concatenates two strings but adds two integers. Try adding "2" to "3" first as strings and then as integers.
- Swift doesn't allow the use of -, *, or / in strings (but you may use them freely in integers). Try subtracting "ice" from "icecream".
- You can concatenate strings only with other strings; you can't mix strings and numbers in concatenation. Try adding the integer 2 to "dogs".

Converting data

NOTE You can find the code for this application in the Chapter03_Ex2playground file inside the Hello-Swift-Code-master folder that you downloaded from GitHub. If you haven't downloaded the code from GitHub, go to: https://github.com/tanmayb123/Hello-Swift-Code/archive/master.zip. You should download the code only once for all chapters.

Sometimes you'll be working with data that is a string, but you need to turn it into an integer.

Suppose that you made an app that asks a user to input two numbers, and your app adds them together. You get string input from users (*always* true by default). You have to convert the strings that the user gives you as input to integers or decimals, which you can mathematically add together.

This example is one reason why you may need to convert data. If you don't convert to integers and add, you get the *literal* output (such as `"2" + "18" = "218"`) because Swift thinks you're concatenating two strings.

With the types of variables you've learned, here are some conversions you can do:

- `String` to `Double` or `Int`

  Examples: `String "42"` to `Int 42`, `String "3.50"` to `Double 3.50`
- `Int` to `Double` or `String`

  Example: `Int 2015 to Double 2015.0, or Int 2015 to "2015"`
- `Double` to `Int` or `String`

  Example: `Double 3.14 to Int 3, or Double 3.14 to String "3.14"`

Now look at some code that converts two strings to two integers. This code has some new keywords that you haven't seen before, and I explain them soon. For now, see whether you can figure out how the keywords in listing 3.2 work.

Listing 3.2 Convert strings to integers

```
var string1: String = "12"
var string2: String = "34"
```

Creating the String values "12" and "34"

```
print("\(string1 + string2)")

var int1: Int = Int(string1)!
var int2: Int = Int(string2)!

print("\(int1 + int2)")
```

Printing the two String values added (concatenated) together

Creating two new Integers int1 and int2, which get the String values converted to Int type

Adding the two integers and printing the result

Figure 3.5 shows what you'll see if you try this code in the playground.

```
Ready | Today at 3:31 AM
MyPlayground003

//: Playground - noun: a place where
    people can play
import UIKit

var string1: String = "12"                 "12"
var string2: String = "34"                 "34"

print ("\(string1+string2)")               "1234\n"

var int1: Int = Int(string1)!              12
var int2: Int = Int(string2)!              34
print ("\(int1+int2)")                     "46\n"

1234
46
```

Figure 3.5 Converting strings to integers in the playground

What happens if I try to convert a string like "Fred" to an integer?

Simple: the app will crash. (Because "Fred" can't be converted to an integer, it has no numeric value.) For a string to be converted to an integer, it has to consist of all digits—and nothing else, such as "123", "-256", or even "23.41". You learn how to counter this problem in chapter 5.

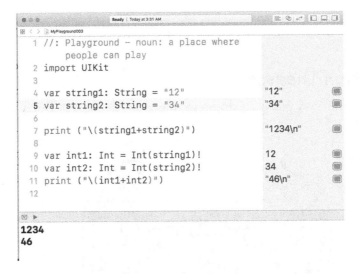

What else can I convert, and are there types that I can't convert?

I'm not going to get into this topic yet, but as an appetizer, here's a tip: when you convert something, it has to make sense. Example: you can convert a decimal to an integer, but Swift chops off the decimal part. You'll find other problems, such as memory sizes of different variable types, but it's too early in the book for me to describe them in detail. For example, if you try to convert 3.14 to Int, you will get 3. Swift will chop off .14 part of it.

Math Operation Theater

In this section, you learn to do some more math (sorry, but you have to) in Swift.

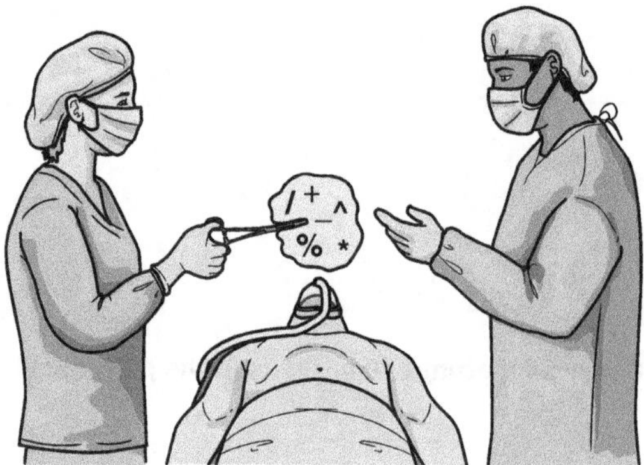

What is an operation?

NOTE You can find the code for this application in the Chapter03_Ex4.playground file inside the Hello-Swift-Code-master folder that you downloaded from GitHub. If you haven't downloaded the code from GitHub, go to: https://github.com/tanmayb123/Hello-Swift-Code/archive/master.zip. You should download the code only once for all chapters.

An *operator* (no, not the surgical one, the mathematical one) is something like +, -, *, or /. Here, * stands for multiplication, and / stands for division. An operation uses these operators on numbers such as `5 + 2 = 7`.

The operators can work with numbers or variables. Instead of writing `5 + 2` to get `7`, you can create code that writes a sentence for you.

Figure 3.6 shows code that you'll type in the playground and its output.

```
//: Playground - noun: a place where
    people can play
import UIKit

var a: Int = 5                                5
var b: Int = 2                                2
var c: Int = a + b                            7

print ("The value of c is\(c)")               "The value of c is7\n"

The value of c is7
```

Figure 3.6 Using an operator with numbers in the Playground

Here's an explanation of that code:

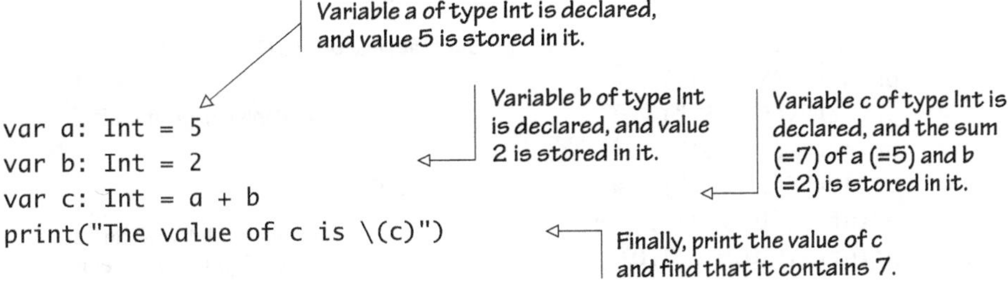

Now if you spy on the value of variable `c`, you get 7, as you'd get from `5 + 2`.

Swift has many more operators, and in the next section, I discuss the most common ones.

Do basic math with Swift (+, -, *, /)

In this section, I teach you how to do basic math in Swift. You're going to do a little bit of math in the playground so that you can see how easy it is. You'll add, subtract, multiply, and divide some integers and decimals.

```
//: Playground - noun: a place where
    people can play
import UIKit

print ("\(5+5)")        "10\n"
print ("\(5-5)")        "0\n"
print ("\(5*5)")        "25\n"
print ("\(5/5)")        "1\n"
print ("\(10/4)")       "2\n"
print ("\(10.0/4.0)")   "2.5\n"
```

```
10
0
25
1
2
2.5
```

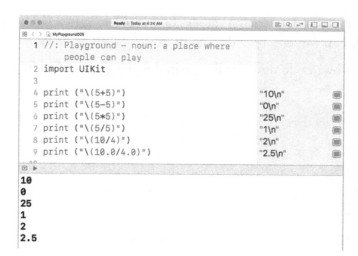

Figure 3.7 Doing math in the Playground

First, read the code in figure 3.7 without looking at the output. Can you predict the output?

Here's what each line of code was supposed to do. Were you able to figure out the output?

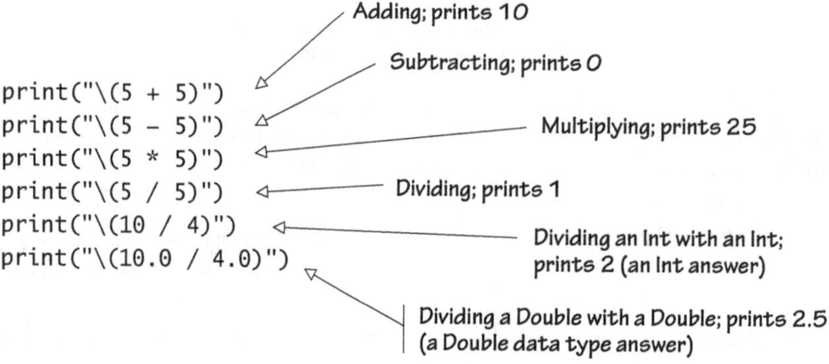

The operators +, –, *, and / are known as *binary operators* because they work on two numbers. The numbers on which these operators work are called *operands*.

You've learned basic operations in Swift. Wasn't that a piece of cake?

Doing math in a print() function

Can you do math only in a `print()` function? Not really. You can use math in lots of places in your code. You could use math to give a value to a variable, for example:

```
var myAnswer1: Double = 153 * 3
var myAnswer2: Double = myAnswer1 / 2
```

Why does this example use `Double`?

Caution! Sometimes you get unexpected results

Think about what 15 divided by 2 equals. Take a look at this code:

```
print("\(15 / 2)")
```

This line prints the result `15 / 2`, which is 7, not 7.5 as expected. Why?

You get 7 because both 15 and 2 are integers. Swift gives you back only the integer part of the answer if it finds an integer being divided by an integer. Swift doesn't do any rounding, either; it leaves off the decimal part of the answer. To prevent this situation, make sure that all your variables are the right types.

Back to the point: for any operation, use the number, its symbol, and the other number to get the result. Slightly more advanced operations may not work this way, however. You find out more in the next section.

Step up in math with Swift (square root, power, modulus)

You may not know or remember what some of these operators are: square root, power, and modulus. Table 3.3 explains.

Table 3.3 Some advanced math operators in Swift

Math operator and how it works	Explanation	Swift code
Square root $\sqrt{25}$ = 5, because 5x5 = 25 $\sqrt{16}$ = 4, because 4x4 = 16	What number times itself is equal to the number you're finding the square root of	`sqrt(25.0)` `sqrt(16.0)`

Table 3.3 Some advanced math operators in Swift *(continued)*

Math operator and how it works	Explanation	Swift code
Power 5^3 = 125, because 5x5x5=125 2^4 = 16, because 2x2x2x2=16	How many times to use the number in multiplication to get the answer	`pow(5.0, 3.0)` `pow(2.0, 4.0)`
Modulus 25 mod 4 = 1, because remainder of 25 / 4 is 1 15 mod 3 = 0, because remainder of 15 / 3 is 0	The remainder of a division problem	`25 % 4` `15 % 3`

Hands on!

Try these lines in the Playground:

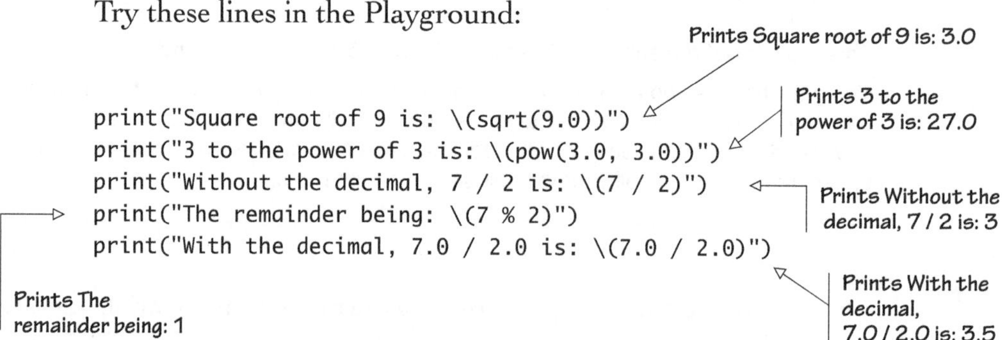
Prints Square root of 9 is: 3.0
Prints 3 to the power of 3 is: 27.0
Prints Without the decimal, 7 / 2 is: 3
Prints The remainder being: 1
Prints With the decimal, 7.0 / 2.0 is: 3.5

```
print("Square root of 9 is: \(sqrt(9.0))")
print("3 to the power of 3 is: \(pow(3.0, 3.0))")
print("Without the decimal, 7 / 2 is: \(7 / 2)")
print("The remainder being: \(7 % 2)")
print("With the decimal, 7.0 / 2.0 is: \(7.0 / 2.0)")
```

The first example gives you the square root of 9, which is equal to 3. The second example gives you 3 to the power of 3, which is equal to 27. The third example gives you how many times 2 goes into 7. The next example gives you the remainder when you divide 7 by 2, using the % operator called *modulus*; the result is 1 because you get the remainder 1 when you divide 7 by 2. Finally, you get 3.5 when you divide 7.0 by 2.0, because Swift knows that you're dividing a `Double` with a `Double`. The result is a `Double`: 3.5.

Advanced math in the playground

NOTE You can find the code for this application in the Chapter03_Ex6.playground file inside the Hello-Swift-Code-master folder that you downloaded from GitHub. If you haven't downloaded the code from GitHub, go to:

https://github.com/tanmayb123/Hello-Swift-Code/archive/master.zip. You should download the code only once for all chapters.

The code in this playground lets you try out these operations, some of which you'll use in your apps soon.

Open a new playground, and copy the following lines into it:

```
var squareRootOf9 = sqrt(9.0)
var power5to3 = pow(5.0, 3.0)
print("5 + 5 = \(5 + 5)")
print("5 - 5 = \(5 - 5)")
print("5 X 5 = \(5 * 5)")
print("5 / 5 = \(5 / 5)")
print("SQUARE ROOT of 9 = \(squareRootOf9)")
print("5 to the POWER of 3 = \(power5to3)")
print("5 MODULUS 3 = \(5 % 3)")
```

You'll see a lot of output pop up on the side, as shown in figure 3.8.

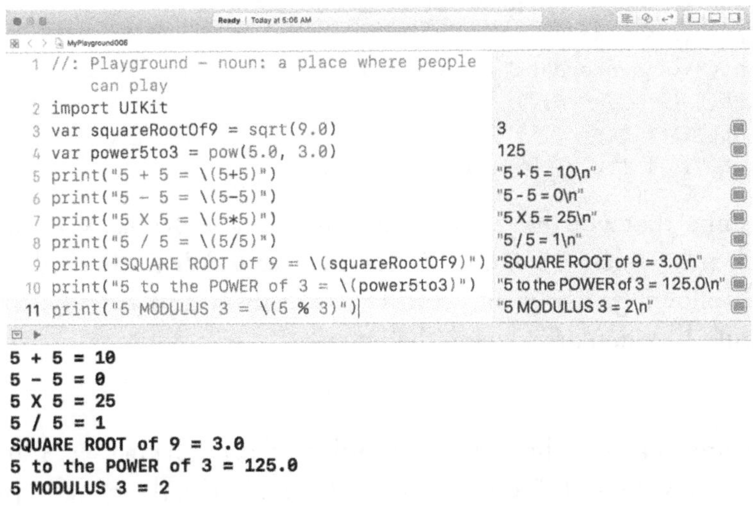

Figure 3.8 Advanced math in the playground

With this chapter, you've completed your third milestone: learning about variables and doing math. You're about to leave the playground level and move to coding apps.

Check your app knowledge

Try the following:

1 What are variables?

2 What is putting two strings together called?

3 Why is a variable called a variable?

4 What does *data conversion* mean?

5 Why might you need to convert data?

6 Write code to declare variables that hold these pieces of data:

```
"That pizza was so good!"
17
2.23
"15.49"
```

7 What is the output of the following commands? (Hint: some of them won't work. Can you figure out what's causing the errors?)

```
print("\("moon" + "light")")
print("\(25 % 4)")
print("\("Squarepants"-"pants")")
print("\(2 + 3 * 4)")
print("\("fifty" + 5)")
print("\("fifty" + "5")")
```

8 Assume that you have two variables of type `String`, `var1` and `var2`, with the values "13" and "25", respectively. Write the code to print the following, using only the two variables and `print()`. The sum should be calculated inside the `print()`.

```
13+25=38
```

9 Assume that you have two variables of type `String`, `var3` and `var4`, with the values "15" and "4", respectively. Write the code to print the following, using only the two variables and `print()`. The remainder should be calculated inside the `print()`.

```
If you divide 15 by 4, you get a remainder of 3.
```

4

I/O laboratory

Now we're going to learn how to make your users and your apps communicate with each other.

This chapter covers

- *Input: how your users communicate with your apps*
- *Output: how your app communicates with your users*
- *How to get input from a text field and show it as output*
- *What to do when things go wrong*

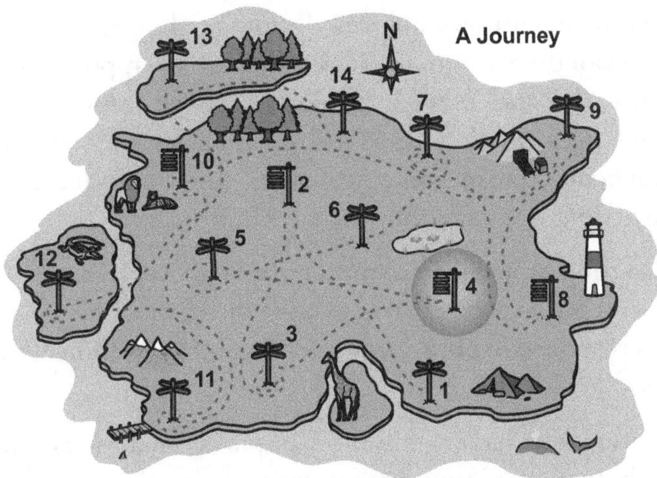

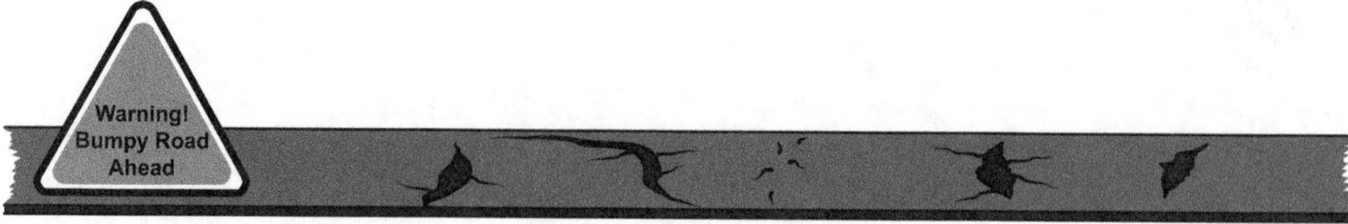

You've learned how to set up an app. Now that you know the basics, you can create apps that produce output in response to the input your users give them. In this chapter, you focus on input and output. And because you're going to be adding code to an app, now is a great time to learn how to fix your apps when you make mistakes and break rules.

When you're done creating apps in this chapter, you'll know how to get input from your user and display that input on the screen. Lots of steps are involved, so you'll build your app in chunks. Along the way, I'm going to show you what errors look like on purpose. Don't worry—I'll show you how to fix these errors. Here's what your path looks like:

1 Build an app that outputs text.
2 Run the app, and see an error.
3 Fix the error.
4 Add a text field.
5 Add code that lets your user input some text.
6 Display the input as output.

That's a lot of pieces, but they're all easy.

How apps and users interact

Every day, computers help us do lots of things, such as browsing the web, responding to email, reminding us of appointments, interacting with friends, and playing games. Each of these tasks begins when someone presses a key, taps a screen, clicks a mouse button, types on the keyboard, or in some way tells the computer to do something. These actions are called input.

After getting input, the computer starts processing and then shows you the result, plays a song, prints a document, or sends an email. The computer's response to your input is called *output*. Figure 4.1 describes this process.

Computers also have some built-in parts, or devices attached to them, that help them get input from users and give the users output. A mouse,

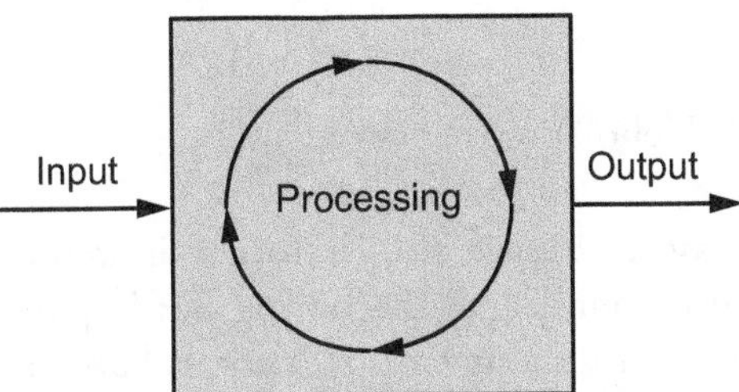

Figure 4.1 A computer takes input, does the processing, and gives output.

for example, is an input device; so are keyboards, cameras, and microphones. For output devices, think of printers, monitors, and speakers. Some devices can be both input and output devices. A touchscreen, for example, is both an input and an output device.

How users get output

NOTE You can find the code for this application in the Chapter04_MessageMagic file inside the Hello-Swift-Code-master folder that you downloaded from GitHub. If you haven't downloaded the code from GitHub, go to: https://github.com/tanmayb123/Hello-Swift-Code/archive/master.zip. You should download the code only once for all chapters.

Output is produced by the code in your app. You're about to start building apps that give users output, which means that you'll be changing and adding code.

In this section, you're going to build an app that gives the user output, and you'll name this app Message Magic.

Start with Hello World!

You're going to start where you left off with the Hello World! app you created in chapter 1 and add some code to it.

If you don't remember how you built Hello World!, take a few minutes to reread the instructions, and build it again from scratch—only this time, change the label's text to Message Magic and the name of the app to Message Magic.

Why do I have to build Hello World! over again?

Sometimes, the best way to learn a skill is to use it again. Practice makes perfect! Do you remember all the boring but important steps you had to go through to set up a new app? You probably remember more than you think you do. This task is a good chance for you to get some extra practice going through the setup steps for new apps. Here's a little cheat sheet for you, and if you've forgotten, all the steps are in chapter 1.

Here's a quick reminder of the steps you need to take to get started:

1 Create a new project.
2 Choose the project options.
3 Save the project.
4 Open the main storyboard.
5 Change the screen size.
6 Drag a label to the view.

Add a variable to hold the label

Here's where you change your Message Magic app by customizing a few things on the main screen.

Right now, when you start the app, you see the label Message Magic. You want the screen to display a new message: Hey, Frank! Although you could change the label to say Hey, Frank!, you want to be able to change the label in your code.

To make Hey, Frank! show up, you need to add two lines of code to one of your app's files.

OPEN THE VIEW CONTROLLER

In Xcode, with your app open, click the file named ViewController.swift, as you see in figure 4.2. You'll see a bunch of code. Don't panic! You're only going to add two lines.

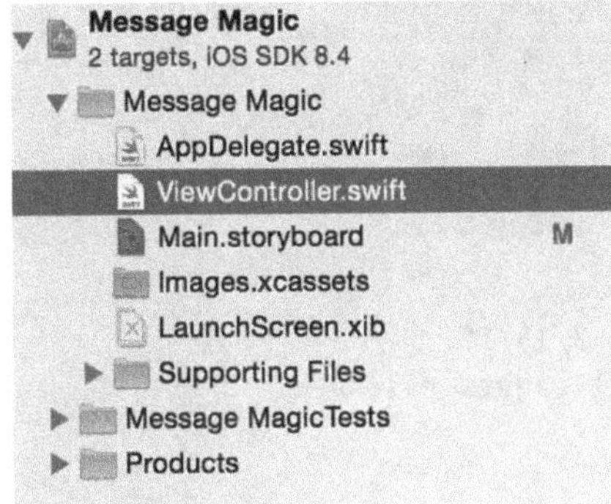

Figure 4.2 This file is listed in the pane on the left side of Xcode in the Project Navigator. After you click it, you see code in the main panel. That panel is where you'll add new code.

ADD CODE FOR THE LABEL

You'll be adding the following two lines of code. Take a look; then I'll tell you where to put them. You're creating a variable where you can store the text that you want your label to display:

```
@IBOutlet var outputLabel: UILabel!     <- Declaring the outputLabel IBOutlet of type UILabel

outputLabel.text = "Hey, Frank!"        <- Storing Hey, Frank! in the text of the variable outputLabel
```

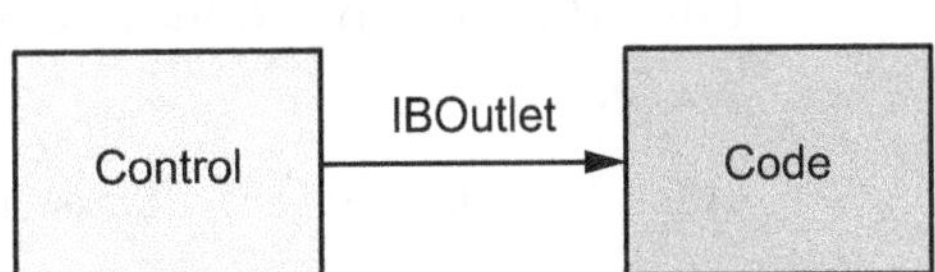

Figure 4.3 Controls must be linked to the code through `IBOutlets` so you can use the code to make the label control's text change. `UILabel` is a control. `UIButton`, `UITextField`, and `UITextView` are also controls.

The first line declares a variable called `outputLabel` of type `UILabel`. Think of `UILabel` as meaning *user interface label*. The exclamation point (`!`) tells Swift that the label's value isn't yet known. `@IBOutlet` is a keyword that helps link controls from the interface builder to the code you'll write. `IBOutlet` stands for *interface builder outlet*. Figure 4.3 shows the relationship between controls and the code through `IBOutlets`.

The second line sets the text stored in the new variable `outputLabel` to Hey, Frank!

EDIT THE VIEWCONTROLLER.SWIFT FILE

You should see this code:

```
//
//  ViewController.swift
//  MessageMagic
//
//  Created by Tanmay Bakshi on 2/13/15.
//  Copyright (c) 2015 TBSS. All rights reserved.
//
import UIKit

class ViewController: UIViewController {

    override func viewDidLoad() {
        super.viewDidLoad()
        // Do any additional setup after loading the view, typically
        ➥ from a nib.
    }

    override func didReceiveMemoryWarning() {
        super.didReceiveMemoryWarning()
        // Dispose of any resources that can be recreated.
    }
}
```

Find this line of code, and put your cursor after the opening curly brace:

```
class ViewController: UIViewController {
```

Press the Return key twice, and type this code on a blank line:

```
@IBOutlet var outputLabel: UILabel!
```

You have one more line to add to the code. Find the end of this line:

```
super.viewDidLoad()
```

Press the Return key one time and type this line in the blank space you created:

```
outputLabel.text = "Hey, Frank!"
```

Now your code, with the two lines added, should look like that in listing 4.1.

Listing 4.1 Message Magic code with `outputLabel`

```
import UIKit

class ViewController: UIViewController {

    @IBOutlet var outputLabel: UILabel!              // The first line of code is inserted here.

    override func viewDidLoad() {
        super.viewDidLoad()
        outputLabel.text = "Hey, Frank!"             // The second line of code is inserted here.
        // Do any additional setup after
        ➥ loading the view, typically from a nib.
    }
    override func didReceiveMemoryWarning() {
        super.didReceiveMemoryWarning()
        // Dispose of any resources that can be recreated.
    }

}
```

WARNING If you were to run the app at this point, you'd get an exception. An exception happens when something wrong in your program causes it to break when it's running.

What is an exception, and how is it different from an error?

An *exception* is a crash in your program caused by a mistake that can be found *only* during runtime (when your app is running). If your code has an error, you can't run your app if the error is still there. In the case of an exception, you can still run your app, but it will stop as that line of code is run and the exception occurs.

An *error* is some mistake in the code: a misspelled word, a missing bracket, or some other kind of typographical error. Errors can also be mistakes, such as declaring variables incorrectly or assigning an integer value to a variable that's been declared as being of the `String` type.

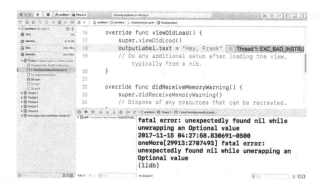

```
override func viewDidLoad() {
    super.viewDidLoad()
    outputLabel.text = "Hey, Frank"   Thread 1: EXC_BAD_INSTRU
    // Do any additional setup after loading the view,
        typically from a nib.
}

override func didReceiveMemoryWarning() {
    super.didReceiveMemoryWarning()
    // Dispose of any resources that can be recreated.

fatal error: unexpectedly found nil while
unwrapping an Optional value
2017-11-15 04:27:58.830691-0500
oneMore[29913:2707493] fatal error:
unexpectedly found nil while unwrapping an
Optional value
(lldb)
```

Figure 4.4 The exception you receive when you run Message Magic for the first time

WHEN YOU RUN THIS CODE, YOU'LL GET AN EXCEPTION, BUT YOU'RE GOING TO FIX IT

That's it for the code, but you're not done yet. If you try to run the program, you'll get an exception that looks like figure 4.4. When you get this exception, your app freezes on the simulator or device, and a green line appears on a line of code. This green line is where the code stopped, but the line sometimes doesn't tell you exactly where the mistake is.

You also see an error message in the bottom-right corner of your screen: `Swift compiler: fatal error: unexpectedly found nil while unwrapping an Optional value (lldb)`

The exception happened because you don't have anything inside the outputLabel variable and you are trying to set its text to `"Hey, Frank!"`. You're trying to tell a label control to change its text, but you haven't connected your code with the actual control. You can get rid of this exception after you connect your label control with your `IBOutlet`.

What's a compiler?

A *compiler* is a behind-the-scenes "miracle" program that translates the code that you write in English into code called *machine language* or *binary* that your computer understands.

Connect your label variable to a label in the view

To fix the exception, you must connect the label control to the outlet, IBOutlet, to give outputLabel a text value.

OPEN THE MAIN STORYBOARD

Open Main.storyboard by clicking it (refer to figure 4.2).

CONNECT THE LABEL AND THE VARIABLE

Right-click and drag from the yellow icon (View Controller) to the label, as shown in figure 4.5. This step draws a temporary blue line from the View Controller to the label with the text `Message Magic`.

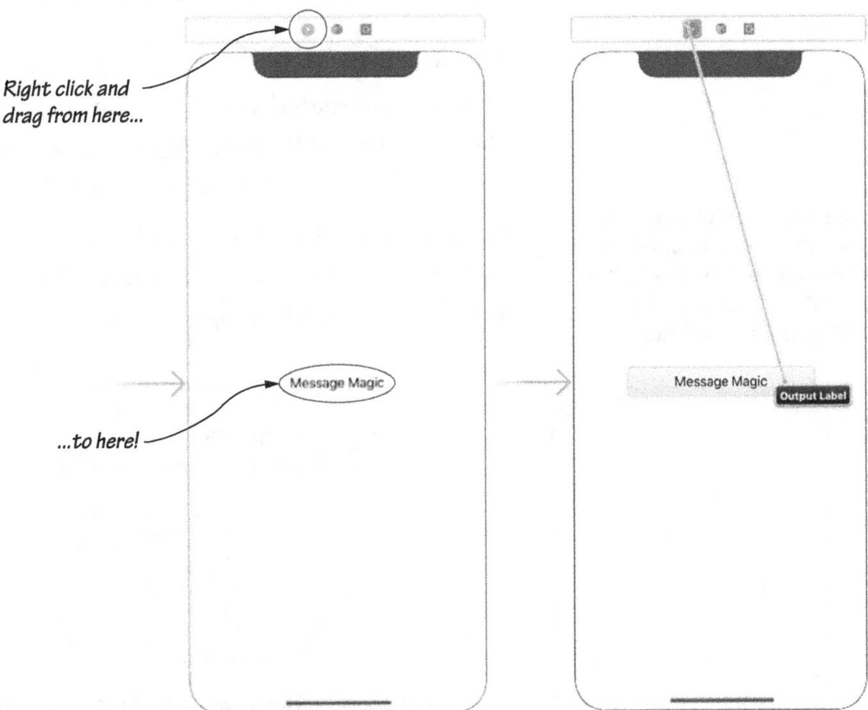

Figure 4.5 Connect the `UILabel` to the `IBOutlet`. Right-click and drag to connect your `Label` to `IBOutlet`.

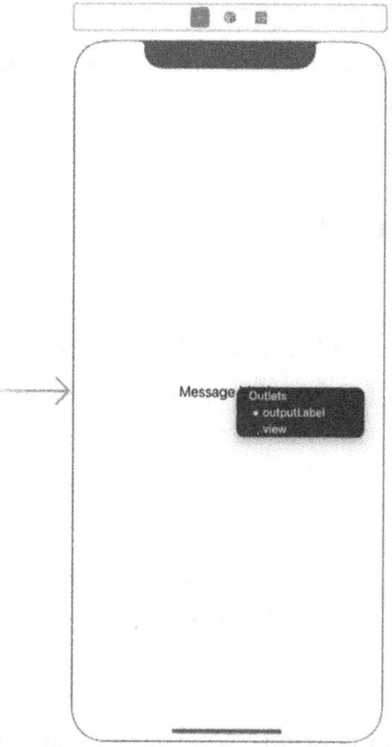

Figure 4.6 Select `outputLabel` as the `IBOutlet` to connect to. Remember `outputLabel`? You added this variable to the ViewController.swift file.

A dark list pops up, and the blue line disappears when you release the mouse button. This dark list shows you the `outputLabel` variable you created (figure 4.6).

Click outputLabel, which is the first option in the list.

RUN THE APP; THE EXCEPTION SHOULD BE GONE

Now when you run your app (you shouldn't get an error or exception), you see the text you stored in the variable show up as the label text. The label text Message Magic is replaced by the text in your variable, as shown in figure 4.7.

The Interface Builder

When you created this app, you set the text of the label to say `Message Magic`. What happened to it? Why is it showing `Hey, Frank!`?

`Message Magic` has been replaced because the code you added is executed after the Interface Builder, as shown in figure 4.8.

Figure 4.7 The main screen

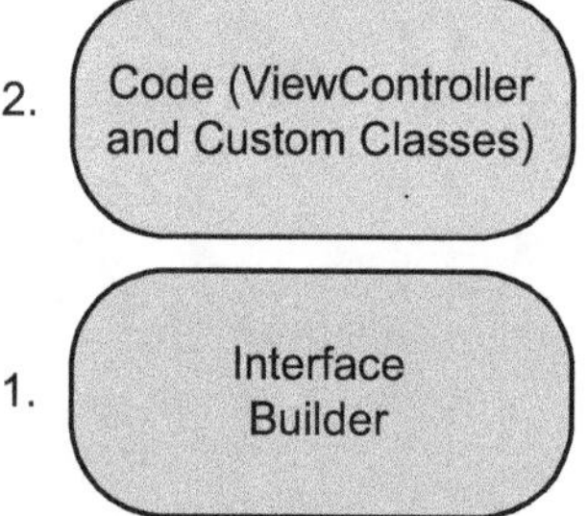

Figure 4.8 The sequence of the execution of IB (Interface Builder) and code is controlled by Xcode priority levels. The IB is executed first. Your code is executed after the IB loads, so, if you make a change in your code to a control that was already in the IB, that change is overridden by your code.

TIP You put your code in a function called `viewDidLoad()`. When you run the app and the view loads, whatever code is inside that function will execute.

Now your app is able to change the text of a label to the text you saved in a variable in the code. This capability is useful if you want to change the label's text while the app is running, but it's not so useful if you need user input for the label's text. To solve this problem, change the app to let your users type words, and then use those entries to change the label's text.

Users give apps input

Input is some data or response that the user gives an app so that the app can perform a task or work on that data. Table 4.1 shows some examples.

Table 4.1 App and input examples

App	Input
Calculator	Numbers and operators, such as +, -, x, and ÷
Notes	Text to store
Greeting Generator	Your name
Health	Your age and weight
Timer	Time to count down from

You should be able to think of lots more examples. Look at your favorite apps, and notice what kind of input they ask you for when you use them.

If you want your users to be able to enter text as input, you need to give them a place to type (a text box) and a button to click when they're done, so you'll know when to grab their input text.

To see how this process works, you'll modify Message Magic to create Catch & Throw: an app that catches the user's input and throws it back at him.

NOTE You can find the code for this application in the Chapter04_Catch-Throw file inside the Hello-Swift-Code-master folder that you downloaded from GitHub. If you haven't downloaded the code from GitHub, go to: https://github.com/tanmayb123/Hello-Swift-Code/archive/master.zip. You should download the code only once for all chapters.

In the next few sections, you learn how to

- Add a text field to an app so that the user can type some text.
- Add a button, that when clicked, tells the app to grab what the user typed in the text field.
- Link the new text field to the code.
- Add a function to grab the text input from the text field and display it as the label's text when the button is clicked.

Add a text field and button to the app

You need to add a text field so that your users can give you input.

OPEN THE MAIN STORYBOARD

Open Main.storyboard by clicking it (refer to figure 4.2).

ADD A TEXT FIELD AND BUTTON

Find and click the Object Library in the bottom-right pane, as shown in figure 4.9. Scroll down until you find Text Field; then click and drag a text field to the view in the main storyboard.

Find Button, then click and drag a button to the view in the main storyboard.

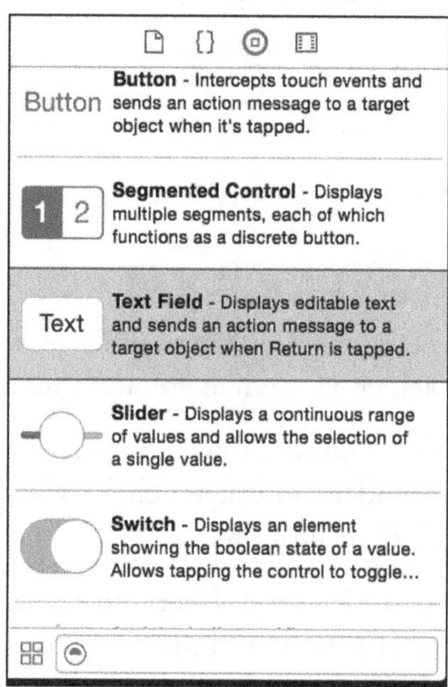
Button
Button - Intercepts touch events and sends an action message to a target object when it's tapped.
1 2
Segmented Control - Displays multiple segments, each of which functions as a discrete button.
Text
Text Field - Displays editable text and sends an action message to a target object when Return is tapped.
Slider - Displays a continuous range of values and allows the selection of a single value.
Switch - Displays an element showing the boolean state of a value. Allows tapping the control to toggle...

Figure 4.9 Getting a text field from the Object Explorer

Add code to connect the text field to code

In this section, you add a line to your code.

CREATE AN IBOUTLET

First, you create a variable (an `IBOutlet`) that stores what the user types in the text field. This variable should look familiar:

```
@IBOutlet var userInput: UITextField!
```

Edit your ViewController.swift file so that it looks like this:

Listing 4.2 The code to add the `userInput` text field

```
import UIKit

class ViewController: UIViewController {

@IBOutlet var outputLabel: UILabel!   //You added this earlier for
➥ your label.
@IBOutlet var userInput: UITextField!
//This is what you'll link to
➥ the text field.

    override func view DidLoad() {
        super.viewDidLoad()
        outputLabel.text = "Hey, Frank!" //added 4.1 -- This is what
➥ the Label will say before you change it to what the user types.
        // Do any additional setup after loading the view, typically
        ➥ from a nib.
    }

override func didReceiveMemoryWarning() {
        super.didReceiveMemoryWarning()
        // Dispose of any resources that can be re-created.
    }
}
```

This line declares an IBOutlet called userInput of type UITextField. Think of UITextField as standing for user interface text field. The exclamation point tells Swift that the value isn't yet known.

Don't I have to add an `@IBOutlet` line for the button?

Great question. The button doesn't need to store anything as a variable, so you don't need to create one for it. You do need to add a function and connect the button to it, but you're not there quite yet.

CONNECT THE IBOUTLET TO THE CODE

To finish setting up the text field, you need to connect it to the code you've already added, as follows:

1 Click the Main.storyboard file to open the main storyboard.
2 Control-click the yellow circle (View Controller), drag to the text field, and then release the mouse button.
3 Choose userInput from the dark menu.

Now the text field has the name `userInput` and is connected to your code. Figure 4.10 shows you how this connection will look in your app and in your code.

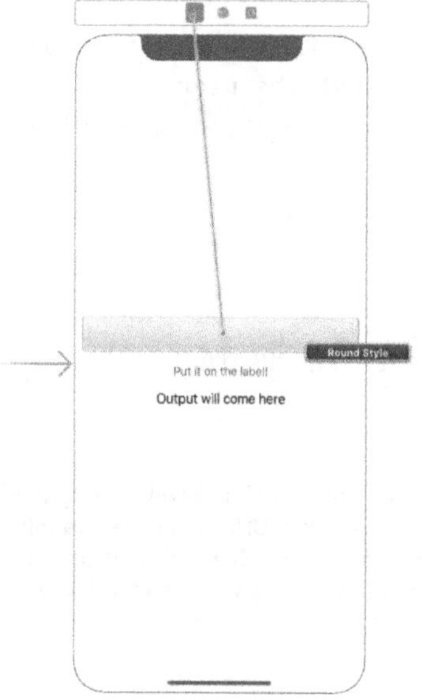


```
class ViewController: UIViewController {

    @IBOutlet var outputLabel: UILabel!
    @IBOutlet var userInput: UITextField!
```

Figure 4.10 Connecting the `TextField` to its `IBOutlet`

Before you can use the Text Field to grab input from the user, the Text Field control needs to be linked to the code. To do this, give your controls names that you can use in your code to call them.

Add the function to change the label text to input text

You're ready for the last bit of code you need to change. Add a function that says, "When someone clicks the button, change the text of the label to whatever is in the text field."

You'll be adding only the little bit of code that's shaded gray in listing 4.3. Ready?

Listing 4.3 Implementing the `UIButton`

```
import UIKit

class ViewController: UIViewController {

    @IBOutlet var outputLabel: UILabel! //added 4.1
    @IBOutlet var userInput: UITextField! //      <- This is what you'll link to the text field.

    override func viewDidLoad() {
        super.viewDidLoad()
        outputLabel.text = "Hey, Frank!"
        // Do any additional setup after loading the view, typically
        ➥ from a nib.
    }

    @IBAction func displayToLabel() {
        outputLabel.text = userInput.text
    }

    override func didReceiveMemoryWarning() {
        super.didReceiveMemoryWarning()
        // Dispose of any resources that can be recreated.
    }

}
```

In this code, you declared the `IBAction` with the `@IBAction` tag and then the keyword `func`. `@IBAction` says you want to create an action for a button, and the `func` part tells Swift that you're creating a function. After the opening brace, you're telling Swift that the code you'll type in will be executed by a button click; in other words, this opening brace indicates the start of the function code. The closing brace tells Swift that you're no longer typing code for that button; in other words, this closing brace is the end of the function code. (You learn more about functions in chapter 8.) The `displayToLabel()` part is the name of the function. This name is what you use to access it in the IB (like the name of the `IBOutlet`).

NOTE To connect the `IBAction` to a button, you right-click and drag from the button to the View Controller, not the other way around, as you do for `IBOutlets`.

To connect your button to the function you've added, do the following:

1. Click the Main.storyboard file to open the main storyboard.
2. Control-click the button, and drag up to the yellow circle (View Controller).
3. Choose displayToLabel from the dark menu, as shown in figure 4.11.

Figure 4.11 Selecting which `IBAction` to link the button to

Can I make the button say something other than "Button"?

Sure. Double-click it and then type what you want it to say—maybe something like Change Text.

When you're done with all that, you're ready to run your app; the results should look like figure 4.12.

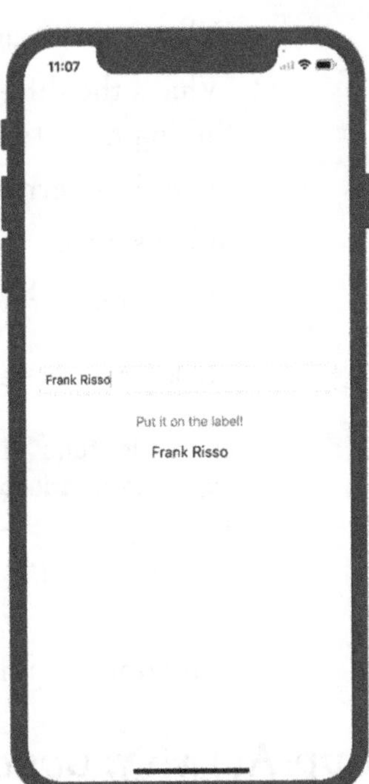

Figure 4.12 Running the Catch & Throw app

You may wonder how your app knew when to get the text from the text field. This is where an `IBAction` (Interface Builder Action) kicks in, as shown in figure 4.13. An `IBAction` handles Button Click actions. Button Click actions are special functions that can be linked to a button in the IB. The IB recognizes the `IBAction` and allows you to link it to a button so that the button performs the code in the function whenever it's clicked.

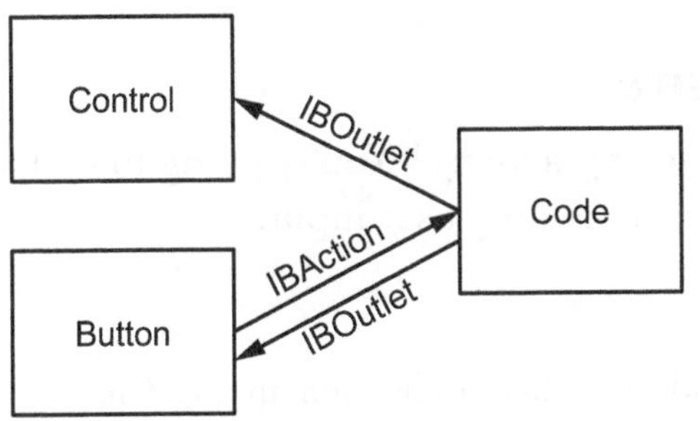

Figure 4.13 Buttons and other controls must be linked to the code.

Check your app knowledge

1 Fill in the blanks in the following sentences:

A A(n) ________ connects controls from the Interface Builder to the ViewController.

B. A(n) ________ allows the code to receive actions from buttons.

C. A(n) ________ occurs when the code breaks unexpectedly during runtime; this couldn't have been caught during compilation.

2 What's the difference between input and output? What's the difference between input devices and output devices? What are some devices that can take input *and* give output?

3 What is an `IBOutlet`, and what is an `IBAction`?

4 What's the difference between linking a button with an `IBAction` and linking a control with an `IBOutlet`?

5 What is an error, and what is an exception?

6 What's wrong with the following code?

```
class ViewController: UIViewController {

@IBOutlet var textField: UITextField

override func viewDidLoad() {
super.viewDidLoad()
}

}
```

7 Why don't you need `IBOutlets` for `UIButtons`?

App-Activity: Concatenate

It's time for the Concatenate app-activity! You're going to build an app dedicated to concatenating and adding user input.

What does this app do?

NOTE You can find the code for this application in the Chapter04_App-Activity file inside the Hello-Swift-Code-master folder that you downloaded from GitHub. If you haven't downloaded the code from GitHub, go to: https://github.com/tanmayb123/Hello-Swift-Code/archive/master.zip. You should download the code only once for all chapters.

This app has two text fields in which the user can enter two words *or* two numbers. If the user clicks the Concatenate button, the app should concatenate the numbers or words and display them in the label `Output Comes Here`. For concatenation to happen, the user can input any alphabetic characters or numbers. If the user enters `5` and `Stars`, for example, the label should display `5Stars`. But if the user clicks the Add button, the app should add the numbers and display the result in the label. For the Add button to function, the user should input digits only.

Create the UI

In this app-activity, you create an app with the UI (user interface; remember?) shown in figure 4.14.

You can customize this UI to look the way you want.

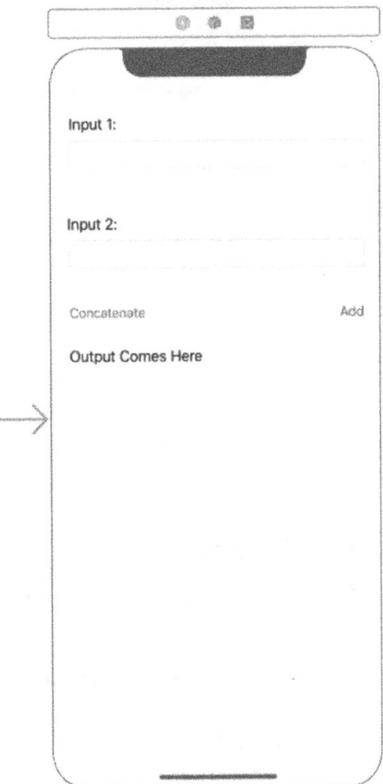

Figure 4.14 The UI you need to make

Code the app

If you're wondering where the code is, it isn't here! This problem is a challenge for you to complete. Try your best to create the code. If you have trouble, you can refer to or copy the code you just downloaded for this app.

App-Exercise: Greeting Generator

Now it's time for the Greeting Generator app-exercise! You're going to build an app dedicated to greeting people.

What does this app do?

NOTE You can find the code for this application in the Chapter04_Greeting-Generator file inside the Hello-Swift-Code-master folder that you downloaded from GitHub. If you haven't downloaded the code from GitHub,go to: https://github.com/tanmayb123/Hello-Swift-Code/archive/master.zip. You should download it only once for all chapters.

In the Greeting Generator, you type a name (input), and when you click a button, the app displays a greeting addressed to the name you typed. That is, your app takes input, has a button, and provides output.

Create the UI

Let's start! Create a new app, and make a UI that looks like figure 4.15.

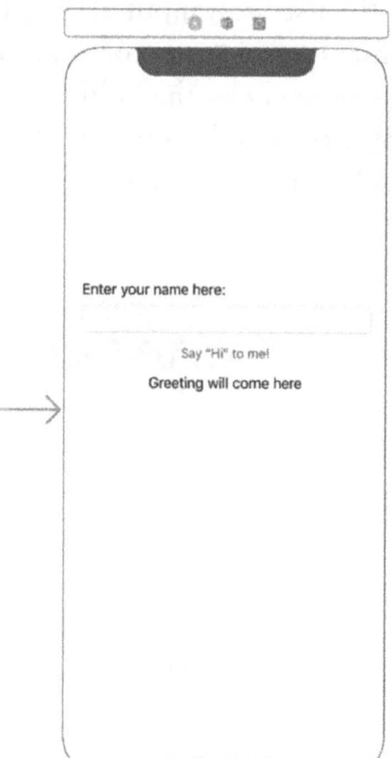

Figure 4.15 Greeting Generator UI

Code the app

Now go to your code, and make it look like this:

Listing 4.4 *Greeting Generator code*

```
import UIKit

class ViewController: UIViewController {

    @IBOutlet var input: UITextField!
```

The IBOutlet for the input text field, in which the user provides input

```
    @IBOutlet var output: UILabel!

    override func viewDidLoad() {
        super.viewDidLoad()
        // Do any additional setup after loading
        ➥ the view, typically from a nib.
    }

    @IBAction func displayGreeting() {

        output.text = "Hi, \(input.text)"
    }

    override func didReceiveMemoryWarning() {
        super.didReceiveMemoryWarning()
        // Dispose of any resources that can be re-created.
    }
}
```

The IBOutlet for the output label, in which the application provides output to the user

The declaration of the displayGreeting IBAction—the code that will be called when the user clicks the button

This line of code sets the output label's text to Hi and then whatever the user put in the input textfield.

CONNECT IBOUTLETS AND IBACTIONS

Now go to your Interface Builder and connect your label to the output `IBOutlet` and your text field to the input `IBOutlet`. After that, connect your button to the `displayGreeting IBAction`.

Run the app

Done! Run your app. You should see output similar to figure 4.16 after entering a name in the text field and clicking the button.

In chapter 5, the computer decides what to and what not to do.

Figure 4.16 The Greeting Generator app in action!

5

Computers make decisions, too!

This chapter is all about how to write code that makes decisions.

This chapter covers

- *What conditions are*
- *How to use conditions to make decisions in programming*
- *How to use a basic* `if` *statement in condition checking*
- *How to use the* `else` *and* `else if` *clauses with the* `if` *statement*
- *What the basic conditional operators are*
- *What the* `switch` *statement is and how to use it*

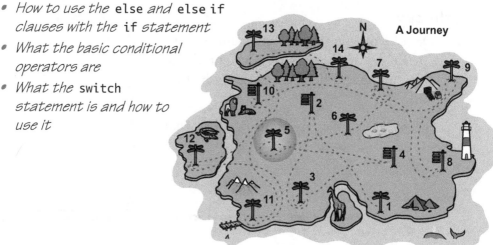

You're all set to cover your fifth milestone: Computers make decisions, too! You make decisions all the time. You decide to do something depending on some bit of information in life. If it's raining, for example, you use an umbrella. You make the decision to carry an umbrella based on whether or not it's raining.

Your code needs to make decisions, too. Imagine an app that can tell you whether you need an umbrella. This app checks to see whether it's raining. If so, the app outputs the information that you need an umbrella.

Conditions with the `if` statement

Think of a *condition* as a question that can have only a true or false answer. If the answer, or *result*, of the condition is *true*, you do something. You use conditions all the time without even noticing. Table 5.1 shows some examples of simple conditions.

Table 5.1 Examples of simple conditions

Condition	Result
If the weather is cold = TRUE	Wear a coat.
If I am thirsty = TRUE	Drink something.
If I am sick = TRUE	Don't go to school.

Pop quiz

Try to come up with some missing conditions and results:

Condition	Result
If ____________________ = TRUE	Put on pajamas.
If my hair is too long = TRUE	____________________.
If ____________________ = TRUE	Study all evening.

IF THIS IS TRUE, DO SOMETHING

Your code can also use conditions to figure out whether it needs to do something. Using an `if` statement, your code can

- Check whether a user answered correctly in a math game and then give him a point.
- Check whether a user entered the correct password and then let her play the game.

Here are a few more examples of conditions you might use in code:

- If your number of coins is greater than 150, you get a powerup.
- If your score is more than 90 percent, your grade is A+.
- If your score is less than 50 percent, you have the option of a retest.

Until now, the conditions you've seen in this book are mostly of the type "if this equals something." The conditions I'm going to show you are different. They're math comparisons, such as > (greater than) and < (less than).

App: Which Number Is Bigger?

Now that you know how `if` statements let you make decisions, you're ready to learn how apps can use them.

Here's a quick reminder of the steps you need to take to get started:

1 Create a new project.
2 Choose the project options.
3 Save the project.
4 Open the main storyboard.
5 Change the screen size.
6 Drag a label to the view.

What does this app do?

You're about to create an app that takes two numbers and tests this condition: which number is bigger?

NOTE You can find the code for this application in the Chapter05_a1-_WhichNumberIsBigger file inside the Hello-Swift-Code-master folder that you downloaded from GitHub. If you haven't downloaded the code from

GitHub, go to: https://github.com/tanmayb123/Hello-Swift-Code/archive/master.zip. You should download the code only once for all chapters.

The Which Number Is Bigger? app will do the following:

- Get two numbers as input.
- Use an `if` statement with a condition that compares the numbers.
- Display whichever number is bigger.

The user interface (UI) looks like figure 5.1.

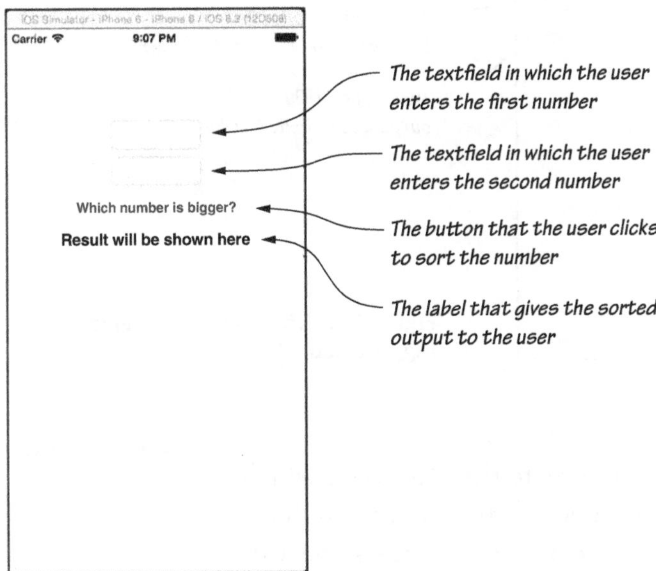

Figure 5.1 Overview of UI for the Which Number Is Bigger? app

Set up the project

To start, create a project:

1. Go to Xcode.
2. Click Create a New Xcode Project.
3. Fill out the info.

Create the UI

Next, make a UI that looks like the one in figure 5.2. Drag two text fields, a label, and a button to the view. (Check out chapter 4 if you've forgotten how.) The details for each control are in figure 5.2.

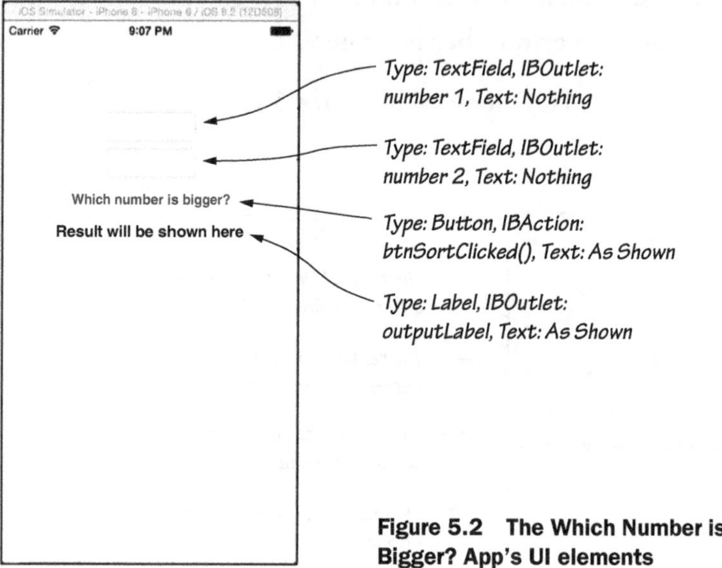

Figure 5.2 The Which Number is Bigger? App's UI elements

Code the app

Now you have to create the `IBOutlets`, which allow controls such as text fields to have names your code can use, to access the values your users will enter in them. You also have to create the `IBActions`, which let you connect controls such as buttons to the code to be executed when they're clicked.

Figure 5.3 shows you how your app will look when it's done if you use the numbers 8 and 6 as inputs.

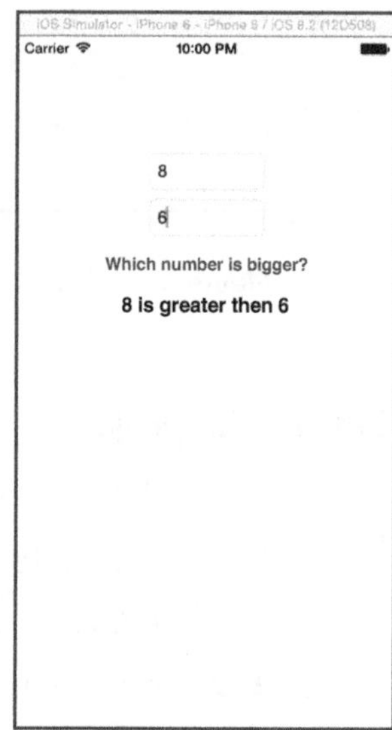

Figure 5.3 Your completed app and output if you use the numbers 8 and 6 as inputs

Open the ViewController.swift file, which is where you'll add your code. You may remember from chapter 4 where to put the `IBOutlets` and `IBActions`, but in case you don't, I've put them in listing 5.1 so that you can check your work.

Here's the code you need to add to create `IBOutlets`:

```
@IBOutlet var number1: UITextField!
@IBOutlet var number2: UITextField!
@IBOutlet var outputLabel: UILabel!
```

This line creates a variable, number1, that holds the number your user enters in the top text field.

This line creates the variable named number2 that holds the number in the bottom text field.

Can you guess what this variable does? You'll find out soon!

And here's how to create `IBActions`:

```
@IBAction func btnSortClicked() {
    if Int(number1.text!)! > Int(number2.text!)! {
        outputLabel.text = "\(number1.text!) is greater than
        ➥ \(number2.text!)"
    }
}
```

Here's the condition "Is number1 greater than number2?"

Take a close look at the code. See this?

```
Int(number1.text!)!
```

Here's what's going on. First, the variable name tells the code that you want to know what's in the `UITextField` you named `number1`. The .text part says you want to know what text the user entered into the `UITextField`. If you were simply displaying the text, you could stop here. But you're going to use a math comparison, so you have to turn the text into an actual number: an integer. That's what the `Int()!` part around `number1.text!` does.

Check out listing 5.1 to see where you need to put this code. You should add all the text that's highlighted. Everything that isn't highlighted is already there when you create a project.

Listing 5.1 Which Number Is Bigger? app, version 1

```
import UIKit

class ViewController: UIViewController {
    @IBOutlet var number1: UITextField!
    @IBOutlet var number2: UITextField!
    @IBOutlet var outputLabel: UILabel!

    override func viewDidLoad() {
        super.viewDidLoad()
        // Do any additional setup after loading the view,
        ➥ typically, from a nib.
    }

    @IBAction func btnSortClicked() {
        if Int(number1.text!)! > Int(number2.text!)! {
            outputLabel.text = "\(number1.text!) is greater than
                                ➥ \(number2.text!)"
        }
    }

    override func didReceiveMemoryWarning() {
        super.didReceiveMemoryWarning()
        // Dispose of any resources that can be re-created.
    }

}
```

Add the IBOutlet statements, one for each UI element. Remember that these statements give variable names to the labels and text fields so that you can access them in your code.

This IBAction is linked to the Which Number Is Bigger? button. When that button is clicked, the code compares the number in the top box with the number in the bottom box and then displays the result in the label below the bottom box.

Connect IBOutlets to controls and IBActions to buttons

Before you go any further, you need to connect the `TextFields`, `Label`, and `Button` to the code you added. You need to make the following connections:

- Connect `IBOutlet number1` to your first `TextField`.
- Connect `IBOutlet number2` to the second `TextField`.
- Connect `IBOutlet outputLabel` to the `Label`.
- Connect the button to the `btnSortClicked IBAction`.

If you forgot how to connect `IBOutlets` to controls, here are the steps:

1 Open the Main.storyboard file.
2 Right-click and drag from the View Controller button at the top of the view to your control.
3 Select the name of the `IBOutlet` you want to connect it to.

And here's how to link your buttons to your `IBActions`:

1 Go to your Main.storyboard file.
2 Right-click and drag from the button you made to the View Controller button.
3 Select the name of the `IBAction` you want to connect to (in this case, `btnSortClicked`).
4 Learn how the code works.
5 Suppose that you try the app by entering the numbers 8 and 6. What does the code do?

First, take a close look at the `if` statement in the code (figure 5.4).

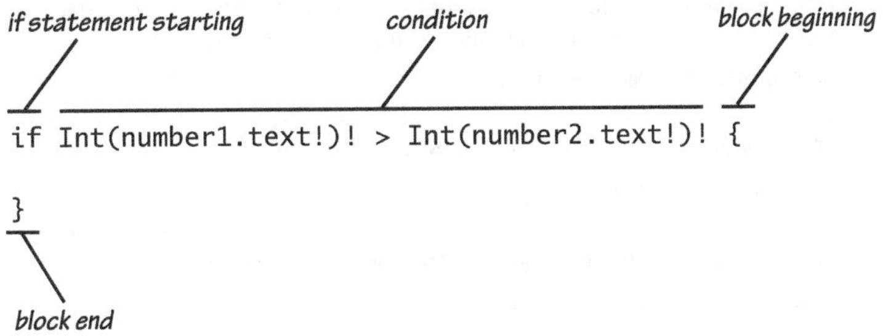

Figure 5.4 The parts of an `if` statement

The `if statement` is checking whether the first number (`number1`) is greater than the second number (`number2`). If so, the code changes the output label's text to `8 is greater than 6`. (You entered `8` in the first `TextField` and `6` in the second `TextField`.) The `Int(number1.text!)!` part gets text that the user gave you in the `TextField` (`number1.text!`) and converts it to an integer (`Int()!`).

You do this to compare the numeric value of `number1` with the numeric value of `number2`. A similar operation is done on the string value the user entered in the second `TextField`.

NOTE Notice the opening and closing braces—{ and }—after the condition. The code inside these braces is called a *block* of code. This block of code that follows your condition is like saying "If the condition is true, do the stuff in the braces."

This example uses the greater-than operator. Table 5.2 lists some more conditional operators that you can use in `if` statements. Many more conditional operators are available, and you learn them a little later in your journey of learning Swift.

Table 5.2 Conditional operators

Symbol	Used For
==	Checks whether values are equal to each other (not to be confused with =, which means to set a value of a variable) Example: `if num1 == num2`
!=	Checks whether values aren't equal to each other (not to be confused with !, which means to unwrap an Optional; the ! here means *not*) Example: `if num1 != num2`
<	Checks whether the first value is less than the other Example: `if num1 < num2`
>	Checks whether the first value is greater than the other Example: `if num1 > num2`
<=	Checks whether the first value is less than or equal to the other Example: `if num1 <= num2`
>=	Checks whether the first value is greater than or equal to the other Example: `if num1 >= num2`

Note that there are no spaces between the two operators in ==, <=, and >=.

Pop quiz

Figure out whether these conditions are true or false:

- `23 == 23`
- `10 >= 11`
- `2 <= 2`
- `-9 == 9`

Run the app

Right now, if you were to run the app, you'd see the two `TextFields` waiting for you to enter numbers in them, as shown in figure 5.5. Enter `8` in the first and `6` in the second; then click the Which Number Is Bigger? button. Did that work?

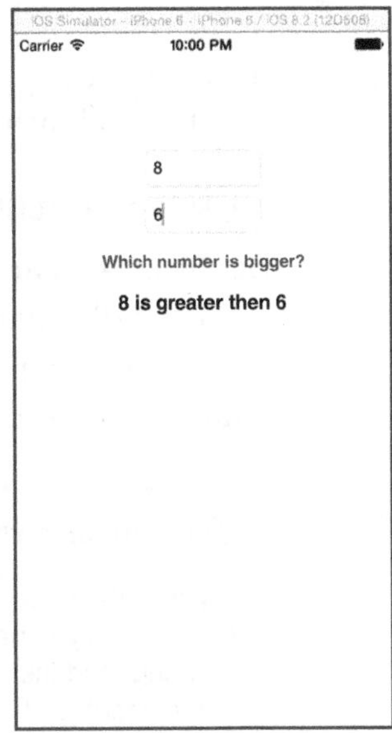

Figure 5.5 Which Number Is Bigger? app, trial 1

Yay—it works!

Now, for fun, try to break it. Can you guess which of these pairs of values entered in your app will break it and which won't? Why?

First number	Second number
`8`	`six`
`10`	`-10`
`2+`	`8`
`Dog`	`cat`
`1000`	`.10`

What if I put `8` in both the `TextFields`?

Remember: Don't enter anything that's not a number in `TextFields`. You shouldn't enter `eight` or `six`, or any other alphabetical character, because the code isn't capable of handling anything that's not a number except the minus (-) sign for negative numbers. You may enter a plus sign (+) for positive numbers. Also, take care that you never enter a space between the - symbol and a negative number. If you want to enter negative 8, type `-8`, not `- 8`. If you do the latter, the app will crash.

NOTE If the app crashes, you can restart it by going to Xcode, pressing Command-R, and then pressing Return (or clicking Stop).

OH, NO—A GLITCH!

But wait—what if the second number is equal to the first? Your app can't handle that situation yet! At present, if you put `8` in both `TextFields`, you won't get any message, Can you guess why? It's time to issue a patch for this glitch.

This glitch is frustrating, but that's good!

Think of the glitches you encounter as being . . . well, your friends. Don't get bogged down when you have troubles while programming. Each time you fix a glitch, you're learning, and the next time you see the same one, you'll fix it a lot faster. You'll become capable of solving more problems this way.

NOTE A *patch* is something that fixes a glitch in your code or an app.

PATCH THAT GLITCH!

To catch whether the first number is equal to the second, use an `else` clause. (If you're intrigued by what a *clause* is, it's part of a statement.) This `else` clause executes if the `if` condition is `false`.

NOTE You can find the code for this application in the Chapter05_a2 _WhichNumberIsBigger file inside the Hello-Swift-Code-master folder that you downloaded from GitHub. If you haven't downloaded the code from GitHub, go to: https://github.com/tanmayb123/Hello-Swift-Code/archive/master.zip. You should download the code only once for all chapters.

Here's what the patch will do:

```
if number1 > number2
        display - number1 is bigger than number2
else
        display - number1 is equal to number2
```

After your `if` statement, type this:

```
else {
    outputLabel.text = "\(number1.text!) is equal to \(number2.text!)"
}
```

Done! Your `IBAction` should look like this:

```
    @IBAction func btnSortClicked() {
        if Int(number1.text!)! > Int(number2.text!)! {
            outputLabel.text = "\(number1.text!) is greater than
                                ➥ \(number2.text!)"
        } else {
            outputLabel.text = "\(number1.text!) is equal to
                                ➥ \(number2.text!)"
        }
    }
```

Here's what's going on: if the condition in the `if` statement (`number 1 > number 2`) turns out to be `true`, the block of code in the first set of curly braces executes and shows you the message:

```
8 is bigger than 6
```

There's nothing new here, but if the condition is `false` because the first number is equal to the second number, the block of code in the `else` clause executes. This situation happens if you put `8` in the first `TextField` and `8` in the second `TextField`. The `else` clause puts `8 is equal to 8` in the label called `outputLabel`.

Run the app again!

Run the app to see whether your patch worked. Good news; it worked! Now continue testing to make the code better. This time, try putting `6` in the first `TextField` and `8` in the second one. What happened?

OH, NO—A GLITCH AGAIN!

Another problem: what if the second number is bigger? If you test the app now by entering `6` in the first `TextField` and `8` in the second, and then clicking the button, the app displays `6 is equal to 8`. The code can't handle this situation because the `else` statement executes whenever the `if` statement fails to execute for any reason. It's time to issue another patch!

PATCH THAT GLITCH!

This time, you use the `else if` clause. Here's what you're going to do in Englishy code:

```
if number1 > number2
        display - number1 is bigger than number2
else if number1 < number2
        display - number1 is smaller than number2
else
        display - number1 is equal to number2
```

NOTE This plain-English code isn't really called *Englishy*; it's known in the programming world as *pseudocode*. Pseudocode isn't actual code; it explains what the code does.

The `else if` clause executes if the `if` statement fails *and* its own condition is `true`.

NOTE You can find code for this application in the Chapter05_a3_WhichNumberIsBigger file inside the Hello-Swift-Code-master folder that you downloaded from GitHub. If you haven't downloaded the code from GitHub, go to: https://github.com/tanmayb123/Hello-Swift-Code/archive/master.zip. You should download the code only once for all chapters.

Now make your code look like this.

```
@IBAction func btnSortClicked() {
    if Int(number1.text!)! > Int(number2.text!)! {
        outputLabel.text = "\(number1.text!) is greater than
                        ➥ \(number2.text!)"
        } else if Int(number1.text!)! < Int(number2.text!)! {
        outputLabel.text = "\(number1.text!) is smaller than
                        ➥ \(number2.text!)"
    } else {
        outputLabel.text = "\(number1.text!) is equal to
                        ➥ \(number2.text!)"
    }
}
```

After your if statement and before your else statement, type

```
else if Int(number1.text!)! < Int(number2.text!)! {
    outputLabel.text = "\(number1.text!) is smaller than
  \(number2.text!)"
}
```

Your bug-free code should look like this:

Listing 5.2 The code for the Which Number Is Bigger? app, version 2

```
import UIKit

class ViewController: UIViewController {
    @IBOutlet var number1: UITextField!
    @IBOutlet var number2: UITextField!
    @IBOutlet var outputLabel: UILabel!

    override func viewDidLoad() {
        super.viewDidLoad()
        // Do any additional setup after loading the view, typically
        ➥ from a nib.
    }

    @IBAction func btnSortClicked() {
        if Int(number1.text!)! > Int(number2.text!)! {
            outputLabel.text = "\(number1.text!) is greater than
                            ➥ \(number2.text!)"
```

```
        } else if Int(number1.text!)! < Int(number2.text!)! {
            outputLabel.text = "\(number1.text!) is smaller than
                              ➥ \(number2.text!)"
        } else {
            outputLabel.text = "\(number1.text!) is equal to
                              ➥ \(number2.text!)"
        }
    }

    override func didReceiveMemoryWarning() {
        super.didReceiveMemoryWarning()
        // Dispose of any resources that can be re-created.
    }

}
```

This time, you're also checking whether the first number is smaller than the second. If so, you're showing the message `6 is smaller than 8`. If not, the `else` clause executes and shows the message `8 is equal to 8`.

Run the code again

This code is ready to help you do your homework! You can also show this app to your friends to make sure that your app is capable of comparing two integers. The app can compare huge negative *and* positive integers.

Recapping the if, else, and else if statements

Now that you have hands-on experience, here's the simplified syntax of an `if` statement:

```
if <CONDITION> {
} else if <CONDITION> {
}
. . .
. . .
. . .
  else {
}
```

This block of code executes when the condition in the if <CONDITION> line is true.

This code executes when the if statement's condition fails and the condition in the else if <CONDITION> line is true. The ellipses (. . .) after the closing brace show that there can be multiple else if conditions.

If the condition in the if statement and the condition in the else if statement are both false, this code executes no matter what.

Angular brackets (<>) in code show you something you need to fill to customize your code. `<Condition>`, for example, means any condition you need to check, and `<INT_VALUE>` means any integer value you want to use.

Here's what the `if` / `else if` / `else` code does:

- `if`—This statement is the heart of condition checking and is required for condition checking in Swift. If the condition is `true`, it runs the code inside its opening and closing braces.
- `else if`—This is another `if` statement after the initial `if` block. If the condition in the initial `if` clause is `false` and the condition in the `else if` clause is `true`, only then will the `else if` statement run the code inside it.
- `else`—This statement is part of the `if` statement that executes code *only* if the `if` clause's condition and the `else if` clause's condition are *both* false. It runs no matter what as long as all the earlier conditions are `false`.

Enough is enough for the else ifs!

The problem with `else if` is that it starts making your code hard to read. Imagine if you needed a bunch of them—which can happen. You can have multiple `else if` statements if you need to check a few conditions one after the other. Your code gets messy fast. Fortunately, the next statement that you'll learn is easier to code and to read.

You know the basics of the `if` statement. Next, you learn the `switch` statement.

NOTE If you're having trouble with any of the code, including `IBOutlets`, refer to chapters 3 and 4. If you're having trouble with any of the UI elements (not including `IBOutlets`), refer to chapter 2.

Exercise

Take a walk through the following code. Pretend that you're an iDevice running this app. Walk through the code and figure out the output for each of the four sets of numbers in the table.

```
if Int(number1.text!)! > Int(number2.text!)! {
    outputLabel.text = "\(number1.text!) is greater than \(number2.text!)"
} else if Int(number1.text!)! < Int(number2.text!)! {
    outputLabel.text = "\(number1.text!) is smaller than \(number2.text!)"
} else {
    outputLabel.text = "\(number1.text!) is equal to \(number2.text!)"
}
```

First number	Second number	Output
8	1000000	
-11	-10	
2345	8	
-1000	-10	

switch statements

The `switch` statement is available in most programming languages. You use it when you need to branch out to take an action depending on which one of numerous conditions is `true`. You've probably made decisions like these in your own life but didn't realize it.

Suppose that you have an app that can detect the temperature. Depending on how hot or cold the temperature is, the app prints different messages about the weather on the screen.

Depending on the temperature (in degrees Fahrenheit), the app prints these messages:

- `temp < 20` `It's too cold. Stay inside!`
- `temp < 30` `It's below freezing. Wear a warm coat, hat, and gloves.`

- `temp < 40`   `It's cold but not freezing. Wear a warm coat.`
- `temp < 50`   `It's brisk. You should take a sweater.`
- `temp < 70`   `It's about right. Wear long sleeves if you want to.`
- `temp < 100`   `Wow, is it hot! Wear short sleeves.`
- `anything else`   `It's way too hot. Stay inside; there's a heat warning!`

As you notice, your app branches out to display a different message depending on which of the many conditions turns `true` first, which is what *branching out* means. Imagine trying to perform this task with `if/else` statements. Your code would be a mess!

Suppose that you're working on an app, and you have to create code that converts the numbers 1 to 4 to words. You create the following code with an `if` statement:

```
let x: Int = 3
if x == 1 {
    print("You entered One, didn't you?")
} else if x == 2 {
    print("You entered Two, didn't you?")
} else if x == 3 {
    print("You entered Three, didn't you?")
} else if x == 4 {
    print("You entered Four, didn't you?")
} else {
    print("Uh-oh, you did not enter the number 1, 2, 3, or 4!")
}
```

You're declaring x because you need a variable for the if statement to check. It also enables you to run this code in the playground.

But why does this code use `let` instead of `var`?

You have yet another way to store data apart from using `var` for the variable. If you use `var`, the system assumes that the value will change. (*Variable* means that the value will vary.) But in some cases, if you need to store data that will never change and will be set only once, you can use a constant by using the `let` keyword. As the name implies, a *constant* means that the computer assumes that the value will never change.

Type this code in the playground, and look at the output. Try changing the value of x from 3 to a different number, and observe how the output changes. This first line won't be in the app because you get this number from the user in one of the TextFields.

But the code looks messy, with too many else if statements. Code like this becomes difficult for you (or another programmer) to debug and maintain later. And if you had 20 conditions to check, you'd need to write at least 40 lines of code.

Another reason why using too many else if statements is a bad idea is that code like this makes your app slower. You want a cleaner, more readable way of doing things. How? You can use the switch statement.

The switch statement looks like this:

```
let x: Int = 3

switch x {
    case 1: print("You entered One, didn't you?")
    case 2: print("You entered Two, didn't you?")
    case 3: print("You entered Three, didn't you?")
    case 4: print("You entered Four, didn't you?")
    default: print("Uh-oh, you did not enter the number 1, 2, 3, or 4!")
}
```

You're declaring x because you need a variable for the switch statement to check. It also enables you to run this code in the playground.

Try changing the value of x from 3 to other numbers, and observe the output.

Now take a closer look at this code.

You should recognize the first line of the code from chapter 3, where you created variables. Here, you're declaring a variable named x of type Int with a value of 3. Then you're doing something called a switch case. Inside the switch case, you have many conditions to check whether x is equal to some number:

- case 1: means "Is the variable x equal to 1?"
- case 2: means "Is the variable x equal to 2?"
- case 3: means "Is the variable x equal to 3?"

And so on.

But wait—where did the variable `x` come from? (You should be able to guess.) When you started the `switch` case, you typed `switch x {`. The `x` after `switch` in the statement tells Swift that you're referring to that variable.

In the next section, you learn how these statements work by creating an example.

App: The Mystery of the Entered Number

Get ready, because it's time to build The Mystery of the Entered Number app!

What does this app do?

In this section, you create an app that converts the numbers 1 through 4 to words by using a `switch` statement. When you enter `1`, `2`, `3`, or `4` in the `TextField` and click the button, you get the number you entered as a word as output in the label.

NOTE You can find the code for this application in the Chapter05_MysteryOfEnteredNumber file inside the Hello-Swift-Code-master folder that you downloaded from GitHub. If you haven't downloaded the code from GitHub, go to: https://github.com/tanmayb123/Hello-Swift-Code/archive/master.zip. You should download the code only once for all chapters.

If you enter another number in the `TextField` and click the button, however, you get `"Uh-oh, you did not enter 1, 2, 3, or 4!"`, as you can see in listing 5.3. That's how `switch` cases make the app work!

The UI for this app is shown in figure 5.6.

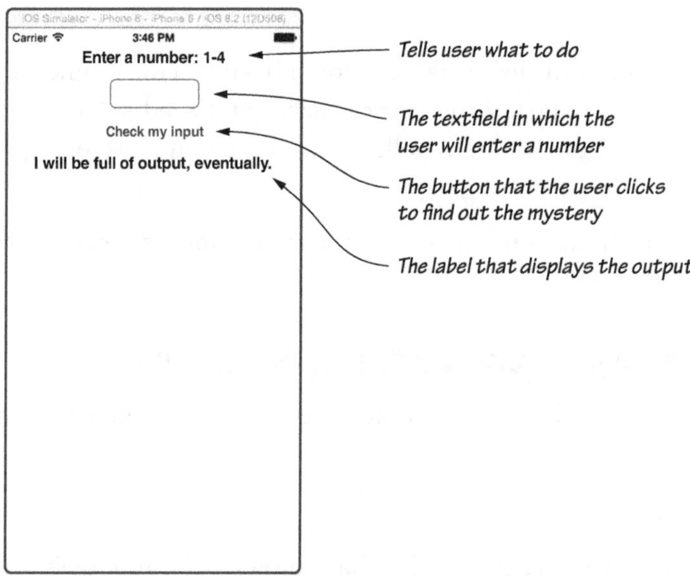

Figure 5.6 The Mystery of the Entered Number app

For this app, you use the same `switch` statement code that you used earlier in this chapter, the only difference being that you change the label's text instead of using `print()` to display it.

Create the UI

It's time to set up the project and build the UI for the Mystery of the Entered Number application!

SET UP THE PROJECT

Create a new Xcode project, and name it The Mystery of the Entered Number.

CREATE THE UI

Go to the Main.storyboard file, and make a UI that looks like figure 5.7.

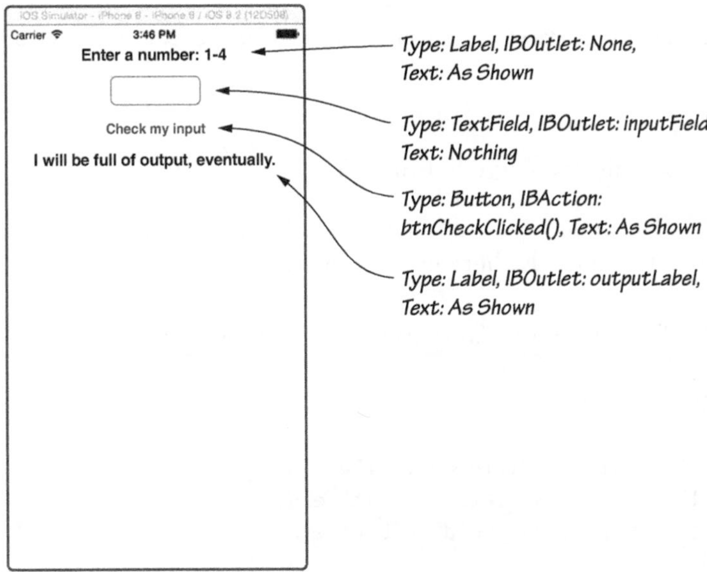

Figure 5.7 The Mystery of the Entered Number UI

Code the app

When you've done that, go to your code, and make the following `IBOutlets`:

```
@IBOutlet var inputField: UITextField!
@IBOutlet var outputField: UILabel!
```

Finally, create this `IBAction`:

```
@IBAction func btnCheckClicked() {
    var userInput: Int = Int(inputField.text!)!
    switch userInput {
    case 1:
        outputField.text = "You entered One, didn't you?"
    case 2:
        outputField.text = "You entered Two, didn't you?"
    case 3:
        outputField.text = "You entered Three, didn't you?"
    case 4:
        outputField.text = "You entered Four, didn't you?"
```

```
    default:
        outputField.text = "Uh-oh, you did not enter 1, 2, 3 or 4!"
    }
}
```

Your code should look like listing 5.3.

REMINDER The code with gray background is what you need to insert. The remaining code is already there in your .swift file.

Listing 5.3 The code for The Mystery of the Entered Number app

```
import UIKit

class ViewController: UIViewController {
    @IBOutlet var inputField: UITextField!
    @IBOutlet var outputField: UILabel!

    override func viewDidLoad() {
        super.viewDidLoad()
        // Do any additional setup after loading the view, typically
        ➥ from a nib.
    }

    @IBAction func btnCheckClicked() {
        var userInput: Int = Int(inputField.text!)!
        switch userInput {
        case 1:
            outputField.text = "You entered One, didn't you?"
        case 2:
            outputField.text = "You entered Two, didn't you?"
        case 3:
            outputField.text = "You entered Three, didn't you?"
        case 4:
            outputField.text = "You entered Four, didn't you?"
        default:
            outputField.text = "Uh-oh, you did not enter 1, 2, 3 or 4!"
        }
    }

    override func didReceiveMemoryWarning() {
        super.didReceiveMemoryWarning()
```

```
        // Dispose of any resources that can be re-created.
    }

}
```

CONNECT IBOUTLETS AND IBACTIONS

If your code looks like listing 5.3, connect the `IBOutlet inputField` to the `TextField` in your UI. Next, connect `IBOutlet outputField` to the label on your UI. Finally, connect the `IBAction btnCheckClicked` to your button in the UI.

Run the app

You should see this display in the simulator or on your device (figure 5.8).

When you enter `1, 2, 3,` or `4` in the `TextField` and click the `Button`, you get the number you entered as a word as output in the `Label`.

If you enter other numbers in the `TextField` and click the `Button`, you get `"Uh-oh, you did not enter 1, 2, 3, or 4!"` That's how the `switch` cases make the app work!

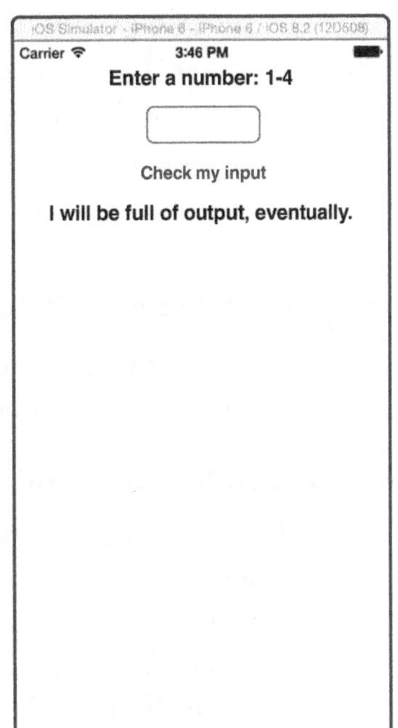

Figure 5.8 The Mystery of the Entered Number app

Check your app knowledge

1 What is the difference between `else` and `else if`?

2 Create code that uses a `switch` case to tell whether the user entered + or - or * or /. You may display messages in a label or by using `print()`.

3 What is a block of code?

4 What are glitches, or bugs, and how are patches and fixes related to them?

5 What's wrong with this code, and how can it be fixed? (Hint: The code has two mistakes.)

```
var x = 10
if x = 11 {
    print("X is equal to eleven.")
} else if x = 9 {
    print("X is equal to nine.")
} else {
    print("X is neither eleven nor nine.")
}
```

6 What do you think will be printed after the code is fixed? Run it in the playground to check.

7 What is an alternative way of doing the same thing for the corrected code as shown in question 5? Try this method in the playground or as an app.

8 What are the conditional operators, and what are they used for?

App-Exercise: Gold, Silver, Bronze

Flex your fingers and warm up for the first app-exercise of this chapter: Gold, Silver, Bronze.

What does this app do?

In this app-exercise, I teach you how to create an app that ranks numbers as Gold, Silver, and Bronze (figure 5.9). You enter three numbers, and the app lists them in the order greatest to least.

Figure 5.9 A visual representation of the app you're about to create

This app requires a lot of `if` statements to be checked, so get ready!

NOTE You can find the code for this application in the Chapter05_GoldSilverBronz file inside the Hello-Swift-Code-master folder that you downloaded from GitHub. If you haven't downloaded the code from GitHub, go to: https://github.com/tanmayb123/Hello-Swift-Code/archive/master.zip. You should download the code only once for all chapters.

Set up the project

Go to Xcode, and create a new project called Gold, Silver, Bronze.

Create the UI

Make a UI like the one in figure 5.10.

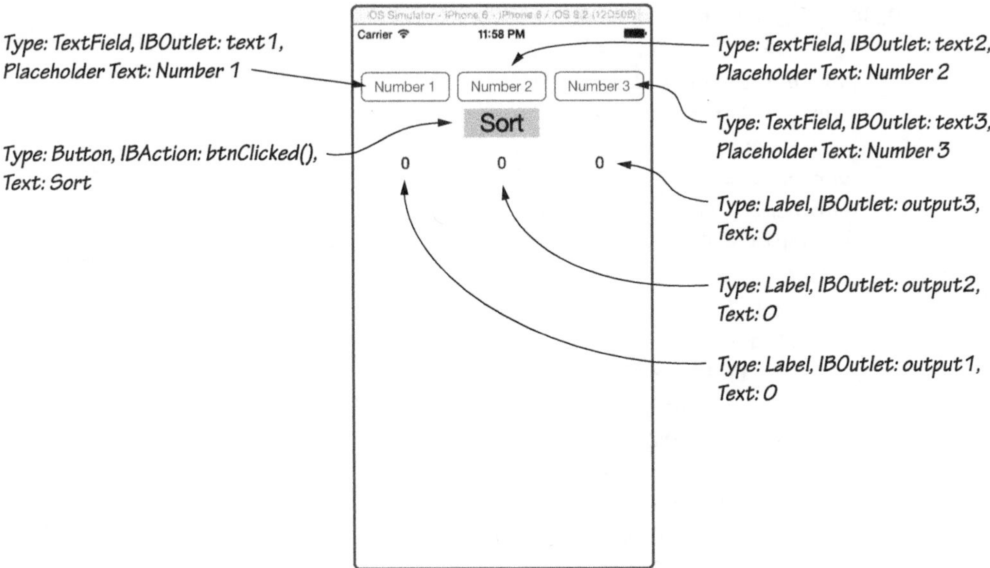

Figure 5.10 Gold, Silver, Bronze UI

Code the app

Now code the Gold, Silver, Bronze application.

ADD THE IBOUTLETS

Add these `IBOutlets` to your code.

```
@IBOutlet var text1: UITextField!
@IBOutlet var text2: UITextField!
@IBOutlet var text3: UITextField!

@IBOutlet var output1: UILabel!
@IBOutlet var output2: UILabel!
@IBOutlet var output3: UILabel!
```

ADD IBACTION

Add this `IBAction`:

```
@IBAction func btnClicked() {
    var a = Int(text1.text!)!
    var b = Int(text2.text!)!
    var c = Int(text3.text!)!

    var num1 = 0
    var num2 = 0
    var num3 = 0

    if a < b {
        if a < c {
            if b < c {
                num1 = a
                num2 = b
                num3 = c
            } else {
                num1 = a
                num2 = c
                num3 = b
            }
```

```
            } else {
                num1 = c
                num2 = a
                num3 = b
            }
        } else {
            if b < c {
                if a < c {
                    num1 = b
                    num2 = a
                    num3 = c
                } else {
                    num1 = b
                    num2 = c
                    num3 = a
                }
            } else {
                num1 = c
                num2 = b
                num3 = a
            }
        }

        output1.text = "\(num3)"
        output2.text = "\(num2)"
        output3.text = "\(num1)"
    }
```

CONNECT THE `IBActions` AND `IBOutlets` WITH CONTROLS

Now hook up the `IBAction` with the `Button` and the `IBOutlets` called `text1`, `text2`, and `text3` with the `TextFields`, respectively. Also, connect the `IBOutlets` `output1`, `output2`, and `output3` to the `Labels`, respectively.

Run your app

Next, run your app and, finally, enjoy the happiness of having created a three-number sorter app. (You may want to test it now.)

Figure 5.11 shows what the app looks like when it's running.

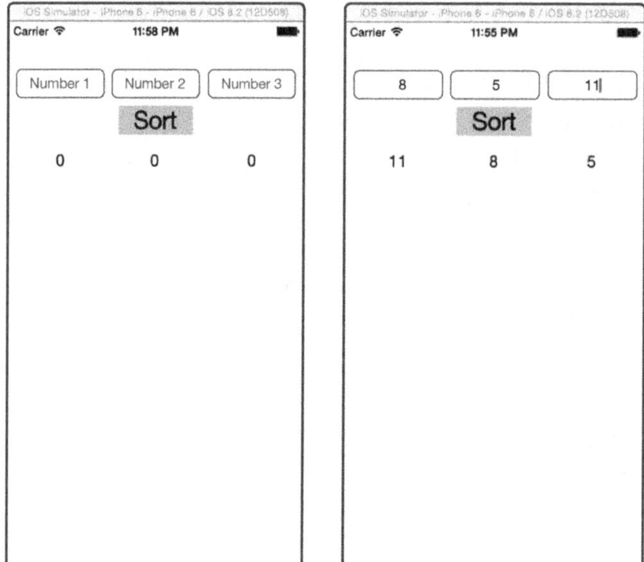

Figure 5.11 The Gold, Silver, Bronze app

This app is another one that can help you do your homework and test your answers.

App-Exercise: tTables the Times Tables Bee!

Now it's time for a personal favorite of mine: the Times Tables Bee app, called tTables. I'm sure that it's going to help you a lot!

What does this app do?

In this section, you create a times-tables helper app. The app generates two random numbers, of which you have to find the product. (By *product*, I mean the answer you get if you multiply the first number by the second number.)

NOTE You can find the code for this application in the Chapter05_tTables file inside the Hello-Swift-Code-master folder that you downloaded from

GitHub. If you haven't downloaded the code from GitHub, go to: https://github.com/tanmayb123/Hello-Swift-Code/archive/master.zip. You should download the code only once for all chapters.

You'll build tTables, a multiplication-table helper app. tTables does the following things:

1 Shows you two random numbers to multiply.
2 Gets your answer as input.
3 Uses an `if` statement with a condition that checks your answer against the real one.
4 Displays `correct` or `wrong` and repeats.

Along the way, this app also keeps track of your score.

Set up the project and create the UI

Open Xcode, and create a new project called tTables. Make a UI like the one in figure 5.12.

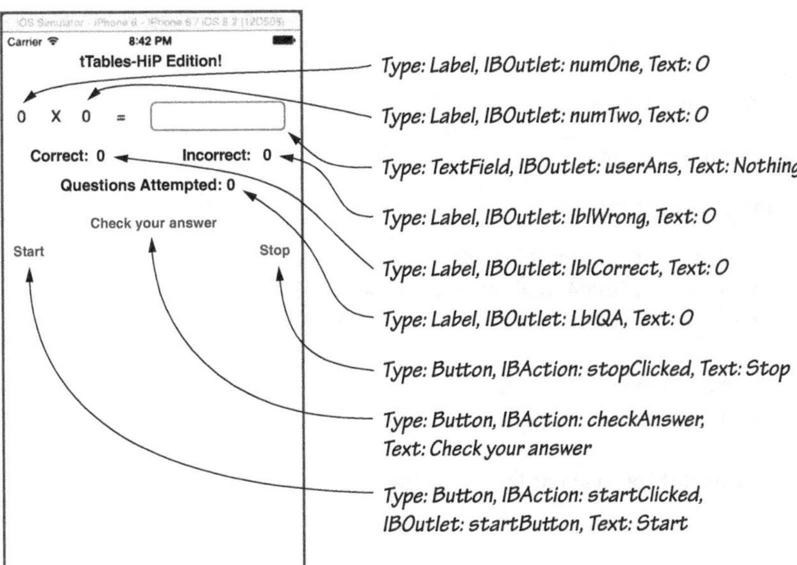

Figure 5.12 tTables UI

NOTE If this UI is a little too complicated for you to understand and create, you can refer to the UI in the app you downloaded.

Code the app

Now code the tTables application.

CREATE IBOUTLETS

Go to the ViewController.swift file, and create these seven `IBOutlets`.

```
@IBOutlet var numOne: UILabel!
@IBOutlet var numTwo: UILabel!
@IBOutlet var userAns: UITextField!
@IBOutlet var lblCorrect: UILabel!
@IBOutlet var lblWrong: UILabel!
@IBOutlet var lblQA: UILabel!
@IBOutlet var startButton: UIButton!
```

CREATE VARIABLES

Next, create these six variables:

```
var correct:Int = 0
var wrong:Int = 0
var QA:Int = 0
var num1:Int = 0
var num2:Int = 0
var numUser:Int = 0
```

CREATE IBACTIONS

Finally, create these three `IBActions`:

```
@IBAction func startClicked() {
    num1 = Int(arc4random() % 12) + 1
    num2 = Int(arc4random() % 12) + 1

    numOne.text = "\(num1)"
    numTwo.text = "\(num2)"

    startButton.isEnabled = false
}

@IBAction func checkAnswer() {
    numUser = Int(userAns.text!)!
    var realAns:Int = num1 * num2
```

```
    if numUser == realAns {
        correct += 1
        lblCorrect.text = "\(correct)"
        QA += 1
        lblQA.text = "\(QA)"
        userAns.text = ""
        num1 = Int(arc4random() % 12) + 1
        num2 = Int(arc4random() % 12) + 1
        numOne.text = "\(num1)"
        numTwo.text = "\(num2)"
    } else {
        wrong += 1
        lblWrong.text = "\(wrong)"
        QA += 1
        lblQA.text = "\(QA)"
        userAns.text = ""
        num1 = Int(arc4random() % 12) + 1
        num2 = Int(arc4random() % 12) + 1
        numOne.text = "\(num1)"
        numTwo.text = "\(num2)
    }
}

@IBAction func stopClicked() {
    correct = 0
    wrong = 0
    QA = 0
    num1 = 0
    num2 = 0
    numUser = 0
    lblCorrect.text = "0"
    lblWrong.text = "0"
    lblQA.text = "0"
    numOne.text = "0"
    numTwo.text = "0"
    userAns.text = ""
    startButton.isEnabled = true
}
```

Learn how the code works

You're declaring seven `IBOutlets`, and table 5.3 shows what they're used for.

Table 5.3 The IBOutlets for tTables

Name of IBOutlet	Type	Use
`numOne`	`UILabel`	The first number that the user sees in the multiplication question
`numTwo`	`UILabel`	The second number that the user sees in the multiplication question
`userAns`	`UITextField`	The user's answer typed in a `TextField`
`lblCorrect`	`UILabel`	The label that shows how many correct answers the user got in the current round
`lblWrong`	`UILabel`	The label that shows how many wrong answers the user got in the current round
`lblQA`	`UILabel`	The label that shows how many questions the user attempted in the current round
`startButton`	`UIButton`	The button that starts the quiz

You're also creating six `Int` variables (table 5.4.).

Table 5.4 The variables for tTables

Name of variable	Type	Use
`correct`	`Int`	The number of correct answers the user submitted.
`wrong`	`Int`	The number of wrong answers the user submitted.
`QA`	`Int`	The total number of answers the user submitted.
`num1`	`Int`	The first random number that the user gets in the question. (I explain random numbers soon.)
`num2`	`Int`	The second random number that the user gets in the question. (I explain random numbers soon.)
`numUser`	`Int`	The user's answer to the question.

Finally, you're creating three `IBActions` (table 5.5).

Table 5.5 The IBActions for tTables

Name	What it does
`startClicked`	This button starts the test. It generates two random numbers and stores them in `num1` and `num2`. It also prevents the user from clicking Start again (`startButton.enabled = false`).
`checkAnswer`	The user's answer is put in the `numUser` variable as an `Int`, and the correct answer (calculated by the computer) is put in the `realAns` variable. The app checks whether the user's answer is correct by checking whether the `numUser` variable is equal to the `realAns` variable. If the variables match, the user is correct. The app increments `correct` answers and `QA` (questions attempted) variables; it also generates two new random numbers. If the variables don't match, the user is wrong, The app increments wrong answers and QA variables; it also generates two new random numbers.
`stopClicked`	This button stops the test. It resets all the variables and text of all `UILabels`, and it makes sure that the user can click Start again (`startButton.enabled = true`).

RANDOM NUMBERS

A *random number* is a number chosen randomly from a list or range that you specify. Computers are used to generate random numbers for many purposes, such as these:

- Choosing the winning ticket of a lottery
- Choosing one of the six numbers in a roll of a die
- Choosing a number to practice times tables as though someone else is randomly asking the times-tables questions

To get a random number, you can use this statement (which generates a number from 1 to 12):

```
Int(arc4random() % 12) + 1
```

You can try this statement in a playground. It gives you a new random number if you refresh your playground by clicking first Editor and then Execute Playground.

Here, `Int(arc4random() % 12)` is code that generates a random number from 0 to 11. But in your app, you want to get random numbers from 1 to 12 to practice times tables, so add 1 to get random numbers from 1 to 12.

To make this random-number generation clearer to you, here's an example of generating a random number from 1 to 6 to simulate a common six-sided die:

```
Int(arc4random() % 6) + 1
```

This code generates random numbers from 0 to 5 and adds 1 to these numbers to get random numbers from 1 to 6. This code gives you the same results as though you rolled a six-sided die.

For now, that's all you need to know. You learn more about generating random numbers when you create a virtual dice app in chapter 8.

Run your app

If you run your app, you should see the interface in figure 5.13.

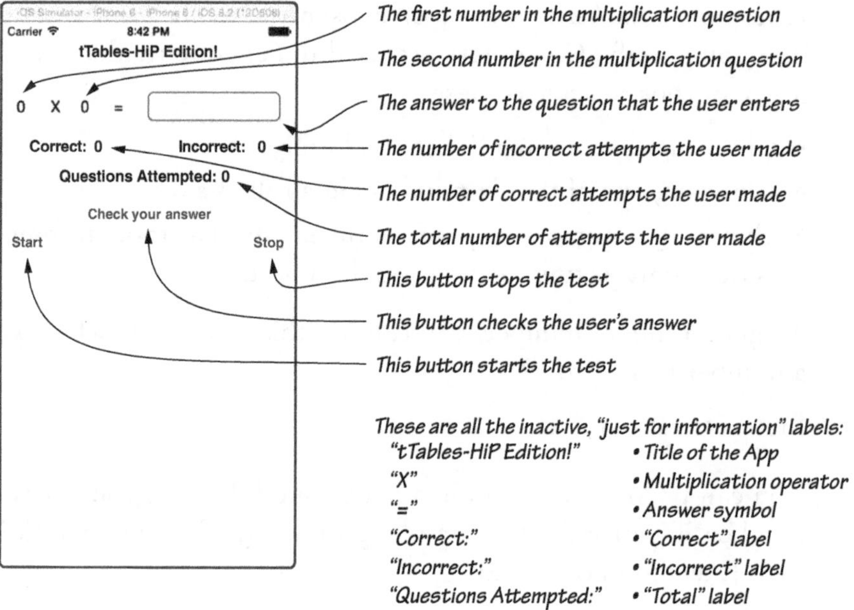

Figure 5.13 The tTables app

Pop quiz

1. What is a random number? Give five examples of when you'd need random numbers.
2. How do you generate a random number in these situations?

   A. 0 to 49 to generate a probable lottery number

   B. 2 to 12 to simulate rolling a pair of dice

6

Let computers do repetitive work

In this chapter you'll learn how to make your app repeatedly perform an action using a *loop*.

This chapter covers

- *What are repetitions or iterations, and how are they used in programming?*
- *What are loops, and how do you use the three types of loops?*
- *Why do you need to repeat the same block of code multiple times?*

Milestone 6, learn about loops, helps you write more efficient code. You've come a long way on your journey of programming in Swift. Chapter 1 gave you a head start. Chapter 2 introduced you to the user interface (UI). Chapter 3 taught you about the iPhone's memory—as a matter of fact, the memory of most computers—and variables. You had hands-on experience with input/output (I/O) in chapter 4. Then chapter 5 made you feel like an app developer because you started to make apps decide, at runtime, what to do next based on data and situations.

Loops are constructs provided by Swift and other programming languages that allow you to run the same block of code a number of times.

Controlling repetition

Take a look at a loop you might perform in real life. You're in physical-education class, and the teacher tells you to run three laps. As you run, you keep track of how many laps you've done. When you finish the third lap, you stop running. It's important to know how many times you've gone around the track so that you don't do too few laps or too many.

Here are some more real-life examples:

- You're taking a test in which you have to answer 15 questions. You keep answering questions until you've finished all 15. When you've done that, the test is over.
- You have to find the sum of a set of ten numbers. You loop through 1 to 10 and keep adding each number, and when all ten numbers are summed, you stop.
- You have to clean a part of the floor where you spilled some milk. You keep mopping while the floor is still dirty with milk.
- Your bicycle tire is low. You keep pumping the air pump until the tire is full.

In all these examples, you have to perform the same activity more than once while a condition remains true, and until the condition becomes false. Sometimes, you want your code to do the same thing more than once. Next, I show you how to do this without a loop and then how to do it with one.

Imagine an app that's like your physical-education teacher, telling you to do exercises. This app may tell you to do five laps. Suppose that you want to write code that prints out each lap you're supposed to run, one at a time. Using a playground, you could do this:

```
print("Run a lap.")
print("Run a lap.")
print("Run a lap.")
print("Run a lap.")
print("Run a lap.")
```

This code works, but it doesn't seem to be a good method. It's time-consuming and lengthy to print five times. What if you wanted to print 50 or 100 times?

Printing the same thing again and again seems silly. Why would I want to do that?

I agree; you won't need to print the same thing. But I'm about to show you how the same block of code—in this case, `print()`—can be repeated. Usually, your apps need to repeat code blocks that do more important things than print text. I'll get to that topic soon.

Although printing the same text isn't common, lots of times you'll need to repeat some code. When you need to repeat the same commands, you can use *loops*. There are several types of loops, and you'll dive into all of them in this chapter.

for-in loop statements

I'll start with the most commonly used loop in Swift: the `for-in` loop.

Suppose that you want to create code that prints `Do a situp.` ten times. What do you do? As you saw in the preceding section, you can type `print("Do a situp.")` ten times, but this method isn't efficient. Fortunately, you have a much easier way: the `for-in` loop.

Try it yourself

Open the playground, and write the following code, which I'll explain in a minute. Can you guess what it does?

```
for counter in 1...10
{
    print("Do a situp.")
}
```

This line initializes the loop, declares the variable that controls the loop, and tells it how many times to execute.

This line is the block of code that the for-in loop repeats.

Take another look at this line of code:

```
for counter in 1...10
```

Here, `1...10` means "Repeat the loop ten times, making the variable `counter` go from 1 through 10." If it were

```
for counter in 4...6
```

`4...6` would mean "Repeat the loop three times, making the variable `counter` go from 4 through 6 in three steps." In each repetition, the variable `counter` takes on the values `4`, `5`, and finally `6`. Although these ranges are uncommon, there are situations in which they can be useful! If you needed to print Report Cards for Grades 4 to 6 for a student, for example, these ranges would come in handy.

In the preceding examples, I used a variable called `counter` to keep track of the values each time you go through the loop. You can call the variable whatever you want. In programming, you often see the letter `i`, `j`, `k`, or `n` used for this kind of variable. Programmers use these single-letter variable names on purpose because they keep the loop's structure compact and also give you a feel for variable `i` or `n` being an integer or number in use.

Now you've seen a simple loop. A variable keeps track of how many times you've gone through a loop, and code inside the curly braces gets executed each time the loop runs. Next, I show you something important that you can use a loop variable for.

How does it work?

Look at the following lines of code, which print numbers 1 through 5 on five lines, one below the other:

```
for cupcakeCount in 1...5 {
    print(“\(cupcakeCount)”)
}
```

This code shows that in the `for-in` loop, the variable `cupcakeCount` takes values from `1` through `5` in five iterations.

So far, you've seen a loop that prints the same text each time it executes. You can use a loop variable to make what you print change each time through the loop. This code keeps track of putting icing on five cupcakes:

```
for cupcakeCount in 1...5 {
    print("Icing put on cupcake \(cupcakeCount)")
}
```

And this is the output:

```
Icing put on cupcake 1
Icing put on cupcake 2
Icing put on cupcake 3
Icing put on cupcake 4
Icing put on cupcake 5
```

Figure 6.1 is a screenshot of the code and output from Xcode.

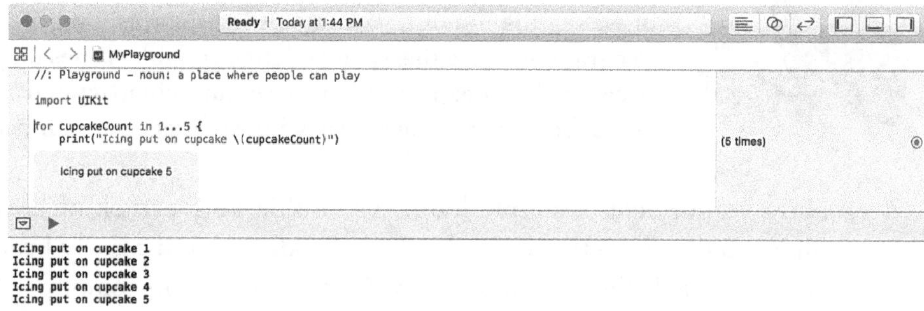

Figure 6.1 Icing-on-cupcake code example viewed in the playground

If your Xcode Playground doesn't look like figure 6.1 and you don't see the output, choose View> Debug Area > Activate Console.

Take a closer look at the parts of a loop. Here's the basic syntax of a `for-in` loop:

```
for <variablename> in <range> {
    <code>
}
```

Table 6.1 shows what each part of this code means.

Table 6.1 Syntax definitions for the `for-in` loop

Syntax block	Definition
`<variablename>`	The name of the variable that the computer increases in each repetition of the loop, called the *loop control variable* Examples: `i`, `j`, `n`, `num`, `counter`, or any valid variable name
`<range>`	The range of numbers to go through. The format is `<startingnumber>...<endingnumber>`. The loop starts at the first number in the range and goes all the way to the last one. If you want 42 loop cycles, you can use `1...42`. For 13 loops, use `1...13`. Examples: `1...53`, `1...100`
`<code>`	The block of code that the loop executes each time. Examples: `print("6 x 7 = 42")` `print("\(i) x \(j) = \(i * j)")` Assume that in the second code example, `i = 6, j = 7`. Run these examples to see what they do.

Playground example

Open a new playground, and name it loops_in_swift. Next, type this code:

```
    for i in 1...5 {
        print("Loop number \(i)")
}
```

This line is where you start the loop.

This line of code is executed every time the loop repeats.

Now open the debug pane in the playground. You should see output like this:

```
Loop number 1
Loop number 2
Loop number 3
Loop number 4
Loop number 5
```

Let me explain how the loop works. The `<variablename>` in this case is `i`. As the loop starts, it makes the value of `i` equal to the starting number of your range—in this case, `1`. Every time the loop repeats, the following statement executes automatically, even though you don't write it: `i += 1` (same as `i = i + 1`). You may remember from chapter 3 that this statement adds 1 to the value of `i`. Next, the `<range>` in this case is `1...5`. This range means that the loop executes five times. The variable `i` will be `1`, then `2`, then `3`, then `4`, and finally 5.

I'm still not sure I understand. How am I printing `Loop number 1`, `Loop number 2`, and so on each time? And how is the number getting bigger each time?

You're printing the text `Loop number` followed by the value of `i`. The `for-in` command automatically makes the variable `i` increase by 1 at the end of the loop each time you loop. This process is called *autoincrementing*.

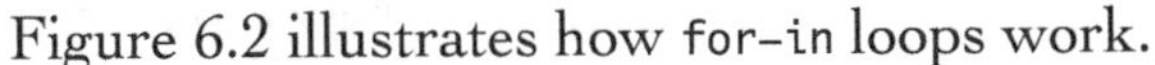

Figure 6.2 illustrates how `for-in` loops work.

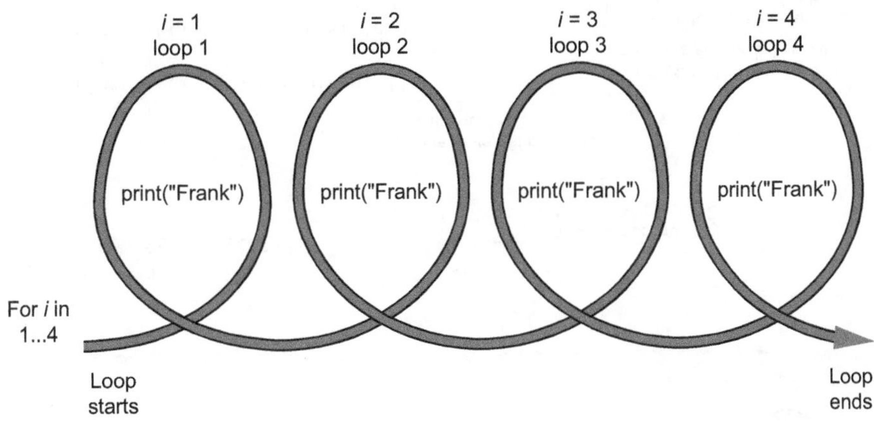

Figure 6.2 How a `for-in` loop works

You use the variable `i` to print the iteration index (number of loops you've done) each time. You may remember from chapter 3 that the `print("\(i)")` part prints the value of the variable `i`.

This kind of iteration with the `for-in` loop isn't the only way you can repeat a block of code. You'll learn about a few more loop types in this chapter. First, though, take a break and try this pop quiz.

Pop quiz

1. Create a `for-in` loop that gives you this output:

   Now it is 2

   Now it is 4

   Now it is 6

   Now it is 8

   Now it is 10

   Hint: You need simple math from chapter 3 and `print()` from chapter 1, combined with the power of loops you've learned in this chapter.

2. This exercise is trickier. Write a program that prints the numbers 1 to 25, and with each number, it prints whether that number is divisible by 4.

   Hint: You need to use both an `if` statement and a math function.

Answers:

1

```
for i in 1...5 {
    print("Now it is \(i*2)")      // You have to multiply the variable i with 2.
}
```

2

```
for i in 1...25 {
    if i % 4 == 0 {                        // This says "if i modulus 4 is equal to 0".
        print("\(i) is divisible by 4")     // This prints the numbers that are evenly divisible by 4.
    } else {
        print("\(i) is not divisible by 4") // This prints the numbers that are not evenly divisible by 4.
    }
}
```

See, I told you it was tricky!

What does *modulus* mean!?

The modulus is the remainder that you get when you divide two numbers. It's a math operator like +, -, *, and /.

while loop statements

Now that you know about `for-in` loops, you're ready to learn about a slightly less common but still useful loop: the `while` loop.

Suppose that you wanted to create a loop that would do something over and over until a condition becomes false (and keeps running as long as the condition is true). How would you do it?

Here's the scenario: the countdown for launching a space shuttle has begun! The computer has to count down until it reaches 0 and then launch the shuttle. So the counter keeps looping down from 10 until it encounters 0. At 0, the space shuttle is launched.

Well, a `for-in` loop can't handle that job. Luckily, `while` loops exist!

Try it yourself

Here's how you can use a `while` loop. As long as the `counter` variable is more than `0` (the condition), the loop keeps counting down:

```
var counter: Int = 10

while counter > 0 {
    print("Space Shuttle Launch Countdown: \(counter)")
    counter -= 1
}
print("Launched!")
```

If you forget the increment or decrement in the body of the `while` loop, you end up with a problem. Why? Well, when you forget the increment or decrement (or forget to update the condition that takes you out of the loop) in a `while` loop, you end up never making the condition of the `while` loop `false`, which means that it's always `true`. And as long as the condition is `true`, the `while` loop continues. So you end up creating an infinite and uncontrollable loop, which results in your iPhone, computer, or Playground crashing.

If you run this loop in a playground and open the debug pane, you'll see

```
Space Shuttle Launch Countdown: 10
Space Shuttle Launch Countdown: 9
Space Shuttle Launch Countdown: 8
Space Shuttle Launch Countdown: 7
Space Shuttle Launch Countdown: 6
Space Shuttle Launch Countdown: 5
Space Shuttle Launch Countdown: 4
Space Shuttle Launch Countdown: 3
Space Shuttle Launch Countdown: 2
Space Shuttle Launch Countdown: 1
Launched!
```

Table 6.2 shows you what this code is saying in English. (You may remember that I called that Englishy code *pseudocode* in Chapter 5.)

Table 6.2 English versus Swift: Analysis of this `while` loop

English language	Swift language
Create a variable, and give it a value.	`var counter: Int = 10`
As long as the variable named `counter` is greater than `0`, run the code in the brackets. This is called loop condition.	`while counter > 0 {`
Print the `counter` variable after the text.	`print("Space Shuttle Launch Countdown: \(counter)")`
Subtract 1 from the counter (decrement).	`counter -= 1`
When the brackets end: If the condition was met, that is, `counter` > `0`, start the loop again. If the condition was not met, run the code after the brackets.	`}`

Here's the syntax of the `while` loop:

```
while <condition> {
    <code>
}
```

Table 6.3 explains each part of the syntax.

Table 6.3 Syntax definitions for the `while` loop

Syntax	Definition
`<condition>`	Any condition. As long as the outcome of this condition is `true`, the `while` loop keeps repeating. When the loop detects that the condition is `false`, it makes no more iterations.
`<code>`	The code inside the `while` statement that's repeated.

Something to think about

In the space-shuttle-launching playground, why do you use `0` (as in the `while` condition `counter > 0`), and why does the countdown go only till 1?

The `while` loop continues only if the condition is `true`, so when the condition becomes `false` (`i` becomes `0`), the `while` loop stops, ensuring that the countdown goes only from 10 to 1.

The not equal to (!=) operator

In the example earlier in this chapter, I used

```
counter > 0
```

for the condition. But I could have used a new operator called not equal to:

```
counter != 0
```

The conditional operators you already know are `<`, `>`, `==`, `<=`, and `>=`. The not equal to operation is two symbols put together: `!=`. The exclamation point means *not*, and the equal sign means *equal to*. So `5 != 6` means "5 is not equal to 6."

This question may be weird, but what happens if my condition is never false? If the earlier example was `while counter < 10`, the condition would always be met!

Excellent question. Your loop would keep going forever and ever, and your computer would break. Okay, not really; your computer would be fine, but you'd have created something called an *infinite loop*. You have to prevent an infinite loop from happening! So when you're using a `while` loop, don't forget to increment or decrement the right way.

CAUTION If you happen to create an infinite loop, it takes up a *lot* of your computer's memory. As a result, the playground, the app on your phone, or your computer may crash. If you create an infinite loop while testing in Xcode, you can press the Command, Option, and Escape (⌘+OPTION+ESC) keys together to bring up a window. In this window, click Xcode and then click Force Quit to kill the Xcode process from memory.

Playground example

Now you're going to turn the `for-in` loop you made in the playground earlier into a `while` loop.

Go back to Xcode, and open the loops_in_swift playground you created earlier. Type this code:

```
var counter: Int = 10

while counter > 0 {
    print("\(counter)")
    counter -= 1
}
```

You should see this output in the debug area:

```
10
9
8
7
6
5
4
3
2
1
```

Figure 6.3 is a screenshot of the output.

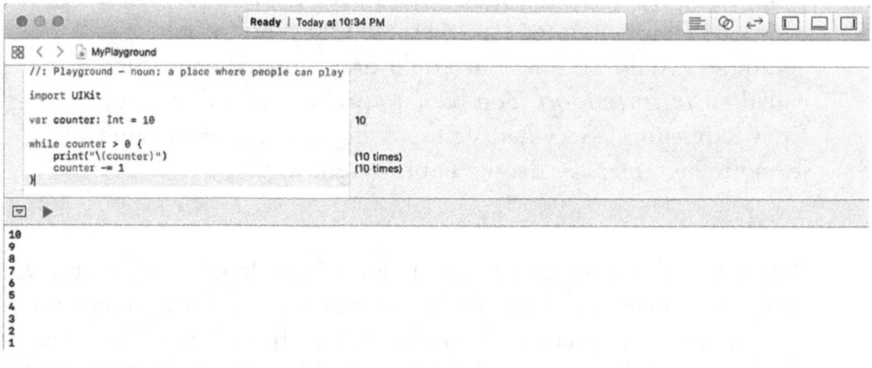

```
//: Playground - noun: a place where people can play

import UIKit

var counter: Int = 10                                10

while counter > 0 {
    print("\(counter)")                              (10 times)
    counter -= 1                                     (10 times)
}

10
9
8
7
6
5
4
3
2
1
```

Figure 6.3 Output of the `while` loop playground exercise

Pop quiz

1. Create a while `loop` that prints multiples of 4 from 1 to 12.
2. Write a small program, using the `while` loop, that prints the numbers 1 to 25 and prints whether e number is divisible by 4.

Answers:

1

```
var i = 1
while i <= 12 {
    print(i*4)
    i += 1
}
```

Remember! "i*4" doesn't actually change the value of "i". In this case, it just prints 4 times the value of "i".

2

```
var i = 1
while i <= 25 {
    if i % 4 == 0 {
        print("\(i) is divisible by 4")
    } else {
        print("\(i) is not divisible by 4")
    }
    i += 1
}
```

This says "if i modulus 4 is equal to 0".

This prints the numbers that are evenly divisible by 4.

This prints the numbers that are not evenly divisible by 4.

The repeat while loop

A variant of the `while` loop is called the `repeat while` loop. Here are the main features of these loops:

- The `while` loop checks a condition, and if the condition is `true`, it runs a block of code. If the condition is false, the block of code doesn't run at all.
- The `repeat while` loop runs a block of code and then checks a condition. If the condition is `true`, the loop continues to run. If the condition is `false`, the loop stops after at least one iteration. So even if the condition is `false`, the loop always executes at least one time. Here's the scenario: you come home from school, and at least once, you clean the study table. After you've cleaned the study table, if it's still dirty, you repeat until the study table is clean.

Here is the syntax of the `repeat while` loop:

```
repeat {
    <code>
} while <condition>
```

Table 6.4 lists syntax definitions for `repeat while` loops.

Table 6.4 Syntax definitions for the `repeat while` loop

Syntax	Definition
`<condition>`	Any condition. As long as the outcome of this condition is `true`, the `repeat while` loop keeps repeating. When the condition becomes `false`, the loop doesn't make another iteration.
`<code>`	The code inside the `repeat while` loop that's repeated.

Playground exercise: repeat while

Here's a simple playground example for the `repeat while` loop:

```
var loopCounter = 1
repeat {
    print("\(loopCounter)")
    loopCounter += 1
} while loopCounter <= 10
```

NOTE Remember that if you're not careful about the counter and the condition, you could end up in an infinite loop.

This code helps you count from 1 to 10. If you were to run this code in the playground right now, you'd get this output:

```
1
2
3
4
5
6
7
8
9
10
```

Pop quiz

Create a `repeat while` loop that prints multiples of 4 from 1 to 12.

How could you write a small program, using the `repeat while` loop, that prints the numbers 1 to 25 and, for each number, whether that number is divisible by 4?

Answers:

1

```
var ctr = 1
repeat {
    print(ctr*4)
    ctr += 1
} while ctr <= 12
```

Remember! "i*4" doesn't actually change the value of "i". In this case, it just prints 4 times the value of "i".

2

```
var ctr = 1
repeat {
    if ctr % 4 == 0 {
        print("\(ctr) is divisible by 4")
    } else {
        print("\(ctr) is not divisible by 4")
    }
    ctr += 1
} while ctr <= 25
```

This says "if i modulus 4 is equal to 0".

This prints the numbers that are evenly divisible by 4.

This prints the numbers that are not evenly divisible by 4.

App: How Many Times?

What this app does

In this app, you make something that takes a number from the user. The app has two buttons. If the user clicks the first button, the app counts from 1 up to that number. If the user clicks the second button, however, the app counts from that number down to 1. Let's get started!

NOTE You can find the code for this application in the Chapter06_HowManyTimes file inside the Hello-Swift-Code-master folder that you downloaded from GitHub. If you haven't downloaded the code from GitHub, go to: https://github.com/tanmayb123/Hello-Swift-Code/archive/master.zip. You should download the code only once for all chapters.

Set up the project and create the UI

To start, create an app called How Many Times. (If you have any trouble doing this, revisit chapter 2.) Next, create a UI like the one in figure 6.4.

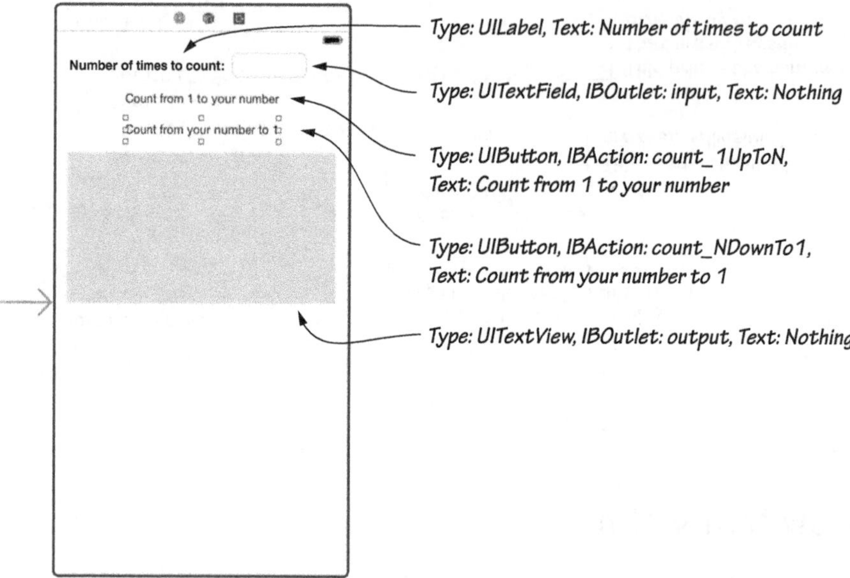

Figure 6.4 The How Many Times? UI

The yellowish, rectangular part in the middle is a TextView, not a TextField. You create a TextView so that you can change the height, not only the width, as with the TextField. If you remember from chapter 2, you can also have multiple-line text with TextViews.

Code the app

Modify your code to look like listing 6.1. (The highlighted parts are what you need to add.)

Listing 6.1 How Many Times? app

```
class ViewController: UIViewController {
    @IBOutlet var input: UITextField!
    @IBOutlet var output: UITextView!

    override func viewDidLoad() {
        super.viewDidLoad()
        // Do any additional setup after loading the view, typically
        ➥ from a nib.
    }

    @IBAction func count_1UpToN() {
        output.text = ""
        var inputNumber = Int(input.text!)!
        for outputNumber in 1...inputNumber {
            output.text = "\(output.text!)\(outputNumber) \n"
        }
    }

    @IBAction func count_NDownTo1() {
        output.text = ""
        var inputNumber = Int(input.text!)!
        while inputNumber != 0 {
            output.text = "\(output.text!)\(inputNumber) \n"
            inputNumber -= 1
        }
    }

    override func didReceiveMemoryWarning() {
        super.didReceiveMemoryWarning()
        // Dispose of any resources that can be re-created.
    }
}
```

Reset the output label's text.

Convert the input the user gave to Integer form and store it in the inputNumber variable.

This for-in loop counts up from 1 to the inputNumber.

Set the output label's text.

Reset the output label's text.

Convert the input the user gave to Integer form and store it in the inputNumber variable.

This while loop counts down from inputNumber to 1.

Tables 6.5 and 6.6 show what the code you added does.

Table 6.5 `IBOutlets` for the How Many Times? app

IBOutlet	Reason
`input`	This `IBOutlet` is where the app gets input from the user for how many times the app should count.
`output`	This `IBOutlet` is the output the App gives to the user: the set of numbers in ascending or descending order.

Table 6.6 `IBActions` for the How Many Times? app

IBAction	Reason
`count_1UpToN`	This `IBAction` executes when the user clicks `Count from 1 to your number`. It creates the variable `inputNumber` with the user's input in it as an integer. Then it uses a `for-in` loop to count from 1 up to the number the user gave it in the variable `inputNumber` and displays these numbers in the TextView.
`count_NDownTo1`	This `IBAction` executes when the user clicks `Count from your number to 1`. It creates the variable `inputNumber` with the user's input in it as an integer. Then it uses a `while` loop to count from the number the user gave it in the variable `inputNumber` down to 1 and displays these numbers in the TextView.

Run your app

When you run the app, it should look like figure 6.5.

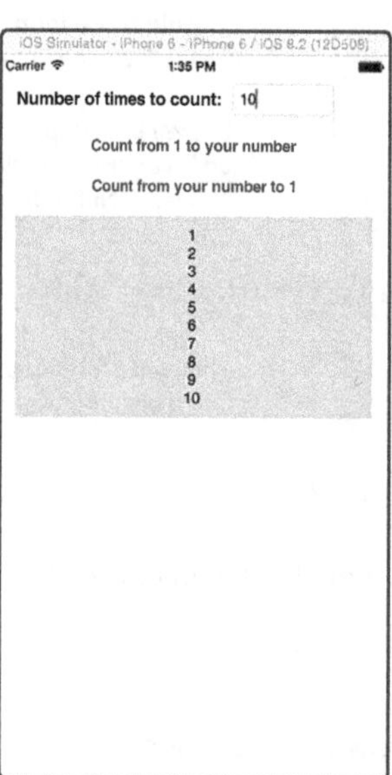

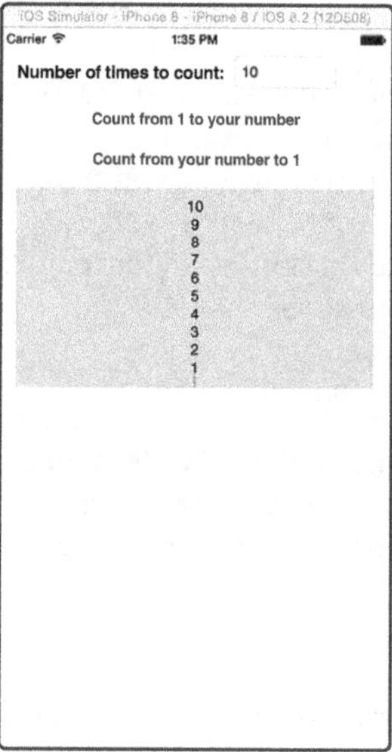

Figure 6.5 The How Many Times? app test

Check your app knowledge

1 What is the most common loop in programming and the most common loop in Swift?
2 What are `for-in` loops used for?
3 If you end up creating an infinite `while` loop, how would you stop it?

4 Create an app similar to How Many Times? that prints only even numbers. (Hint: Refer to chapters 3 and 6, and maybe use a modulus, or an alternative.)

5 Create an app that prints a specific times table that the user asks for. The app should be able to print the times table in reverse order as well.

6 What's the mistake in this code?

```
for i in 2..5 {
    print("Hello!")
}
```

7 If you make a `for-in` loop with the range `25...30`, how many times will it execute?

8 What will these loops print?

Code snippet 1	Code snippet 2

`var i = 0`
`while i != 0 {`
`print("Hello Frank!")`
`}`
	`var i = 0`
	`repeat {`
	`print("Hello Frank!")`
	`} while i != 0`

9 This problem may take a while to complete. Ready? With the help of `for-in` loops, try making a playground that creates a tree graphic made of asterisks (*) that is nine rows high, with a stem that's 2 rows high and 2 columns wide. Your output should look like this:

```
        *
       * *
      * * *
     * * * *
    * * * * *
   * * * * * *
  * * * * * * *
 * * * * * * * *
* * * * * * * * *
       * *
       * *
```

App-Exercise: Hang Your Word Upside-Down

NOTE You can find the code for this application in the Chapter06_HangYourWordUpsideDown file inside the Hello-Swift-Code-master folder that you downloaded from GitHub. If you haven't downloaded the code from GitHub, go to: https://github.com/tanmayb123/Hello-Swift-Code/archive/master.zip. You should download the code only once for all chapters.

What this app does

In this section, you create an app that reverses a string that you provide (such as `"Frank"` to `"knarF"`). You create the code in a Playground to understand it fully and then put it in an app.

Here are the activities you'll go through to create the app:

- Explanation and playground exercise
- Creating the app
- Coding the app
- Running and testing the app

When you're done, your app should look like figure 6.6.

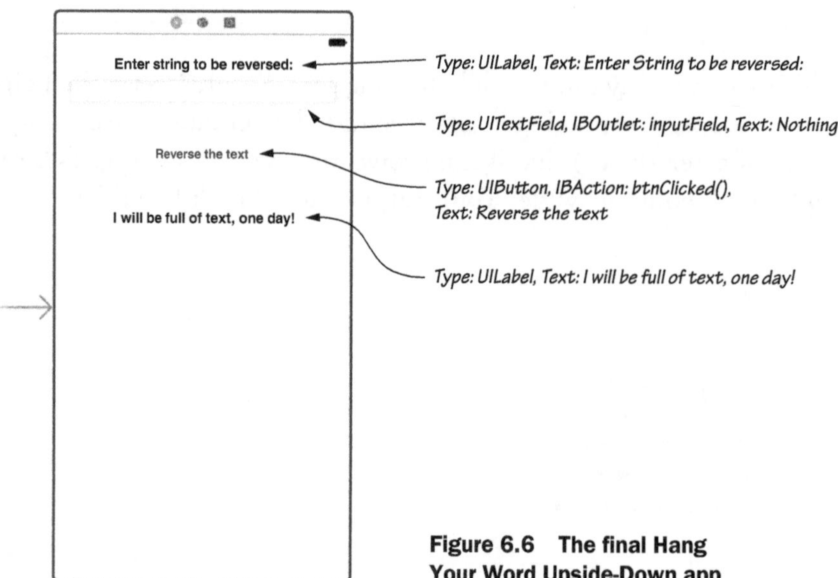

Figure 6.6 The final Hang Your Word Upside-Down app

Explanation, Playground exercise, and helper code

How in the world are you going to do this?

I'll explain how the app works. Don't worry about building it yet; you'll do that in a few minutes. For now, read about how it works.

First, download the starter playground from the website that has the starter code you need. (You learn more about this topic in chapters 7, 8, and 9.) At this point, I want you to include it in your code as is. If you're curious, listing 6.2 is the code that you'll be downloading.

Listing 6.2 `String` **extension for Hang Your Word Upside-Down**

```
extension String {

    subscript(value: Int) -> String {
        get {
            var j = 0
            for i in self.characters {
                if j == (value) {
                    return "\(i)"
                }
                j += 1
            }
            return ""
        }
        set(toSet) {
            var array: [String] = []
            var finalString: String = ""
            for i in self.characters {
                array.append("\(i)")
            }
            array[value] = toSet
            for i in array {
                finalString += i
            }
            self = finalString
        }
    }

}
```

Next, you create two variables: `strStart` and `strEnd`. You set `strStart` to `0` and `strEnd` to 1 less than the number of characters in the string you want to reverse. (You learned about characters and strings in chapter 3.)

Now create a `while` loop that keeps repeating as long as `strStart < strEnd`. Every time the loop executes, the character at number `strStart` in the string and character at number `strEnd` in the string are swapped. Also, in each iteration of the loop, you increase `strStart` by 1 and decrease `strEnd` by 1. Here's the code, which you can try out in the starter playground:

```
var str = "Frankie!"

var strStart = 0
var strEnd = str.characters.count - 1

while strStart < strEnd {
    var temp = str[strStart]
    str[strStart] = str[strEnd]
    str[strEnd] = temp
    strStart += 1
    strEnd -= 1
}

print("\(str)")
```

Table 6.7 gives you a closer look at the variables used in this code.

Table 6.7 Variables for the Hang Your Word Upside-Down app

Variable	Reason
`str`	This string gets reversed by the program.
`strStart`	This integer variable starts at 0 and counts up to the middle of the variable `str`.
`strEnd`	This integer variable starts at the length (end) of `str`, minus 1, and counts down to the middle of `str`. You subtract 1 because strings start from position `0` (not `1`). Take this example: `"ABC"` If you get the count of characters in this string, it's `3`. That is, `A` is at position `0`, `B` is at `1`, and `C` is at `2`. So if the `str` is `"Frank"`, `strEnd` is `4`.

If you were to change the `str` variable, declared at the top of the code, you should see the variable reversed when you print it at the bottom.

Figure 6.7 is a diagram that helps you understand the logic behind reversing a string.

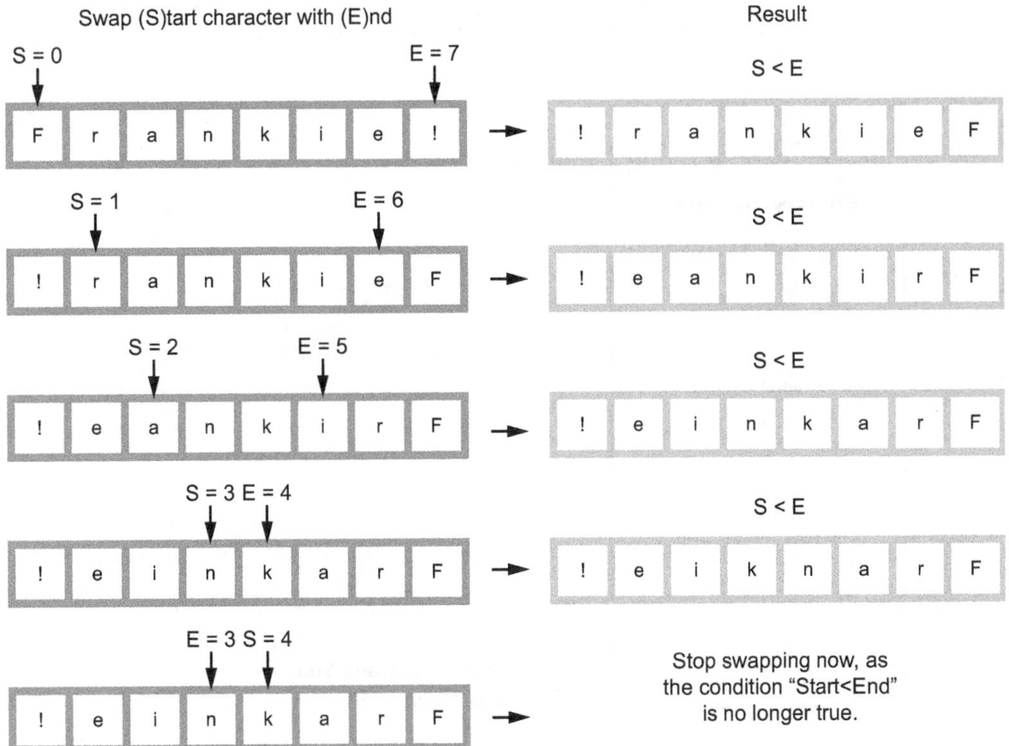

Figure 6.7 Diagram of string-reversing logic

Now use this knowledge to create an app.

Do you need to write a lot of code to make the app work? Not really; Swift provides a function that makes reversing strings easy. In fact, if you were to run the code

```
var name = "Reader"
name = String(name.reversed())
print(name)
```

you'd get "redaeR" (which is the string "Reader" reversed)! It's that simple, but to teach you the concept—how to think logically and reverse the string—I wanted to show you the technique behind it.

Set up the project and create the UI

Create another single-view application called Hang Your Word Upside-Down. Create a UI like the one in figure 6.8.

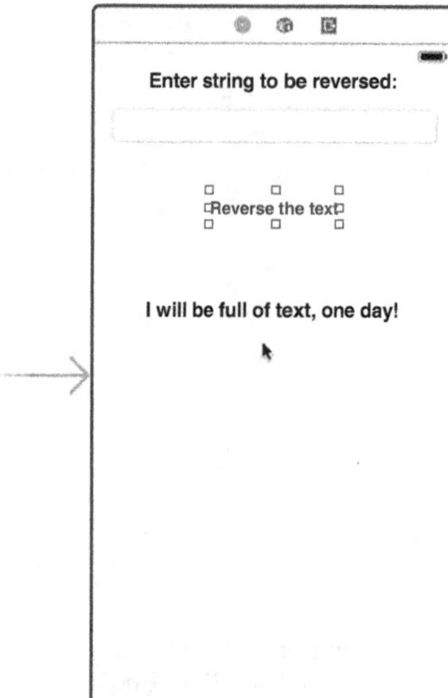

Figure 6.8 The Hang Your Word Upside-Down UI

Code the app

Make your code look like this, and please ignore the following code until you see the following line:

```
class ViewController: UIViewController {
```

Listing 6.3 The Hang Your Word Upside-Down app-exercise

```
import UIKit

extension String {
```

```
    subscript(value: Int) -> String {
        get {
            var j = 0
            for i in self.characters {
                if j == (value) {
                    return "\(i)"
                }
                j += 1
            }
            return ""
        }
        set(toSet) {
            var array: [String] = []
            var finalString: String = ""
            for i in self.characters {
                array.append("\(i)")
            }
            array[value] = toSet
            for i in array {
                finalString += i
            }
            self = finalString
        }
    }
}

class ViewController: UIViewController {
    @IBOutlet var inputField: UITextField!
    @IBOutlet var outputField: UILabel!

    override func viewDidLoad() {
        super.viewDidLoad()
        // Do any additional setup after loading the view, typically
➥ from a nib.
    }

    @IBAction func btnClicked() {

        var str = inputField.text!

        var strStart = 0
        var strEnd = str.characters.count - 1
```

This user input gets reversed by the app.

The strStart counter increments from 0 up.

The strEnd counter decrements from 1 less than the length of the string.

```
        while strStart < strEnd {
            var temp = str[strStart]
            str[strStart] = str[strEnd]
            str[strEnd] = temp
            strStart += 1
            strEnd -= 1
        }

        outputField.text = "Reversed: \(str)"
    }

    override func didReceiveMemoryWarning() {
        super.didReceiveMemoryWarning()
        // Dispose of any resources that can be re-created.
    }
}
```

The logic that reverses the string

You're done!

Run your app

The running app should look like figure 6.9.

Figure 6.9 The final Hang Your Word Upside-Down app

Type a string in the TextField, and click the button labeled Reverse the text. You see the reversed output on the label (figure 6.10).

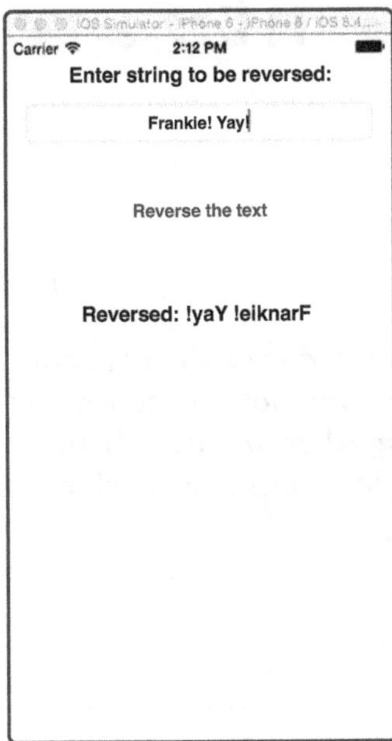

Figure 6.10 Testing the final Hang Your Word Upside-Down app

This chapter concludes the discussion of loops. You learned the following loop types:

- `for-in`
- `while`
- `repeat while`

Tune in next time (chapter 7), when you knit variables together!

7

Knitting variables into arrays and dictionaries

In chapter 3, I introduced the concept of variables to you, and now is the time to put them all together and use them in different ways: in arrays and dictionaries.

This chapter covers

- *What arrays and dictionaries are, and why you need them*
- *How to store data in an array or a dictionary*
- *How to use this data*
- *How to add, delete, and modify your data*
- *How to loop through an array or dictionary*

You've reached milestone 7, knitting variables into arrays and dictionaries. In this chapter, you'll be knitting variables together. You've been using variables in different situations for quite some time. Now you'll learn about using them in arrays and dictionaries. The attendance register that lists your names in order, for example, is an array. Your test scores in the past five quizzes you took are an array as well.

Also, the glossary at the end of your math textbook is a dictionary that lists keywords like *polygon, ratio, data, diagonal,* and *integers* along with their definitions! In fact—which may come as a surprise to you—an English dictionary is a dictionary in programming as well!

Why do we need arrays and dictionaries?

Imagine that ten kids have to give reports to the class. The teacher gives each one a piece of paper with a number from 1 to 10 on it. Frank gets 1, Amy gets 2, Maya gets 3, Tom gets 4, Timmy gets 5, and so on. This list is similar to an array in programming. An *array* is an ordered set of variables. In this example, the values are these kids' names, and the numbers on the pieces of paper control the order:

Name1	Name2	Name3	...	nameN
Tim	Joe	Anna	...	Tanmay

Unlike an array, a *dictionary* lets you assign values other than numbers to order your group of values. I go into more detail on this topic later, but for now, imagine that instead of writing numbers on those slips of paper, the teacher wrote the nicknames of the students. This makes a dictionary, which uses anything except numbers to order the variables.

With what you've learned so far, if you want to number a list of things (suppose that you're teaching Swift to five students and you want to keep a record of their progress by assigning numbers to students), you might do this:

```
var Frank = 1
var Amy = 2
```

```
var Maya = 3
var Tom = 4
var Timmy = 5
```

This code isn't bad if you have only a few variables to assign. But suppose that you need to give numeric order to a much larger group of variables. Can you imagine having to enter 5 or 100 variables this way? Typing all that is time-consuming; you might make a lot of typos; and the list is going to be hard to maintain and use in general. If you want to loop through the values of all these variables, you'd have a tough time. So how do you do it?

Arrays are great for this purpose. You declare an array, loop through it, and give it the correct values, as you see in the next section.

What is an array?

An *array* is a group of multiple variables of the same kind. Consider the example shown in figure 7.1.

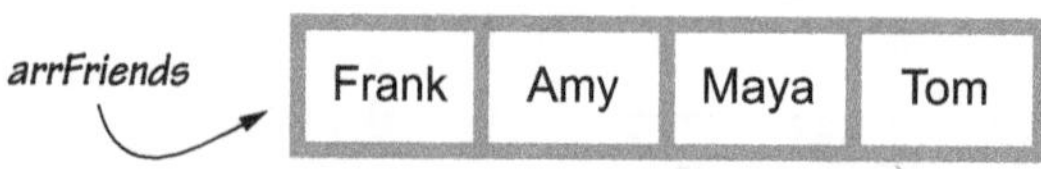

Figure 7.1 Array of names

If you wanted to create this array in code, you could do this:

```
var arrFriends: [String] = ["Frank", "Amy", "Maya", "Tom"]
```

This line of code is an example of creating an array, with `String` values in it. The square brackets (`[]`) around `String` tell Swift that this `String` is an array. Then the code sets values inside the array for Frank, Amy, Maya, and Tom.

As I mention in chapter 3, when Swift is given a value for a variable, it can automatically infer the type, so you don't need to set it manually. Swift can do the same for arrays. You could have written this:

```
var arrFriends = ["Frank", "Amy", "Maya", "Tom"]
```

But this sometimes introduces ambiguity. Suppose that you want a blank array:

```
var arrFriends = []
```

Swift no longer knows the type of the array, because there's no longer any value for Swift to infer a type from. You need to do this:

```
var arrFriends: [String] = []
```

In the real-life example, you give each student a slip of paper with a number. But in this code, there aren't any numbers.

That's the cool thing about arrays. When you put values in it, the array assigns the numbers for you. In this example, these four students end up with numbers assigned in the order in which they're added to the array.

Arrays start counting with 0!

Now I have to tell you something that's really important and kind of confusing. Arrays start counting with 0, not 1. If you think back to the example of the students in class getting slips of paper, the first slip given out says 0, not 1. If ten slips are given out, they're numbered: 0 to 9. This makes sense because digits actually start with 0. It may seem a little weird at first, because in school, you learn to count from 1. You almost forget about zero! (Poor zero.)

You have an array with values, which helps you because it's easy to get the values back out of the array in order.

Think back to the earlier example about the students with numbered slips of paper. Pretend that it's time for the next student to give a report. The teacher may not remember who's next in line, but he knows that the last student who did a report was number 2, so all he has to do is call number 3.

To get the name of someone stored in the array you created, you also (in code) use the number. In programming, this number is called the *index*.

To access some value (friend's name) from the array, you have to type the name of the array and then [<index>]. So to retrieve the first name from the array:

```
print("\(arrFriends[0])")
```

This makes sense because "Tim" is at index 0 of the array. Note that the array indexes start with 0, as 0, 1, 2, 3, and so on. The indexes don't start with 1 as 1, 2, 3, and so on. The index of an array starts at 0, not at 1, as you can see in figure 7.2.

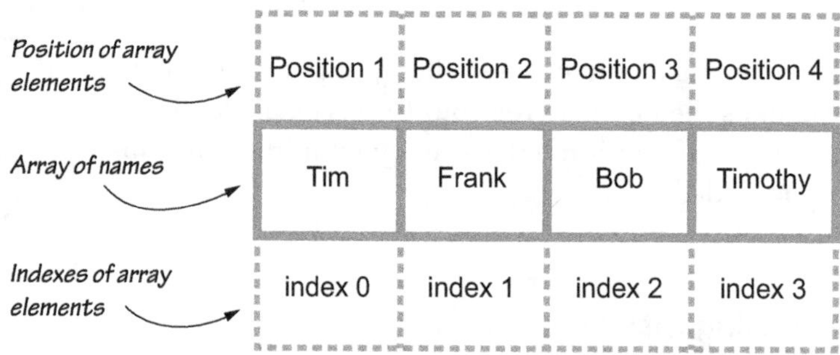

Figure 7.2 Array of names, positions, and indexes

What if you didn't know the index number? What would you do? Well, you learn this in a little while. (Hint: You loop through, check values, and find the index.)

Getting to your data

Now I'll start the official lesson: to get to your data. To get to your data, you need to know the index number of that specific entry. Suppose that you make a list of your pets in the form of an array. You want to access "fish" from that list.

Let's first try this code in the playground!

```
var arrPets: [String] = ["dog", "cat", "fish", "hamster"]

print("\(arrPets[2])")
```

In the playground, the code should print "fish".

The array is illustrated in figure 7.3.

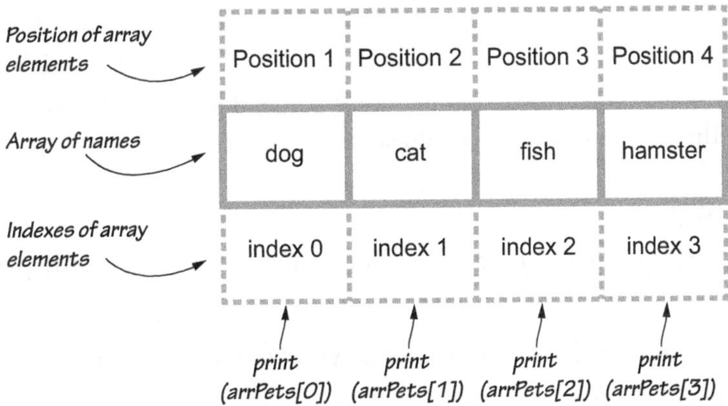

Figure 7.3 Array of pets, positions, indexes, and the print commands

You're grabbing the value at index 2. Why is that "fish" and not "cat"?

Remember, in programming, most ranges start with 0, not 1. If you access index 1, you'd get "cat" which is in fact the second value in the array. If you access index number 0, you get "dog", the first value in the array. So "fish" is at index number 2.

Pop quiz

Take a look at these arrays:

```
var food: [String] = ["pizza", "burger", "salad", "fries"]
var bigNumbers: [Int] = [53000, 24789, 6093, 4949493]
```

What do you think will be printed with these `print()` commands?

```
print("\(bigNumbers[2])")
print("\(food)")
print("\(food[4])")
```

The first command prints 6093. Did you notice that this array contains integers, not strings?

The second command prints all the values in the food array. Try it out!

The third command gives you an error because it's trying to print the fifth value, and the array has only four values.

TIP You can create an array of integers. You need to use the keyword `Int` and leave off the quotes around the values.

Altering the array

Now you're going to store and change data in arrays with programming.

Start by changing the name of one of your friends. The array of friends you already have is

```
var arrFriends: [String] = ["Tim", "Frank", "Ann", "Maya"]
```

What if you need to replace `"Maya"` with `"Tommy"`? How do you change that name in the array?

First, you need to know the index at which to find Maya's name. Maya's name is the fourth one in the list, so her name is at index number 3.

Remember: You know that the index starts with 0, not 1, right? So the fourth name in the list has an index of 3.

You can do this:

```
print("\(arrFriends[3])")
arrFriends[3] = "Tommy"
print("\(arrFriends[3])")
```

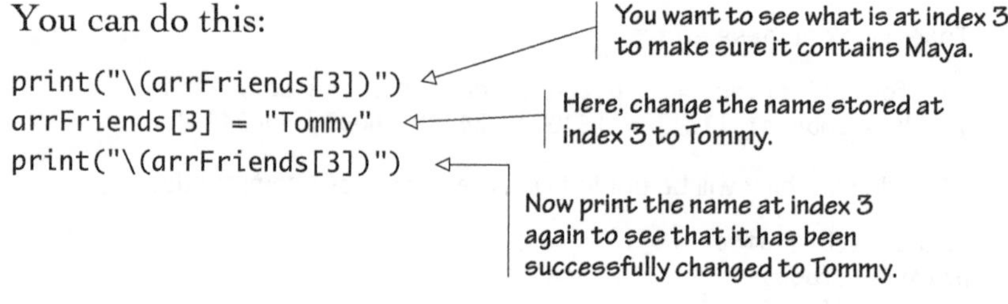

You want to see what is at index 3 to make sure it contains Maya.
Here, change the name stored at index 3 to Tommy.
Now print the name at index 3 again to see that it has been successfully changed to Tommy.

At line 2, you set the third index of the `arrFriends` array to `"Tommy"` the way you'd change the value of any other variable.

Now try it yourself! In this playground exercise, you make an array that lists some of the games you like. Then, in the next section, you loop through it.

To start, open Xcode, and create a new playground. Name this playground arrays_in_Swift. Then remove the first line and type the array code and five games, as in this example:

```
var gamesILike: [String] = ["Basketball", "Soccer", "Hockey",
     "Tetris", "Pacman"]
```

If you want to access the values of the array, type

```
print("\(gamesILike[0])")
print("\(gamesILike[1])")
print("\(gamesILike[2])")
print("\(gamesILike[3])")
print("\(gamesILike[4])")
```

What do you do if you want to add another game to the array? In addition to editing values that are already in the array, you can add more values. To do this, you use the `append` function (method) on an array, as in this example:

```
var gamesILike: [String] = ["Basketball", "Soccer", "Hockey",
  "Tetris", "Pacman"]

gamesILike.append("Agar.io")
```

You can use `.append` after the name of the array along with the value that you want to append to the array, and the value gets added to the array. Remember that as the function name `append` says, the name of this game is put at the end of the array.

After you run this command, the array contains this:

```
["Basketball", "Soccer", "Hockey", "Tetris", "Pacman", "Agar.io"]
```

Now suppose you're bored with hockey and want to remove it from the array. The process is as simple as appending to an array. All you need to do is this:

```
gamesILike.remove(at: 2)
```

There you go! Hockey is no longer in the array.

Looping through arrays

The most interesting part of using arrays is looping through them. Suppose that you create an array and want the names of your friends to be in it. Here's that array:

```
var arrFriends: [String] = ["Tim", "Bob", "Frank", "Tommy", "John"]
```

Now suppose that you want to print every friend's name in the array. How would you do that if you didn't want to list them all by running `print()` five times, with the index changed each time? (And imagine if the array had 100 values in it!)

Instead, you can loop through the array and print every value in the array as you loop. To do this, use what you know about loops from chapter 6 and combine it with what you've learned in this chapter.

In chapter 6, I said that `for in` loops are amazing for iterating or looping through arrays. You're about to find out why for yourself.

The syntax of looping through an array is

```
for <variablename> in <arrayname> {
	<do something>
}
```

Table 7.1 shows what that code means.

Table 7.1 Syntax definitions for the `for in` loop with arrays

Part of syntax	Definition
`<variablename>`	You may remember from chapter 6 that this is the name of the variable that's incremented each time in the loop. But wait—for an array, you don't need to put a range to loop from and to. What will this variable be equal to, and when will it end? Stick around to find out.

Table 7.1 Syntax definitions for the `for in` loop with arrays *(continued)*

Part of syntax	Definition
`<arrayname>`	This is the name of the array that you want to loop through.
`<do something>`	Here, you can write any code you want to run. This is the block of code that gets repeated.

I remember the `for in` loop uses a range that tells it how many loops to do, but this doesn't have one. How does it know how many loops to make?

The `for in` can figure out how long the array is without being told. So instead of `<variablename>` having the value of a `number_from` to `number_to`, the loop knows the length of the array. In the following code example, the code in the loop prints the names of your friends, not `0, 1, 2, 3, 4`.

This code loops through the friends array and prints every name in it:

```
var arrFriends: [String] = ["Tim", "Bob", "Frank", "Tommy", "John"]

for friendname in arrFriends {
      print(friendname)
}
```

But wait—I didn't put the quotes and brackets around the `"friendname"` as `"\(friendname)"` in the `print()` statement. This code couldn't possibly work. Or could it?

Well, it can. I didn't teach you this before, because I didn't want you to be confused, but I think that now is the right time to demonstrate it to you.

You can print variables with `print()` without having to add the quotes, so it's completely valid to use `print(i)`. Try it yourself!

You can put any valid variable name in a `for-in` statement. Instead of having to use `"friendname"`, you could use `i`, `x`, or `myFriends`. You see this output after running that code:

```
Tim
Bob
Frank
Tommy
John
```

Notice that you don't have to use five different variable names to store or print your friends' names!

As you can see, loops help when you're dealing with lots of array elements in an efficient way instead of needing to use a bunch of variable names.

Now that you've seen how arrays work, it's time to create an app.

10 Number Sorter app

In this section, you build the 10 Number Sorter app, which allows you to sort any ten numbers you provide.

What does this app do?

This app lets the user enter ten numbers and sorts them from small to large.

NOTE When you sort from small to large (say, from 1 to 5), the sort is in *ascending* order. If you sort from 5 to 1, the sort is in *descending* order.

NOTE You can find the code for this application in the Chapter07_10Number Sorter file inside the Hello-Swift-Code-master folder that you downloaded from GitHub. If you haven't downloaded the code from GitHub, go to: https://github.com/tanmayb123/Hello-Swift-Code/archive/master.zip. You should download the code only once for all chapters.

Set up the project, and create the UI

To begin, create a user interface (UI) like the one in figure 7.4.

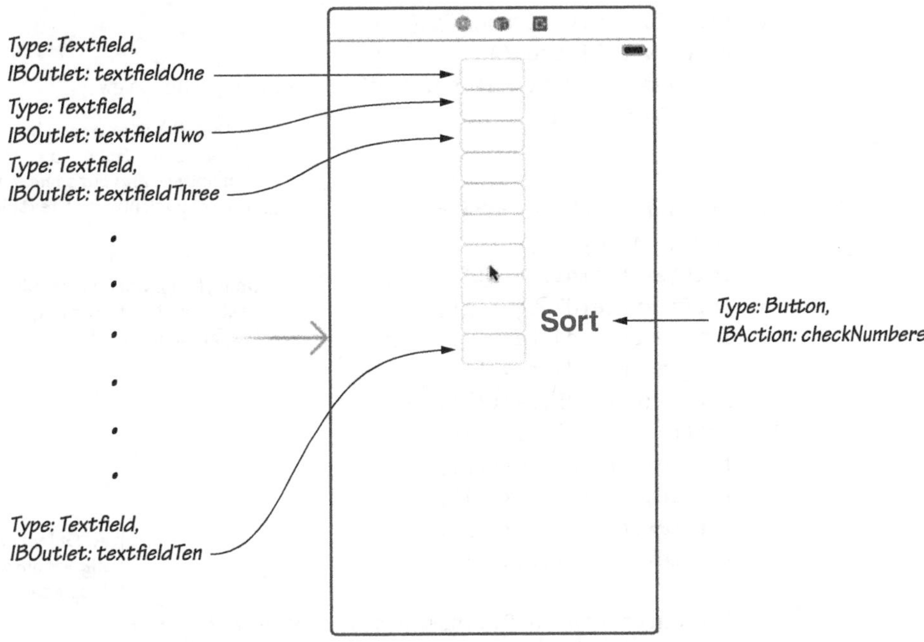

Figure 7.4 The 10 Number Sorter UI

Code the app

Next, modify your code to look like listing 7.1.

Listing 7.1 The 10 Number Sorter code

```
class ViewController: UIViewController {

    @IBOutlet var textfield1:  UITextField!
    @IBOutlet var textfield2:  UITextField!
    @IBOutlet var textfield3:  UITextField!
    @IBOutlet var textfield4:  UITextField!
    @IBOutlet var textfield5:  UITextField!
    @IBOutlet var textfield6:  UITextField!
```

These IBOutlets allow you to get and set the text of the ten TextFields so that you can handle the numbers that the user enters.

```
    @IBOutlet var textfield7:  UITextField!
    @IBOutlet var textfield8:  UITextField!
    @IBOutlet var textfield9:  UITextField!
    @IBOutlet var textfield10: UITextField!

    override func viewDidLoad() {
        super.viewDidLoad()
        // Do any additional setup after loading the view,
➥ typically from a nib.
    }

    @IBAction func checkNumbers() {
        var numArray = [
        Int(textfield1.text!)!,
        Int(textfield2.text!)!,
        Int(textfield3.text!)!,
        Int(textfield4.text!)!,
        Int(textfield5.text!)!,
        Int(textfield6.text!)!,
        Int(textfield7.text!)!,
        Int(textfield8.text!)!,
        Int(textfield9.text!)!,
        Int(textfield10.text!)!
       ]
        for outerLoop in 0...numArray.count - 2 {
            for innerLoop in outerLoop+1...numArray.count - 1 {
                if numArray[outerLoop] > numArray[innerLoop] {
                    var temp = numArray[outerLoop]
                    numArray[outerLoop] = numArray[innerLoop]
                    numArray[innerLoop] = temp
                }
            }
        }
        textfield1.text = "\(numArray[0])"
        textfield2.text = "\(numArray[1])"
        textfield3.text = "\(numArray[2])"
        textfield4.text = "\(numArray[3])"
        textfield5.text = "\(numArray[4])"
        textfield6.text = "\(numArray[5])"
        textfield7.text = "\(numArray[6])"
        textfield8.text = "\(numArray[7])"
        textfield9.text = "\(numArray[8])"
        textfield10.text = "\(numArray[9])"
    }
```

This IBAction uses the "Selection Sort" to sort the numbers and puts the sorted text back into the TextFields.

Using Int(), you convert the text from the text fields (as Strings) to Integers.

A "Selection Sort" algorithm with for loop statements

This code is where you set the text of all the text fields with the sorted numbers.

```
    override func didReceiveMemoryWarning() {
        super.didReceiveMemoryWarning()
        // Dispose of any resources that can be re-created.
    }
}
```

Learn how the code works

The preceding section uses an algorithm called Selection Sort. In this section, I explain it to you.

You're running two loops, one inside the other. You have an outer loop using the variable "outerLoop" and an inner loop using the variable "innerLoop". The outer loop goes through all the numbers except the last one one time. Every time the outer loop repeats, the inner loop loops though the remaining numbers and brings the smallest number to the top by repeatedly swapping the outer loop's number with the smaller numbers below it. This repeats, with the help of "outerLoop", up to the one less than the end of the array, and you get a sorted array in ascending order.

Why do I need to know how to sort things? How can I use this in my own programs?

Although built-in functions can sort your array, it's essential to do this exercise yourself to get familiar with coding techniques and problem-solving.

Knowing when to use sorting in your applications is simple: wherever you need to check for duplicate items in arrays, use sorting. Sorting also makes searching for values faster. Moreover, it's easy to work with numbers that are sorted. You can use sorting in many more ways!

Run your app

Run your app now. To test it, enter numbers in each of the boxes; then click the Sort button.

Go to the second dimension (rows and columns)

In this section, I teach you about the second dimension. Instead of having only rows, your array can have rows and columns. In other words, you get a grid or a matrix.

Table 7.2 shows you a visual example of the arrays you'll be creating.

Table 7.2 Tables showing the two-dimensional arrays

	teamArr array		
	player1	**player2**	**player3**
team1	Ann	Bob	Tim
team2	Todd	Jimmy	Tom
team3	Frank	Amy	Maya

	scoresArr Array				
	student1	**student2**	**student3**	**student4**	**student5**
test1	1	3	5	2	4
test2	1	6	2	2	6

An array with rows and columns is called a *two-dimensional* array. You could also have three- or four-dimensional arrays, but they're a little too complicated to explain right now. In simple terms, a two-dimensional array is an array inside another array, like so:

```
var teamsArr: [[String]] =
[["Ann", "Bob", "Tim"],
 ["Todd", "Jimmy", "Tom"],
 ["Frank", "Amy", "Maya"]]

var scoresArr: [[Int]] = [[1, 3, 5, 2, 4], [1, 6, 2, 2, 6]]
```

NOTE You can see that `teamsArr` is formatted with newlines, whereas `scoresArr` isn't. This doesn't change the functionality of `teamsArr`; it makes the array more readable for the developer.

As you can see, the type of the array changes to

```
[[<TYPE>]]
```

as opposed to

```
[<TYPE>]
```

The difference, if you can't make it out, is that this declaration has two pairs of square brackets around the type, not one pair. You can have as many brackets as you like. The more brackets you use, the more dimensions the array has.

Next, to access the name `"Amy"` in row 3 and column 2 of `teamsArr`, use this code:

```
print(teamsArr[2][1])
```

NOTE The position of `"Amy"` is row index 2 and column index 1 because ranges always start with 0.

Now that you know about arrays, it's time to take your skills to the next level by learning about dictionaries.

What is a dictionary?

A *dictionary* is exactly what it sounds like. You have pairs of items as in an array, but instead of being an integer, the index can be whatever data type you like, as with words and their definitions in a dictionary on your bookshelf.

Turning a dictionary into code

Suppose that you have this excerpt from a real dictionary:

- **Paper** a sheet to write or print on
- **Water** a liquid you drink when you are thirsty
- **Mouse** a pointing & clicking device used in computers
- **Pencil** an instrument you write with on paper

Here's what the code would look like for that dictionary:

```
var meanings: [String: String] = ["paper": "a sheet to write or print
     on", "water": "a liquid you drink when you are thirsty", "mouse":
     "a pointing device used in computers", "pencil": "an instrument
     you write with on paper"]
```

To make the code more readable, you can add extra spaces or newlines:

```
var meanings: [String: String] = [
    "paper": "a sheet to write or print on",
    "water": "a liquid you drink when you are thirsty",
    "mouse": "a pointing device used in computers",
    "pencil": "an instrument you write with on paper"
]
```

TIP As with arrays, you can type inference with dictionaries as well. In the preceding code, you don't need to include ": `[String: String]`".

If you want to access the meaning of "`water`", you could code

```
print(meanings["water"])
```

which prints

```
a liquid you drink when you are thirsty
```

If you want to access the meaning of "`pencil`", this is what you do:

```
print(meanings["pencil"])
```

This code prints

```
an instrument you write with on paper
```

That seems pretty simple. But what can I use a dictionary for besides listing the meanings of words?

Well, you can do a lot of interesting things with dictionaries! You can keep track of players' scores, for example, or the number of days in each month. You can also keep track of data in your science experiments, such as elements' names and their boiling and freezing points.

Creating a dictionary and getting to your data

Suppose that you have a list of people, and you want to make a list of them and indicate whether they're family members or friends. Frank is a friend, for example. Tom is family. Mark is family. Todd is a friend.

You can't do that with an array because you need to store both a name and a relationship, so a number won't work. You're going to use a dictionary.

Here's what the code looks like to make this list a dictionary:

```
var people: [String: String] = ["Frank": "Friend", "Tom": "Family",
  "Mark": "Family", "Todd": "Friend"]
```

You could also do this to make the code easier to read. (Remember, this change doesn't affect the functionality of the code—only makes it more visually appealing.)

```
var people: [String: String] = [
    "Frank": "Friend",
    "Tom": "Family",
    "Mark": "Family",
    "Todd": “Friend"
]
```

The code is easier to read with indenting, isn't it! Here's how this works.

This is the basic syntax to create a dictionary:

```
var <dictionaryName>: [<keytype>: <valuetype>] = [<key1>: <value1>,
  <key2>: <value2>, <key3>: <value3>,  and so on and so forth]
```

Table 7.3 lists the syntax definitions for the preceding code.

Table 7.3 Syntax definitions for dictionaries

Part of syntax	Definition
`<dictionaryName>`	The name of the dictionary you want to declare
`<keytype>`	The type of variable you want your key to be
`<valuetype>`	The type of variable you want your value to be

Table 7.3 Syntax definitions for dictionaries *(continued)*

Part of syntax	Definition
`<key>`	A key, which can be anything, but it must be the type that you listed in `<keytype>`
`<value>`	A value, which can be anything, but it must be the type that you listed in `<valuetype>`

Now that you know how to store the data in a dictionary, you need to be able to get the data out. The syntax is simple:

```
<dictionaryName>[<key>]
```

Suppose that you want to look up whether some name is a friend or a family member. The program could tell you whether that person is a friend or a family member. If you want to know whether `"Frank"` is a friend or family member, enter

```
print(people["Frank"])
```

which should print

```
Friend
```

NOTE A key can't occur twice in a dictionary. "Frank" can't exist in the example dictionary twice, for example. If you make an attempt, Swift replaces the earlier value.

Modifying the dictionary

To store data in dictionaries, you need to have a dictionary. In this section, you use the same people dictionary that you created in the section "Creating a dictionary and getting to your data":

```
var people: [String: String] = ["Frank": "Friend", "Tom": "Family",
    "Mark": "Family", "Todd": "Friend"]
```

Here, if you want to add something to this dictionary, the process is quite different from adding to an array. If you want to add to an array, do this:

```
array.append(value)
```

If you want to add to a dictionary, on the other hand, code

```
<dictionaryName>[<KEY>] = <VALUE>
```

If you want to add "Craig" as your cousin's name, for example, do this:

```
people["Craig"] = "Family"
```

NOTE If the index already exists, Swift doesn't add a new value; instead, it overwrites the previous value.

But what if you want to remove someone from your friends list? This is all you need to do:

```
people["Frank"] = nil
```

NOTE `nil` means *nothing*.

There you go! Frank is no longer in the friends list.

Why doesn't the `append` function work with dictionaries?

When you append, you're adding something to the next spot in an array. If the last index in an array is 5, when you append, the new value gets an index of 6. But dictionaries don't use numbers as indexes, so there isn't a "last" index. If you were to append to a dictionary, Swift wouldn't understand what to set the index to, because you're the one setting the indices!

After you enter Craig's info into the dictionary, if you print the dictionary called `people`, Swift may print

```
["Todd": "Friend", "Craig": "Family", "Frank": "Friend", "Tom":
    "Family", "Mark": "Family"]
```

If you're wondering, printing dictionaries is the same as printing arrays. You can use the `print()` command with the name of the array or dictionary, and you'll get everything in it. To print the preceding dictionary, enter this:

```
print(people)
```

What if you want to read through a dictionary and check for a certain condition before you print an item? You have to use a loop and an if statement for that purpose.

Looping through data in dictionaries

In this section, you learn how to loop through your dictionaries. This process is almost as simple as looping through arrays, except that you have a key and value pair every time, not the value alone.

Suppose that you have a list of fruits and animals. The item (`apple`, `banana`, `cat`, `dog`) is the key. Keys are unique; they can't repeat. You're looking up items (keys) to figure out whether they're animals or fruits. The item you're looking for is the value. Suppose that you want to look through your dictionary for anything with a value of animal and list the key for it. You should get `cat` and `dog` as the keys:

<dictionary> myThings	
<vname1> key	<vname2> value
apple	fruit
banana	fruit
dog	animal
cat	animal

To get your answer, type

```
for (key, value) in myThings {
    if value == "animal" {
        print(key)
    }
}
```

This code says, "For each data pair in my dictionary, if the value is `animal`, print the key." Swift prints

```
dog
cat
```

Here's the syntax:

```
for (<vname1>, <vname2>) in <dictionary> {
    <code>
}
```

Table 7.4 explains all the parts of the syntax.

Table 7.4 Syntax definitions for `for in` loops with dictionaries

Part of syntax	Explanation
`<vname1>`	The first variable name, or the key part of the dictionary
`<vname2>`	The second variable name, or the value part of the dictionary
`<dictionary>`	The actual dictionary to loop through
`<code>`	The code that's executed in each iteration

Pop quiz

1 Create a loop to selectively print only family.
2 Create a loop that changes all "`Family`" to "`Relative`".

Answers:

1
```
for (key, value) in people {
    if value == "Family" {
        print(key)
    }
}
```

2
```
for (key, value) in people {
    if value == "Family" {
        people[key] = "Relative"
    }
}
```

I give you more examples in the next section.

Friend List app

Here's another app!

What does this app do?

This app creates a list of your friends.

NOTE You can find the code for this application in the Chapter07_FriendList file inside the Hello-Swift-Code-master folder that you downloaded from GitHub. If you haven't downloaded the code from GitHub, go to: https://github.com/tanmayb123/Hello-Swift-Code/archive/master.zip. You should download the code only once for all chapters.

Set up the app, and create the UI

Give the app a UI like the one in figure 7.5.

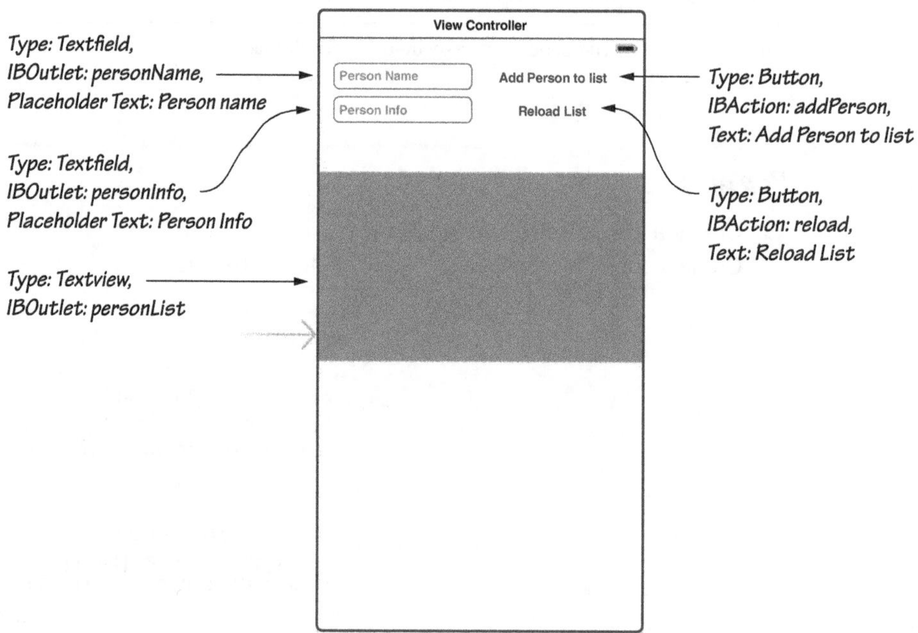

Figure 7.5 The Friend List UI

Code the app

Next, modify the code to look like the following listing.

Listing 7.2 The Friend List code

```
class ViewController: UIViewController {

    var persons: [String: String] = [:]

    @IBOutlet var personName: UITextField!
    @IBOutlet var personInfo: UITextField!
    @IBOutlet var personList: UITextView!

    override func viewDidLoad() {
        super.viewDidLoad()
        // Do any additional setup after loading the view,
➥ typically from a nib.
    }

    @IBAction func reload() {
        var finalString = ""
        for (name, who) in persons {
            finalString = "\(finalString)\(name), \(who)\n"
        }
        personList.text = finalString
    }

    @IBAction func addPerson() {
        persons[personName.text!] = personInfo.text!
        personName.text = ""
        personInfo.text = ""
    }

    override func didReceiveMemoryWarning() {
        super.didReceiveMemoryWarning()
        // Dispose of any resources that can be re-created.
    }
}
```

Here, you're declaring a blank dictionary by enclosing a colon within a pair of square brackets.

You have a dictionary of `String` and `String` type to store the name and info of your friend. Later, you can loop through the dictionary (which is what you do in the `IBAction`) and put that list in the actual `TextView` with a little bit of formatting.

CONNECT THE IBOUTLETS AND IBACTIONS

Table 7.5 lists what all the `IBOutlets` in the app do.

Table 7.5 `IBOutlets` in the Friend List app

`IBOutlet`	What it does
`personName`	The TextField where the user can enter his friend's name. The friend's name also acts as the key in the dictionary called `persons`.
`personInfo`	The TextField where the user can enter his friend's info. The friend's info also acts as the value of the dictionary.
`personList`	The output that the user gets in the TextView.

Table 7.6 lists what all the `IBActions` in the app do.

Table 7.6 `IBActions` in the Friend List app

`IBAction`	What it does
`reload`	This button or `IBAction` reloads the TextView of output and puts whatever is in the dictionary in the TextView.
`addPerson`	This button or `IBAction` puts whatever the user entered in the TextFields into the dictionary.

Now, you can hook up all the `IBActions` and `Outlets` as follows:

1. Connect the "Person Name" TextField to the `personName IBOutlet`.
2. Connect the "Person Info" TextField to the `personInfo IBOutlet`.
3. Connect the "Add Person to list" Button to the `addPerson IBAction`.
4. Connect the "Reload List" Button to the `reload IBAction`.
5. Connect the "Output" TextView to the `personList IBOutlet`.

Run your app! When you do, it should look like figure 7.6.

You should be able to add a person's name to the friend list and display the list, as shown in figure 7.7.

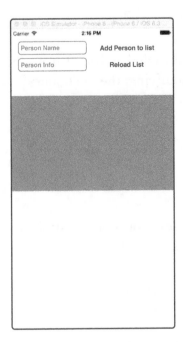

Figure 7.6 Running the Friend List app

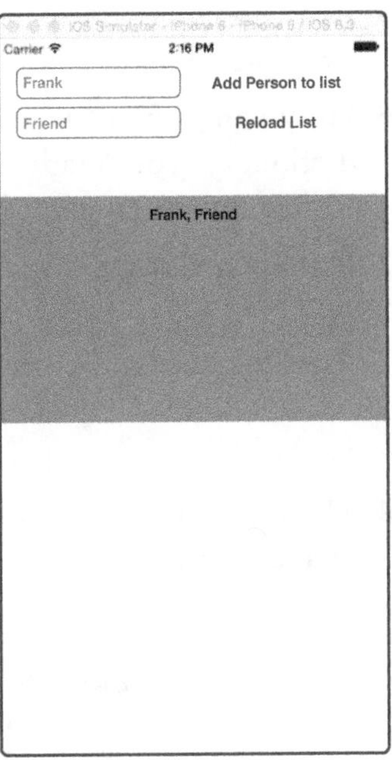

Figure 7.7 Using the Friend List app

Check your app knowledge

1. How do you create an empty array and dictionary?

   Hint: If you're wondering why in the world you'd want to create an empty array or dictionary, there are many reasons. The main reason is that you may want to create an array but don't have the data that goes in it yet. You create a blank array as a placeholder and add the data as it comes in.
2. What are three differences between an array and dictionary?
3. What's wrong with the following line of code?

```
var emptyDictionary: [String: String] = []
```

4 Fill in the blanks for the following code:

```
for ____ in arr {
    print(____)
}
```

5 How do you use a `for in` loop to go through an array? Describe with example code.

6 How can you retrieve every person who's a friend from the `people` dictionary you made in the "Modifying the dictionary" section? Rules: You must use a loop and an `if` statement.

7 Is there a shorter way to do this?

```
var someArray = [1, 4, 23, 6, 7, 2, 8, 9]
for j in 0...someArray.count - 1 {
    print(someArray[j])
}
```

8 The table in figure 7.8 shows the quiz scores of five students in Language, Math, Science, and Social Studies classes.

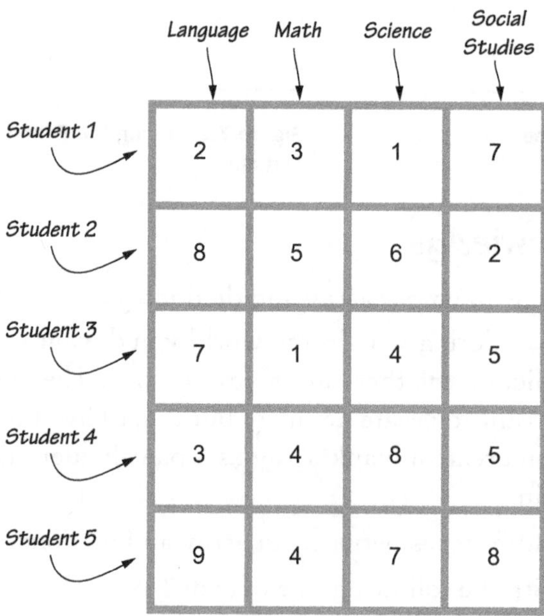

Figure 7.8 Diagram showing the marks in the two-dimensional array

Here's some code that uses the information from the figure in a two-dimensional array:

```
var scores: [[Int]] = [[2, 3, 1, 7], [8, 5, 6, 2], [7, 1, 4, 5],
[3, 4, 8, 5], [9, 4, 7, 8]]

for i in scores {
    print(i)
}
```

Try to find out what the code prints. If you get stuck, test it in the playground to get the correct answer.

App-Exercise: Alphabet Unscrambler

Now you're ready to start building this chapter's first exercise.

What does this app do?

In this section, you make a game: the Alphabet Unscrambler app.

NOTE You can find the code for this application in the Chapter07_Alphabet-Unscrambler file inside the Hello-Swift-Code-master folder that you downloaded from GitHub. If you haven't downloaded the code from GitHub, go to: https://github.com/tanmayb123/Hello-Swift-Code/archive/master.zip. You should download the code only once for all chapters.

In this game, you have nine letters: A, B, C, D, E, F, G, H, and I. The game starts with these letters scrambled. In this game, it's the player's job to put the letters in the correct order by unscrambling them. To unscramble letters, all you can do is click them. When you click a letter, all the letters from the beginning to wherever you clicked are put in reverse order. Continue this process, and you'll be able to unscramble the letters.

Suppose that one scrambled set of letters is

C D I H A B F E G

If you click A, the game reverses the order of the letters C, D, I, H, A to A, H, I, D, C. Then the set of letters looks like this:

A H I D C B F E G

Your job is to click the letters until you get

A B C D E F G H I

The finished app looks like figure 7.9.

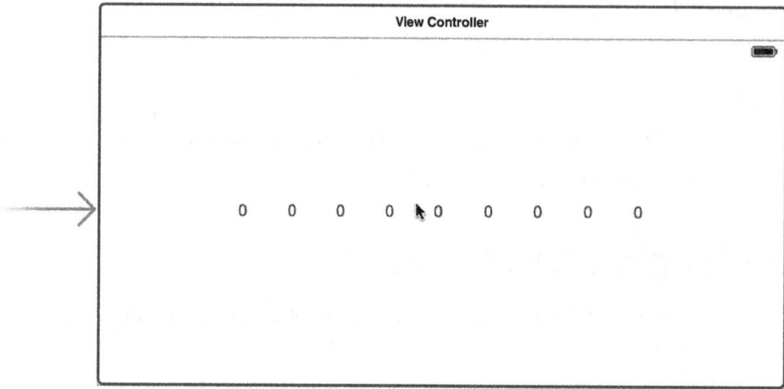

Figure 7.9 The final app

Set up the project, and create a UI

To start, create a UI like the one shown in figure 7.10.

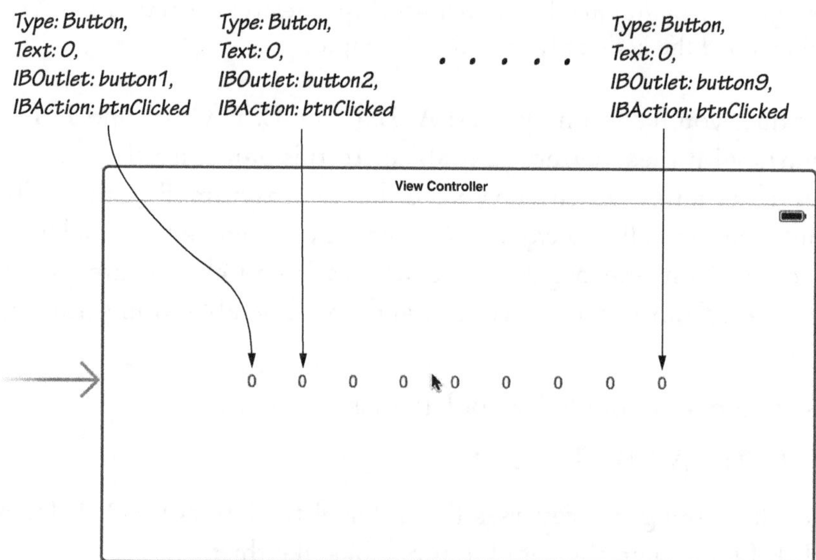

Figure 7.10 The Alphabet Unscrambler game UI

Code the app

Next, modify the code to look like the following listing.

Listing 7.3 The Alphabet Unscrambler code

```
import UIKit

extension Array {
    func shuffle() -> Array {
        var tempArr = self
        for (index, _) in tempArr.enumerated() {
            let rand = Int(arc4random_uniform(UInt32(tempArr.count - 1)))
            let temp = tempArr[rand]
            tempArr[rand] = tempArr[index]
            tempArr[index] = temp
        }
        return tempArr
    }
}

extension UIButton {
    func text() -> String {
        return self.titleLabel!.text!
    }
}

class ViewController: UIViewController {

    var alphabet: [String] = []

    @IBOutlet var button1: UIButton!
    @IBOutlet var button2: UIButton!
    @IBOutlet var button3: UIButton!
    @IBOutlet var button4: UIButton!
    @IBOutlet var button5: UIButton!
    @IBOutlet var button6: UIButton!
    @IBOutlet var button7: UIButton!
    @IBOutlet var button8: UIButton!
    @IBOutlet var button9: UIButton!

    override func viewDidLoad() {
        super.viewDidLoad()
        alphabet = ["A", "B", "C", "D", "E", "F", "G", "H", "I"]
```

This array contains the alphabet from A to I.

These are the IBOutlets for the buttons, so that you can put letters A to I into them.

```
        alphabet = alphabet.shuffle()
        button1.setTitle(alphabet[0], for: .normal)
        button2.setTitle(alphabet[1], for: .normal)
        button3.setTitle(alphabet[2], for: .normal)
        button4.setTitle(alphabet[3], for: .normal)
        button5.setTitle(alphabet[4], for: .normal)
        button6.setTitle(alphabet[5], for: .normal)
        button7.setTitle(alphabet[6], for: .normal)
        button8.setTitle(alphabet[7], for: .normal)
        button9.setTitle(alphabet[8], for: .normal)

        // Do any additional setup after loading the view,
➥ typically from a nib.
    }

    @IBAction func btnClicked(sender: UIButton) {
        var indexTo: Int = 0
        for (index, i) in alphabet.enumerated() {
            if i == sender.text() {
                indexTo = index
            }
        }
        let indexFrom: Int = 0
        var newArray: [String] = []
        for i in indexFrom...indexTo {
            newArray.append(alphabet[i])
        }
        //REVERSE NEW ARRAY!
        var k = 0
        var j = newArray.count - 1
        while k < j {
            let temp = newArray[j]
            newArray[j] = newArray[k]
            newArray[k] = temp
            k += 1
            j -= 1
        }
        //ADD TO OLD ARRAY!
        for i in indexFrom...indexTo {
            alphabet[i] = newArray[i]
        }
        button1.setTitle(alphabet[0], for: .normal)
        button2.setTitle(alphabet[1], for: .normal)
```

Here, you're putting the shuffled alphabet into the buttons one by one.

In this IBAction, you swap all letters from the letter at position 1 to the letter that the user clicked.

Same as in 9 lines of code above, where you set the text of the buttons; it's just after the line in which you called alphabet.shuffle().

```
        button3.setTitle(alphabet[2], for: .normal)
        button4.setTitle(alphabet[3], for: .normal)
        button5.setTitle(alphabet[4], for: .normal)
        button6.setTitle(alphabet[5], for: .normal)
        button7.setTitle(alphabet[6], for: .normal)
        button8.setTitle(alphabet[7], for: .normal)
        button9.setTitle(alphabet[8], for: .normal)
    }

    override func didReceiveMemoryWarning() {
        super.didReceiveMemoryWarning()
        // Dispose of any resources that can be re-created.
    }
}
```

Learn how the code works

NOTE You can ignore the two extensions at the top of the code. Put them in your code, though, to make it work better. You learn about extensions in chapter 9.

Let me explain the code.

First, in the `viewDidLoad` function, you're shuffling all nine letters in the array so that when you start the game, the letters aren't by default already in A, B, C, D, E, F, G, H, I order. (If they are, what's the point of the game?) Then you put the values (the letters A to I) in the buttons in random order one by one, as in this example:

```
button1.setTitle(alphabet[0], for: .normal)
```

This line of code sets the title of the first button to the element at position zero of the array, which could be E or another letter from the set. This way, all the letters gets displayed as clickable buttons in the interface.

Next, all the buttons are connected to an `IBAction` called `btnClicked`. Here, you check what index that button holds, in the array; then you swap all array elements from the beginning to the letter that was clicked. In the last part of the code, you update the text of all the buttons—a repetition of the nine lines of code you wrote in the `viewDidLoad` function. You can avoid this repetition by using functions.

Run the app

Try your game. Does it work as I described it?

That's it! In chapter 8, you learn about functions and get rid of repetition in your code.

8

Reuse your code: Clean it with function detergent

This chapter discusses one of the most interesting and important topics: functions!

This chapter covers

- *What a function is*
- *How a function is created and used*
- *How to pass data to a function*
- *How to receive data from a function*

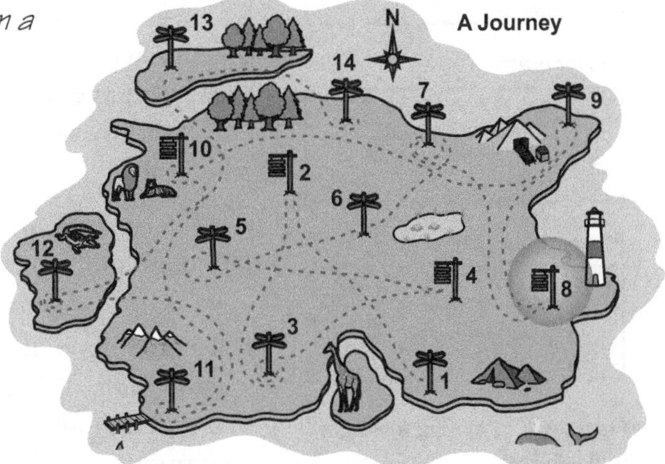

You've reached the eighth milestone: reuse your code. Before you get started, here's the main thing you need to know about functions: functions exist so that you can reuse and clean your code.

Read on, and I'll explain why you might want to have reusable code.

Reuse and clean your code with functions

You're about to find out what a function is. I'll start with a simple example.

Imagine that you're playing a game on your computer. In this game, your character needs to jump over obstacles. You have three ways to make your character jump:

- Press the J key.
- Press the up-arrow key.
- Press the spacebar.

Although it sounds like a simple thing, making a character jump in a game could take 40 lines of code or more.

Player presses J key, so do
lots of code that makes character jump
Player presses up arrow, so do
lots of code that makes character jump
Player presses spacebar, so do
lots of code that makes character jump

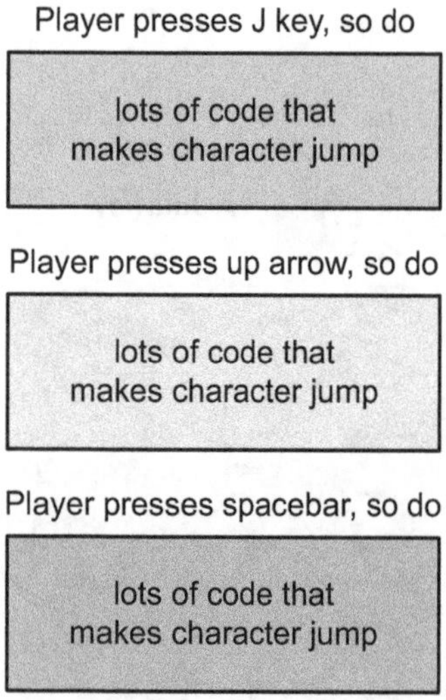

Figure 8.1 Painting a picture of a function

Now think about the jump taking 40 lines of code. I won't put a big block of code here, but look at the diagram in figure 8.1.

All three blocks of code do the same thing: make the character jump. As shown in the figure, you could type the same 40 lines of code for jumping for all three events, but there are a few problems with that:

- It's messy. Your code is long and difficult to understand, and hard to follow later if you want to change it.
- It's not good to update the code to change something. What if you wanted to make the character jump higher? You'd have to find and change the code in all three places, not in one

block. And forgetting to update in all places will make your app buggy and seem to be of bad quality.

Functions are blocks of code that are written once and can be called however many times you need them in your app and wherever the scope allows, so you don't have to type the same lines of code many times. You will learn about scope in chapter 9.

Functions help you keep your code uncluttered and easier to change. If you turn the block of code you used three times into a function, it looks like figure 8.2.

Are you ready to see what a function looks like in code?

Player presses J key, up arrow, or the spacebar, so do

lots of code that makes character jump

Figure 8.2 Understanding functions

Simple functions

You're about to use code to write some simple functions:

- Create a new playground, and call it functions_in_swift.
- Remove the first line of code.
- To create a function, type this code:

```
func sayHello() {
    print("Hello, iOS!")
}
```

Creating a function means

- Giving a name to a function
- Writing the function's code between two curly braces to tell it what to do when it's called
- Take another look at this code, with the lines explained:

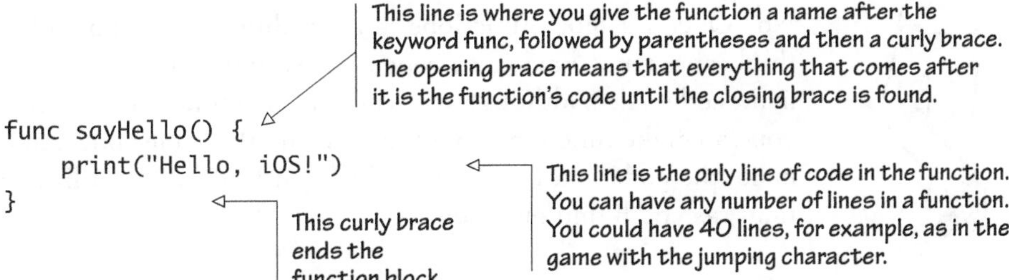

This line is where you give the function a name after the keyword func, followed by parentheses and then a curly brace. The opening brace means that everything that comes after it is the function's code until the closing brace is found.
func sayHello() {
print("Hello, iOS!")
}
This line is the only line of code in the function. You can have any number of lines in a function. You could have 40 lines, for example, as in the game with the jumping character.
This curly brace ends the function block.

This function prints "Hello, iOS" in the playground. To make this happen, you call the function. When you call a function, it carries out the code in its curly braces.

To call this function, type the name of it anywhere in your code. Try this:

```
sayHello()
```

You should see the words "Hello, iOS!" print in the playground.

Now that you have a function in use, here's the basic syntax of a function:

```
func <functionName>() {
    <funcCode>
}
```

Table 8.1 shows what these parts are doing.

Table 8.1 Syntax definitions for simple functions

Part of syntax	Explanation
`<functionName>`	The name of the function, which you use when you call it in your code
`<funcCode>`	The code between the curly braces that runs whenever the function name is called

Why do I need a function to print the same text? It's almost faster to type the code when I need it.

First of all, what if you needed to print 100 lines, and you needed to do this several times? Would you repeat those hundred lines of code? No? Of course not! Functions can have hundreds of lines of code, and think about not having to repeat those lines over and over in your main code. Also, although it's true that this function isn't very useful, you can make functions do more than run the same code. And you can make the code in a function do different things, depending on conditions, as you'll find out soon.

Here are two more functions you can try.

The `enjoy()` function tells Frank to have a good weekend:

```
func enjoy() {
    print("Enjoy your weekend, Frank! See you next week.")
}

enjoy()
```

This line is where you call the function.

Next is the `printDaysOfWeek()` function, which prints the days of the week by using an array:

```
func printDaysOfWeek() {
    let days = ["Sunday", "Monday", "Tuesday", "Wednesday", "Thursday",
    ➥ "Friday", "Saturday"]
    for i in days {
        print(i)
    }
}

printDaysOfWeek()
```

Here, you're calling the function to print the days of the week.

Exercise

1. Create a function that prints the numbers 1 to 10. (Hint: Use a loop in the function block.) Then call the function and check your work.
2. Write a function to print the times table of 3, when called. Check your work from the output it gives.

The functions you've seen so far have limited functionality. They can do the same thing each time they're called. But you can do a lot more with functions. You're about to learn how you can send them data to make them more useful.

Giving info to your reusable code

In this section, you give your functions some data so that they can work with it. You do this with the help of parameters. *Parameters* are the data you give to a function. Think of a parameter as being like input for the function.

Take a look at the simple function in figure 8.3. This function prints whatever the programmer asks it to, using a parameter called `printThis`:

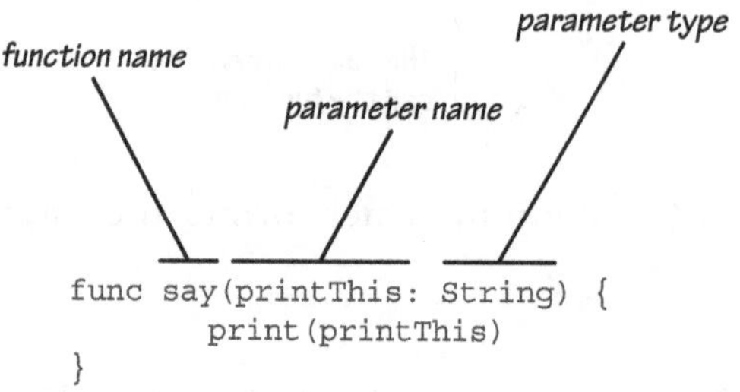

Figure 8.3 Understanding parts of a function

Now try it for yourself! You can use the same playground you created earlier in this chapter.

1 First, type this function in your playground:

```
func say(printThis: String) {
    print(printThis)
}
```

2 Next, call the `say()` function by typing this line:

```
say(printThis: "Hi, my name is Frank.")
```

When you call the function, you're sending it some data. In this example, you're sending it the string `"Hi, my name is Frank."`

When you type the code `say("Hi, my name is Frank.")`, an instruction is sent to the `say()` function to set the parameter `printThis` to that text string. Then this function prints whatever is passed to it by the calling function.

You can send whatever text you want. Try something like this:

```
say(printThis: "Good morning!")
```

This code prints "Good morning!"

This solves the problem of creating a new function every time you need to print something different. You're now using a single function to print different messages depending on what you put in the `printThis` parameter. But functions can do a whole lot more than print whatever they get sent in a parameter.

Here's a taste of what else a function is capable of doing. Imagine a function that takes two numbers as parameters and prints the sum. When you call a function with parameters, even if there's only one, you have to specify each parameter name along with the value that you're passing. In figure 8.4, there are two parameters, `num1` and `num2`, and each has an integer as a value.

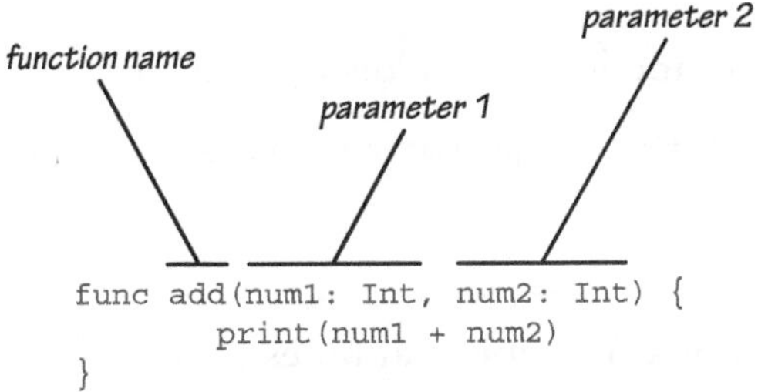

Figure 8.4 Function with parameters

To print the sum of 23 and 5, you can call the function like this:

```
add(num1: 23, num2: 5)
```

This code prints `28`.

Maybe you noticed that in the `say()` function, you used quotes around the parameter value you were passing to the function, and in the `add()` function, you didn't. This is because of the data types you were passing in. The `say()` function needed a string, and strings need quotes. And `add()` takes integers, so you don't need quotes.

Why do I need to put the parameter names? Does this mean I can put the parameters in any order I want?

The parameter names are there to identify the values you're passing to the function. Also, unfortunately, the parameter names and values have to be put in the order in which they were specified in the declaration of the function. But putting those parameters in order does make it easier to go back and understand your code later, when you may have forgotten it.

You can give the `add()` function all kinds of numbers (big or small, negative or positive integers), and it will still work, `add(num1: 294, num2: 357)` prints `651`, for example.

Here's the syntax of such a function that takes parameters:

```
func <funcName>(<parameter1: type>, <parameter2: type>, ...) {
    <funcCode>
}
```

Table 8.2 shows the syntax of a function that takes parameters.

Table 8.2 Syntax definitions for functions with parameters

Part of syntax	Explanation
`<funcName>`	The name of the function and what you use when you call it
`<parameter1: type>,` `<parameter2: type>, ...`	The variables, or values, that the function takes when it's called. Before you pass these parameters (values or variables), you have to declare, in the parentheses, each of the parameters as `<varName>: <varType>`
`<funcCode>`	The code inside the curly braces that runs whenever the function is called

What happens if you have a function that expects two parameters, but you call it with only one?

Xcode gives you a special category of error: a "fix-it." You can click this error, and Xcode will give you the solution and fix it for you automatically.

What types of parameters can you use other than text and integer?

Any valid data type will work as a parameter as it works with a variable or a constant.

Before moving on, you should take another look at the `add()` function, which takes two numbers, adds them, and prints the result. What if the programmer wanted the result back from the function so he could store it in a variable to do other things with it?

Here's an example. Suppose that a cashier is selling pens for 50 cents apiece. At any time, when a person comes to buy pens, the cashier has to calculate the money that the customer needs to pay by multiplying the number of pens by the rate.

The programmer can write a function called `penCost()` that takes two parameters: the number of pens and the rate. Then it returns a value: the money to be charged to the customer for the pens.

But there are taxes on this purchase. The programmer can write another function to compute the tax: `costPlusTax()`. The tax function needs the cost result from the first function, `penCost()`, so it can be used to calculate the taxes with the `costPlusTax()` function.

To capture data from a function, you need to use a return value.

You've learned how to pass some text or a number to a function so that the function can use it. Now you learn how to code a function so that it can return values, or the results of calculations, to the caller.

Next, you learn about return values.

Getting info from your reusable code

Welcome to the final and most interesting stage of learning about functions: return values.

What if you need to receive values returned from a function? Fortunately, this task is simple. I'll begin with an example. Here's a modified version of the `add()` function you saw in the preceding section. Now it returns the result it gets after adding the two numbers:

```
func addNums(num1: Int, num2: Int) -> Int {
    return num1 + num2
}
```

The addNums() function takes two parameters, num1 and num2, and has a return type of Int.

This line returns the sum of the two numbers.

Here's how you can call this function and see the return value:

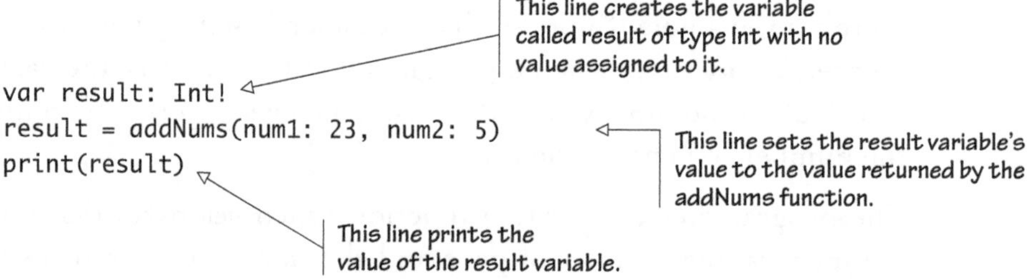

This line creates the variable called result of type Int with no value assigned to it.
var result: Int!
result = addNums(num1: 23, num2: 5)
print(result)
This line sets the result variable's value to the value returned by the addNums function.
This line prints the value of the result variable.

Now try it yourself to get a clearer picture of function syntax. Test the `addNums()` function in the playground:

```
func <funcName>(<parameters>) -> <returnType> {
    <funcCode>
    return <valueToReturn>
}
```

Table 8.3 gives you a closer look at the syntax.

Table 8.3 Syntax definitions for functions with parameters and return values

Part of syntax	Explanation
`<funcName>`	The name of the function and what you use when you call it
`<parameters>`	The variables, or values, that the function takes when it is called. Before you pass these parameters (values or variables), however, you have to declare each of the parameters: `<varName>: <varType>, ...`
`<returnType>`	The type of variable you'll be returning from the function. The -> (arrow) symbol can be read as *returns* in this context.
`<funcCode>`	The code that runs whenever the function is called

`<valueToReturn>`	The value that the function returns, which can be a value or a variable. You can have:
	`return num1 + num2`
	or
	`var answer = 0`
	`answer = num1 + num2`
	`return answer`

Here's another example that calculates the area of a rectangle:

```
func areaOfRectangle(length: Int, width: Int) -> Int {
    return length * width
}
```

Try the function by calling it like so:

```
var area = areaOfRectangle(length: 10, width: 5)
print("The area of the rectangle with length 10 and width 5 is
  \(area)")
```

WARNING You *can* put return statements anywhere in your function block, but you usually won't want to do that, because any code that comes after a return statement in the function block is ignored.

At times, though, you may want to take advantage of this situation. If you put a return statement in an if statement, the function wouldn't stop until the if condition was true. If the if statement weren't executed (with a return statement in it), Swift would continue with the code in the function. Your function would need another return statement, or Swift would give you an error. Here's an example:

```
func franksStatus() -> String {
    let franksAge = 13
      if franksAge >= 18 {
        return "Adult"
    }
}
```

If you try to run this code in the playground, you see an error. Note that the function is programmed to return "Adult" only if Frank's age is greater than or equal to 18. But Frank is 13 at present, so the if statement won't execute. The function won't return anything, which Swift doesn't accept, because this function has been coded to return a string. So Swift gives you an error.

Both of the following code samples compile correctly, however.

```
func franksStatus() -> String {
    var franksAge = 13
    if franksAge >= 18 {
        return "Adult"
    }
    return "Minor"
}

func franksStatus() -> String {
    var franksAge = 13
    if franksAge >= 18 {
        return "Adult"
    } else {
        return "Minor"
    }
}
```

Also, here's a working example of a function that can take two numbers and tell you whether those numbers are equal:

```
func isEqual(num1: Int, num2: Int) -> Bool {
        if num1 == num2 {
            return true
    }
    return false
}
```

Exercise

Try this in your head with these pairs of numbers, and figure out which `return` statement will be called.

```
num1     num2
 2         4
 7         3
10        10
```

NOTE Even though you use `Int` and `Bool` as return types in these functions, you can return any data type that's available in Swift.

Now you know how to create a function, pass parameters, and return values. But (lucky you) you're getting three apps in a row.

Before you dive into these apps, take a few minutes to check your app knowledge.

Check your app knowledge

1 Create a function that takes two numbers as parameters and gives you the product of the two numbers. Do the same thing by creating a function for subtraction and another for division. This function should return a `Double`.

2 What's wrong with the following code?

```
func returnRandom(input: Int) -> Int {
    if input == 5 {
        return 1
    }
}
```

(Hint: After you've made a guess, try the code in the playground to see whether you were right!)

3 What will the following code print? (Trick question!)

```
func customPrint() {
    print("Hello World")
}
```

4 What will the following code print?

```
func a() {
    print("A CALLED")
    b()
}
func b() {
    print("B CALLED")
    c()
}
func c() {
    print("C CALLED")
}
a()
```

5 Create a function that takes three integers and returns the biggest of them.

6 Create a function called `squareIt()` that can take a number as an `Int` and return its squared value. You must print the number returned.

App-Exercise: Virtual Dice

Now you're ready to start the first exercise for this chapter: creating the Virtual Dice app. You'll never need physical dice again!

What does this app do?

In this section, you create a virtual dice application that generates two random numbers from 1 to 6.

NOTE You can find the code for this application in the Chapter08_Virtual-Dice file inside the Hello-Swift-Code-master folder that you downloaded from

GitHub. If you haven't downloaded the code from GitHub, go to: https://github.com/tanmayb123/Hello-Swift-Code/archive/master.zip. You should download the code only once for all chapters.

When the app is done, you'll see output like figure 8.5.

Carrier
5:55 PM
Die #1:
5
Die #2:
3
Randomly Generate Die Numbers

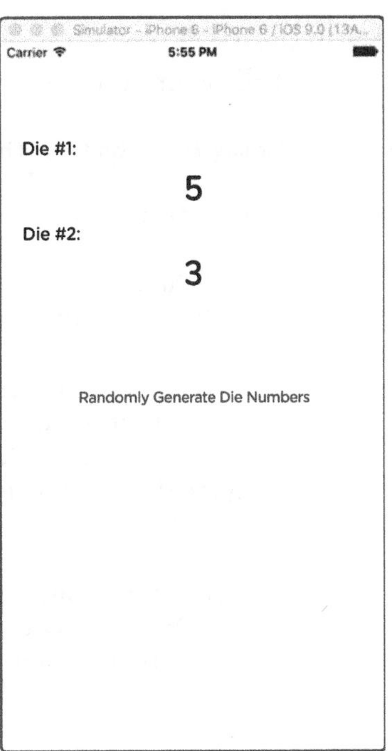

Figure 8.5 Virtual Dice final app

Set up the project and create the UI

For this app, you need a UI like the one in figure 8.6.

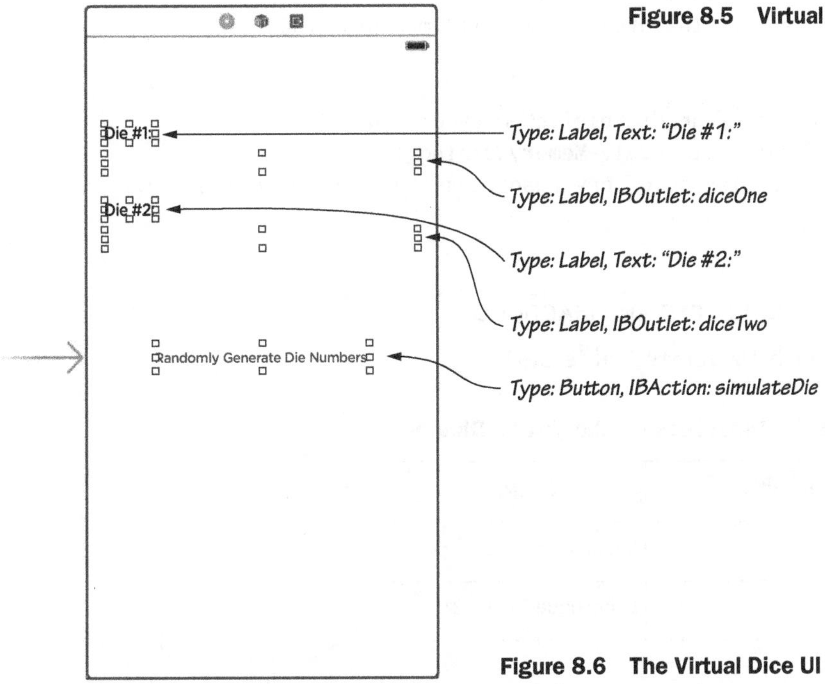

Die #1:
Die #2:
Randomly Generate Die Numbers
Type: Label, Text: "Die #1:"
Type: Label, IBOutlet: diceOne
Type: Label, Text: "Die #2:"
Type: Label, IBOutlet: diceTwo
Type: Button, IBAction: simulateDie

Figure 8.6 The Virtual Dice UI

Code the app

Edit your code to look like this:

Listing 8.1 Code for the Virtual Dice app

```
class ViewController: UIViewController {

    @IBOutlet var diceOne: UILabel!
    @IBOutlet var diceTwo: UILabel!

    override func viewDidLoad() {
        super.viewDidLoad()
        // Do any additional setup after loading the view,
➥ typically from a nib.
    }

    @IBAction func simulateDie() {              <-- This IBAction is called whenever
        diceOne.text = "\(randDice())"              someone clicks the button.
        diceTwo.text = "\(randDice())"
    }

    func randDice() -> Int {                    <-- This function returns a
        return Int(arc4random_uniform(UInt32(6))+1)   random number from 1 to 6.
    }

    override func didReceiveMemoryWarning() {
        super.didReceiveMemoryWarning()
        // Dispose of any resources that can be re-created.
    }
}
```

CONNECT IBOUTLETS AND IBACTIONS

Start with `IBOutlets` (table 8.4).

Table 8.4 `IBOutlets` for the Virtual Dice app

IBOutlet	Control
`diceOne`	Label under `Die #1:`
`diceTwo`	Label under `Die #2:`

Table 8.5 shows the `IBActions`.

Table 8.5 `IBActions` for the Virtual Dice app *(continued)*

IBAction	Button
`simulateDie`	Randomly Generate Die Numbers button

Learn how the code works

Because this app is so small, it's easy to explain in a paragraph. The app waits for you to click the button. When you click the button, it generates two random numbers from 1 to 6 and puts them in the two labels. Observe how the function `randDice()` works to provide you the values as though they're from a real pair of dice. With this app on your phone, you'll never need real dice again!

Run your app

When you run your app, it shows you two random numbers. An example of output is in figure 8.7.

And that's it! Time for the next app.

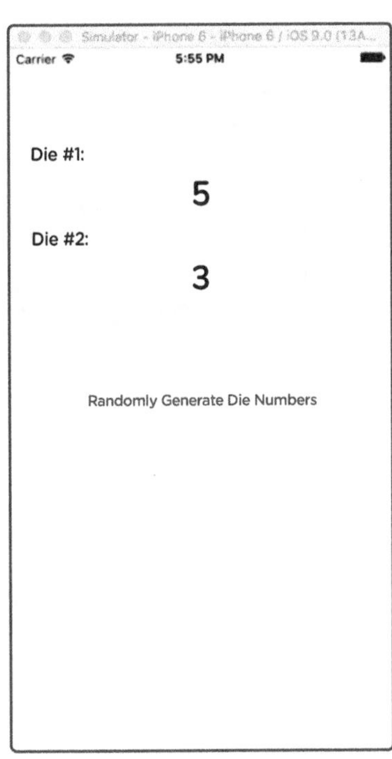

Figure 8.7 Virtual Dice: final app

App-Exercise: Rock Paper Scissors

It's time for the second exercise of this section: creating the Rock Paper Scissors app. You can play Rock Paper Scissors anywhere, any time, with this app.

What does this app do?

You're about to create a Rock Paper Scissors simulator that you can play with me, except that I'll be the computer! In this game, Tanmay (the computer) has as many chances of winning as the real player does, because my moves are 100 percent random.

NOTE You can find the code for this application in the Chapter08_RockPaperScissors file inside the Hello-Swift-Code-master folder that yoGitHub. If you haven't downloaded the code from GitHub, go to: https://github.com/tanmayb123/Hello-Swift-Code/archive/master.zip. You should download the code only once for all chapters.

When you build and run the app, it will look like figure 8.8.

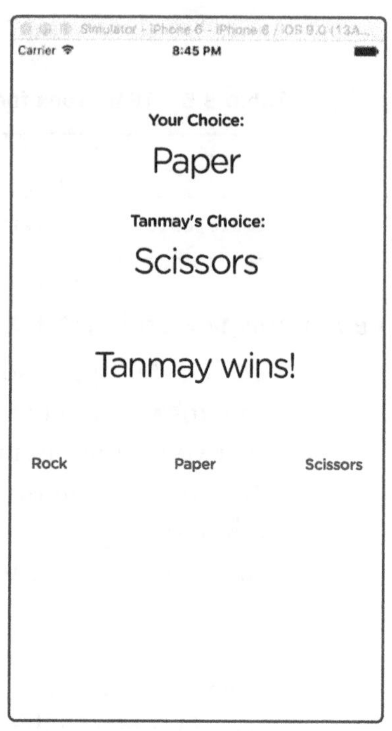

Figure 8.8 The Rock Paper Scissors UI

Set up the project, and create the UI

To start, create a UI like the one in figure 8.9.

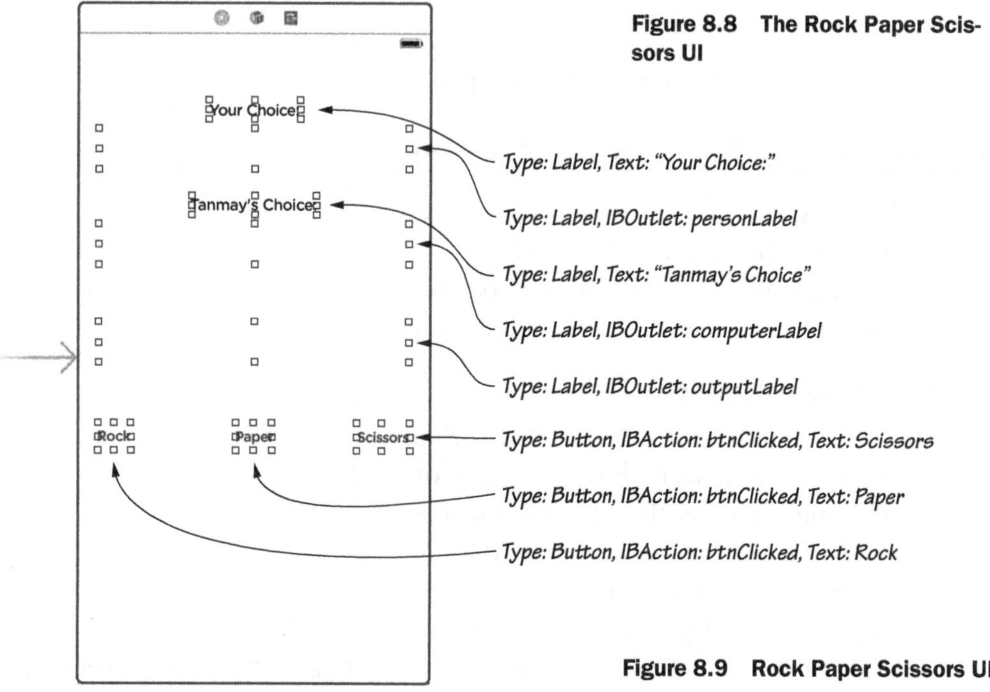

Figure 8.9 Rock Paper Scissors UI

Code the app

Change your code to look like this:

Listing 8.2 Code for the Rock Paper Scissors app

```
import UIKit
extension UIButton {
    var text: String {
        get {
            return self.titleLabel!.text!
        }
        set {
            self.setTitle(newValue, for: .normal)
        }
    }
}

class ViewController: UIViewController {
    @IBOutlet var computerLabel: UILabel!
    @IBOutlet var personLabel: UILabel!
    @IBOutlet var outputLabel: UILabel!

    override func viewDidLoad() {
        super.viewDidLoad()
        // Do any additional setup after loading the view,
➥ typically from a nib.
    }

    @IBAction func btnClicked(sender: UIButton) {
        personLabel.text = sender.text
        computerLabel.text = type()
        if personLabel.text! == computerLabel.text! {
            outputLabel.text = "TIE! Play Again?"
            return
        }
        if checkForPlayerWin(
            humanType: personLabel.text!,
            compType: computerLabel.text!) {
            outputLabel.text = "You win!"
        } else {
            outputLabel.text = "Tanmay wins!"
        }
    }
```

Ignore this extension! Type it, however. You don't need to know yet, but this extension allows you to get the text of your UIButton and set it without lots of code.

This IBAction is called whenever one of the three buttons is clicked.

```
func type() -> String {
    let randNum = arc4random_uniform(UInt32(3))+1
    switch randNum {
    case 1:
        return "Rock"
    case 2:
        return "Paper"
    case 3:
        return "Scissors"
    default:
        return "ERROR"
    }
}
```

This function returns a random move that the computer makes.

```
func checkForPlayerWin(humanType: String, compType: String) ->
➥ Bool {
    if humanType == "Rock" {
        if compType == "Paper" {
            return false
        }
        if compType == "Scissors" {
            return true
        }
    }
    if humanType == "Paper" {
        if compType == "Scissors" {
            return false
        }
        if compType == "Rock" {
            return true
        }
    }
    if humanType == "Scissors" {
        if compType == "Rock" {
            return false
        }
        if compType == "Paper" {
            return true
        }
    }
    return false
}
```

This function checks whether the user wins or loses.

```
    override func didReceiveMemoryWarning() {
        super.didReceiveMemoryWarning()
        // Dispose of any resources that can be re-created.
    }
}
```

Connect the IBOutlets and IBActions

Start with the `IBOutlets` (table 8.6).

Table 8.6 `IBOutlets` for the Rock Paper Scissors app

IBOutlet	Control
`personLabel`	The label under `Your Choice:`
`computerLabel`	The label under `Tanmay's Choice:`
`outputLabel`	The label under `computerLabel`

Table 8.7 lists the `IBActions`.

Table 8.7 `IBActions` for the Rock Paper Scissors app

`IBAction`	Button
`btnClicked`	All three player buttons (Rock, Paper, Scissors)

Learn how the code works

Here's what the app does with the input that you give it:

1. It stores the move the player makes.
2. The app generates a random move by using the `turn()` function.
3. The app saves your move in the `personLabel` and the computer's move in the `computerLabel`.
4. The app figures out who won by using the `checkForPlayerWin()` function, which returns `true` if the player won and `false` if the player lost.
5. The app puts the result in the `outputLabel`.

Run your app

That was simple, wasn't it! When you run the app, make your choice of rock, paper, or scissors, and Tanmay will make his. Your screen will look similar to figures 8.10 and 8.11.

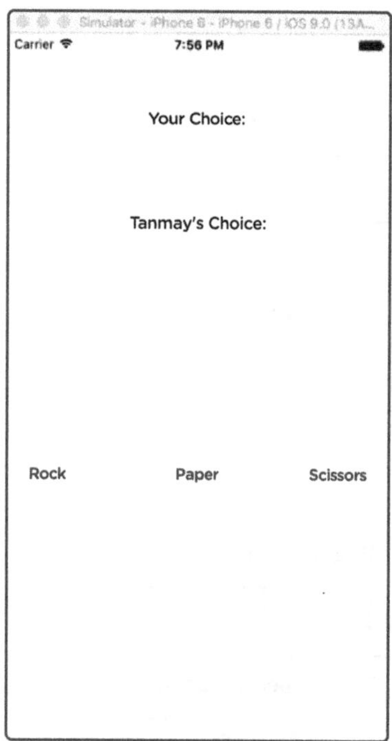

Figure 8.10 The final RPS app

Carrier
8:45 PM
Your Choice:
Paper
Tanmay's Choice:
Scissors
Tanmay wins!
Rock
Paper
Scissors

Figure 8.11 The Rock Paper Scissors UI

App-Exercise: Money Denomination

Get ready for another app-exercise. This exercise will help you to build your programming skills, your math skills, and will be useful in your everyday life.

NOTE You can find the code for this application in the Chapter08_Money-Denomination folder inside the Hello-Swift-Code-master folder that you downloaded from GitHub. If you haven't downloaded the code from GitHub, go to: https://github.com/tanmayb123/Hello-Swift-Code/archive/master.zip. You should download the code only once for all chapters.

Warning: There's a lot of code in this one, so you'll need to be a patient typist. Or you can use the code you downloaded.

What does this app do?

In this section, you create an app that takes a total amount of money from a user (you) and tells you the fewest bills and coins that you'll need to make the total amount of money. This app is based on Canadian currency, which consists of

- $100 bills
- $50 bills
- $20 bills
- $10 bills
- $5 bills
- $2 coins
- $1 coins
- $0.25 coins
- $0.10 coins
- $0.05 coins
- $0.01 coins

When you run the app, you see output like figure 8.12. (This example uses $234.67.)

Simulator - iPhone 6 - iPhone 6 / iOS 9.0 (13A...

Carrier 6:51 PM

234.67

Denominate the money!

$100 bills	2
$50 bills	0
$20 bills	1
$10 bills	1
$5 bills	0
$2 coins	2
$1 coins	0
$0.25 coins	2
$0.10 coins	1
$0.05 coins	1
$0.01 coins	2
TOTAL:	234.67

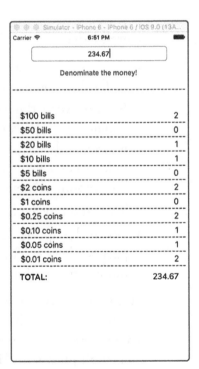

Figure 8.12 Money Denomination: final app

How does this app work?

I'll start by discussing how this app works. It may be a bit challenging, so I created the diagram in figure 8.13 to help you. Take a look at the diagram and then read the explanation after it.

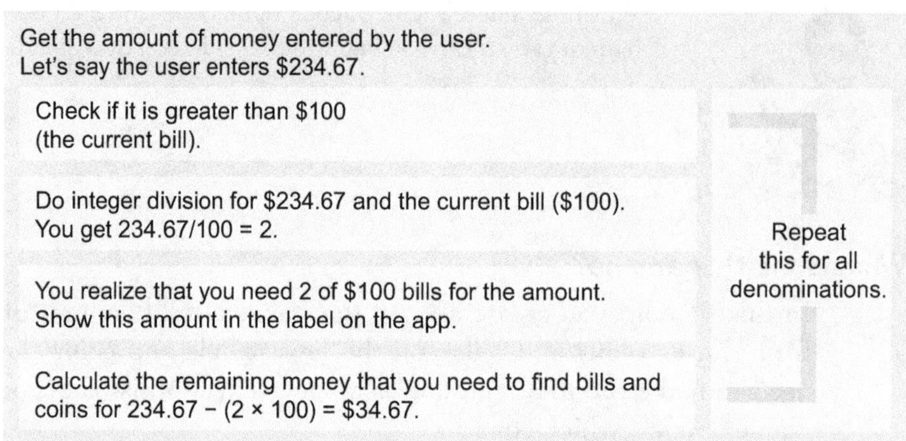

Get the amount of money entered by the user.
Let's say the user enters $234.67.
Check if it is greater than $100
(the current bill).
Do integer division for $234.67 and the current bill ($100).
You get 234.67/100 = 2.
You realize that you need 2 of $100 bills for the amount.
Show this amount in the label on the app.
Calculate the remaining money that you need to find bills and
coins for 234.67 − (2 × 100) = $34.67.
Repeat
this for all
denominations.

Figure 8.13 How the number of bills and coins is calculated

Here's a description of what that figure entails:

1 The code takes an amount of money that a user enters into the app. Call this amount the *starting amount*.
2 Starting with the $100 bills, the code uses the greater-than (>) or equal-to (=) operator to find out whether it can use the bill or coin it's currently checking. If so, it calculates how many of that kind of bills or coins it can use and then subtracts that much from the starting amount of money.
3 This step repeats from the biggest to the smallest denominations.
4 When the app is done with the $1 coin, it gets into the cents. This part is where calculations start to change, and the app has to do a bit more math, so things get trickier!

Suppose that you have $0.40, or 40 cents. You don't want that in decimal form, because it makes the calculations easier when the amount is a whole number. So the code rounds the decimal to hundredths and then multiplies it by 100. As a result, the app gets a whole number that equals the remaining money in cents. Then it continues, and instead of doing math with complicated decimals, it uses simple whole numbers.

Set up the project, and create the UI

Create the UI first. Figure 8.14 shows all the elements you'll need to place in the UI.

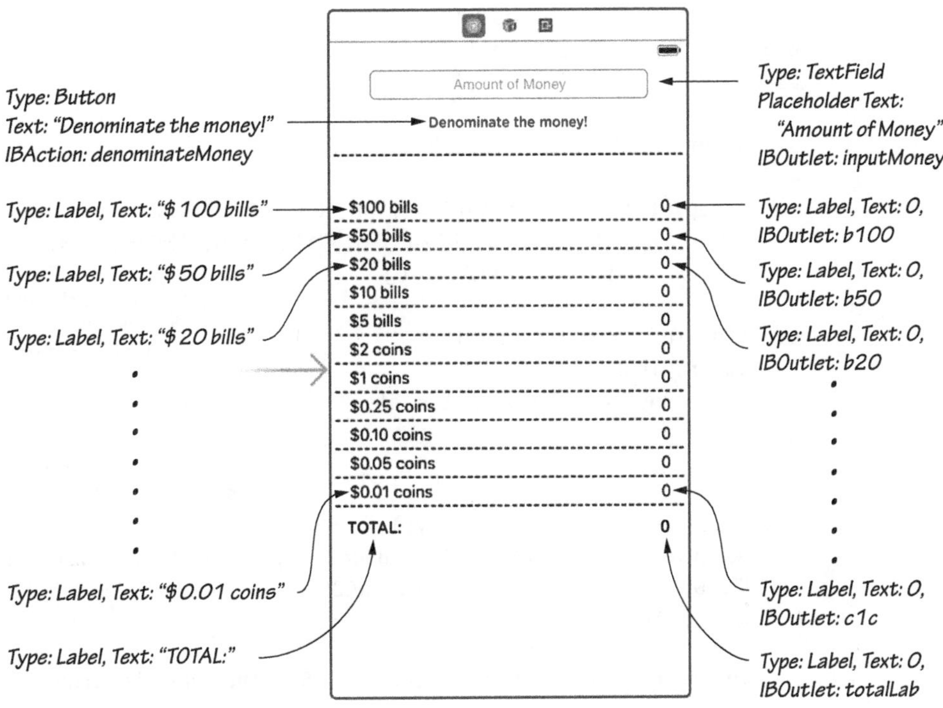

Figure 8.14 Money Denomination UI

Code the app

Type the following code:

Listing 8.3 The code for the Money Denomination app

```
class ViewController: UIViewController {

    @IBOutlet var inputMoney: UITextField!

    @IBOutlet var b100: UILabel!
    @IBOutlet var b50: UILabel!
```

```
    @IBOutlet var b20: UILabel!
    @IBOutlet var b10: UILabel!
    @IBOutlet var b5: UILabel!
    @IBOutlet var c2: UILabel!
    @IBOutlet var c1: UILabel!
    @IBOutlet var c25: UILabel!
    @IBOutlet var c10: UILabel!
    @IBOutlet var c5: UILabel!
    @IBOutlet var c1c: UILabel!

    @IBOutlet var totalLab: UILabel!

    var moneyVals: [String: Int] = ["NB100d": 0, "NB50d": 0, "NB20d":
➥  0, "NB10d": 0, "NB5d": 0, "NC2d": 0, "NC1d": 0, "NC25c": 0,
➥  "NC10c": 0, "NC5c": 0, "NC1c": 0]

    override func viewDidLoad() {
        super.viewDidLoad()
        // Do any additional setup after loading the view,
➥ typically from a nib.
    }

    @IBAction func denominateMoney() {
        moneyVals = ["NB100d": 0, "NB50d": 0, "NB20d": 0, "NB10d": 0,
➥  "NB5d": 0, "NC2d": 0, "NC1d": 0, "NC25c": 0, "NC10c": 0, "NC5c":
➥  0, "NC1c": 0]

        var total = (inputMoney.text! as NSString).doubleValue

        if total >= 100 {
            let nOfBills: Int = Int(total / 100)
            total -= Double(nOfBills * 100)
            moneyVals["NB100d"] = nOfBills
        }

        if total >= 50 {
            let nOfBills: Int = Int(total / 50)
            total -= Double(nOfBills * 50)
            moneyVals["NB50d"] = nOfBills
        }

        if total >= 20 {
            let nOfBills: Int = Int(total / 20)
```

This code is the dictionary that will hold the amount of each bill that's required.

This IBAction denominates the money when the button is clicked.

```
        total -= Double(nOfBills * 20)
        moneyVals["NB20d"] = nOfBills
    }

    if total >= 10 {
        let nOfBills: Int = Int(total / 10)
        total -= Double(nOfBills * 10)
        moneyVals["NB10d"] = nOfBills
    }

    if total >= 5 {
        let nOfBills: Int = Int(total / 5)
        total -= Double(nOfBills * 5)
        moneyVals["NB5d"] = nOfBills
    }

    if total >= 2 {
        let nOfCoins: Int = Int(total / 2)
        total -= Double(nOfCoins * 2)
        moneyVals["NC2d"] = nOfCoins
    }

    if total >= 1 {
        let nOfCoins: Int = Int(total / 1)
        total -= Double(nOfCoins * 1)
        moneyVals["NC1d"] = nOfCoins
    }

    total = round(100 * total) / 100
    total = total * 100

    if total >= 25 {
        let nOfCoins: Int = Int(total / 25)
        total -= Double(nOfCoins) * 25
        moneyVals["NC25c"] = nOfCoins
    }

    if total >= 10 {
        let nOfCoins: Int = Int(total / 10)
        total -= Double(nOfCoins) * 10
        moneyVals["NC10c"] = nOfCoins
    }
```

```
    if total >= 5 {
        let nOfCoins: Int = Int(total / 5)
        total -= Double(nOfCoins) * 5
        moneyVals["NC5c"] = nOfCoins
    }

    if total >= 1 {
        let nOfCoins: Int = Int(total / 1)
        moneyVals["NC1c"] = nOfCoins
    }

    var total__: Double = 0
    total__ += Double(moneyVals["NB100d"]!) * 100
    total__ += Double(moneyVals["NB50d"]!) * 50
    total__ += Double(moneyVals["NB20d"]!) * 20
    total__ += Double(moneyVals["NB10d"]!) * 10
    total__ += Double(moneyVals["NB5d"]!) * 5
    total__ += Double(moneyVals["NC2d"]!) * 2
    total__ += Double(moneyVals["NC1d"]!)
    total__ += Double(moneyVals["NC25c"]!) * 0.25
    total__ += Double(moneyVals["NC10c"]!) * 0.10
    total__ += Double(moneyVals["NC5c"]!) * 0.05
    total__ += Double(moneyVals["NC1c"]!) * 0.01

    totalLab.text = "\(total__)"

    putValuesInLabels()

}

func putValuesInLabels() {
    let b100V = (moneyVals["NB100d"]!)
    let b50V = (moneyVals["NB50d"]!)
    let b20V = (moneyVals["NB20d"]!)
    let b10V = (moneyVals["NB10d"]!)
    let b5V = (moneyVals["NB5d"]!)
    let c2V = (moneyVals["NC2d"]!)
    let c1V = (moneyVals["NC1d"]!)
    let c25V = (moneyVals["NC25c"]!)
    let c10V = (moneyVals["NC10c"]!)
    let c5V = (moneyVals["NC5c"]!)
    let c01V = (moneyVals["NC1c"]!)
```

```
        b100.text = "\(b100V)"
        b50.text = "\(b50V)"
        b20.text = "\(b20V)"
        b10.text = "\(b10V)"
        b5.text = "\(b5V)"
        c2.text = "\(c2V)"
        c1.text = "\(c1V)"
        c25.text = "\(c25V)"
        c10.text = "\(c10V)"
        c5.text = "\(c5V)"
        c1c.text = "\(c01V)"

    }

    override func didReceiveMemoryWarning() {
        super.didReceiveMemoryWarning()
        // Dispose of any resources that can be re-created.
    }

}
```

Connect the IBOutlets and IBActions

Now connect the `IBOutlets` and `IBActions` to their respective controls (tables 8.8 and 8.9).

Table 8.8 The `IBOutlets` for the Money Denomination app

`IBOutlet`	Control
b100	Label beside $100 bills
b50	Label beside $50 bills
b20	Label beside $20 bills
b10	Label beside $10 bills
b5	Label beside $5 bills
c2	Label beside $2 coin
c1	Label beside $1 coin
c25	Label beside $0.25 coin

Table 8.8 The `IBOutlets` for the Money Denomination app *(continued)*

`IBOutlet`	Control
`c10`	Label beside $0.10 coin
`c5`	Label beside $0.05 coin
`c1c`	Label beside $0.01 coin
`inputMoney`	Input TextField
`totalLab`	Label beside `TOTAL:`

Table 8.9 The `IBActions` for the Money Denomination app

`IBAction`	Button
`denominateMoney()`	Denominate the Money!

Run the app

When you run this app, it should look like figure 8.15.

That's it for functions and apps. In chapter 9, you learn how to group your functions and variables to create classes and why you should use them.

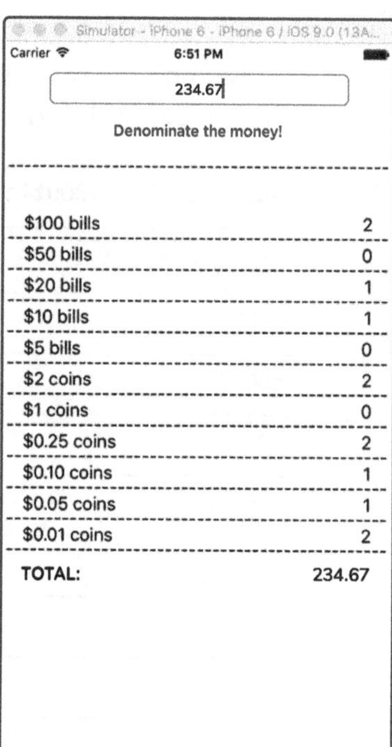

Figure 8.15 Money Denomination app

9

Reduce your code: Use less, do more with class detergent

Congratulations! You've finished all the beginner's topics, and now you move on to intermediate topics. In this first intermediate-level chapter, you learn about classes and how they make your code cleaner, shorter, and easier to reuse.

This chapter covers

- *What is a class?*
- *Why would I use a class, anyway?*
- *What are the benefits of classes?*
- *What are initializers?*
- *How do classes inherit from their parent classes?*
- *What is evolution?*
- *What's scope and how does it apply to your code?*
- *What's the difference between declaring, defining?*

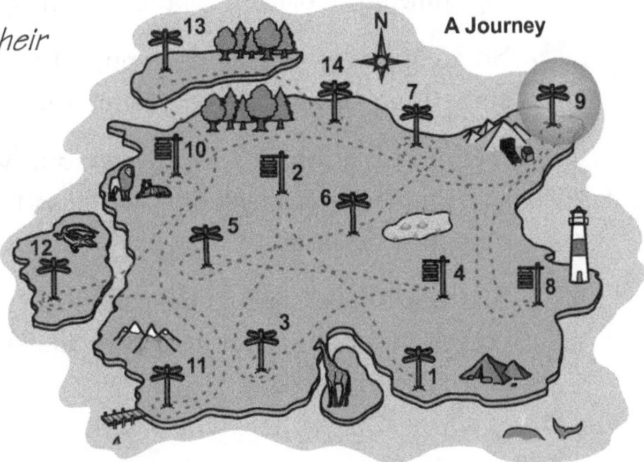

Milestone 9, Reduce your code, is where things get a little more advanced. Classes make your code more portable and easier to maintain.

Reduce and clean your code with classes

I'll start by giving you a bird's-eye view of what classes are and then show you how to code them.

WARNING The topic of classes isn't simple. This chapter has been made easy to understand to help you learn. But some information on classes isn't included or explained in-depth, either because I teach it to you later or you don't need to know it yet.

What is a class?

Think of a class as a collection of related functions and variables, with special features, that are organized into a bundle. Let me give you an example.

To understand the concept of a class, think about what the word *person* means. We're all different in lots of ways—skin color, height, age, hair color, gender, and more—but still, each one of us is a person.

Now suppose that you're making a class called `Person`. This class has many attributes, such as height, age, and eye color. It also contains lots of functions, which are things that a person can do, including breathing, talking, working, playing, eating, and reading this book.

So a *class* is essentially a group of attributes and functions that identify something broadly. Every one of us can be in the `Person` class.

If you talk about a specific person, however, such as Tim Cook, you'd say that he's an *object* of the class `Person`. (I come back to the idea of objects a bit later.)

So the class `Person` can describe every person. Now consider a shark. If you think about what goes into the `Person` class, it's clear that a shark is in a different class.

Similarly, you know that a dog, cat, snake, or plant are in different classes because all these beings have different attributes and functions.

You apply the same concept in your programs. You can take related attributes and functions and organize them into a bundle called a class.

Why you should learn to use classes

You may be thinking, "Okay, I know that a class groups a bunch of related stuff. But I don't see the big deal. Why bother using classes?"

Using classes makes things easier when you have to go back and maintain your code, which you will. (I explain why in a moment.) Here's why you should use classes instead of mushing all your code into one big program. Classes do all the following things:

- Keep code clean and organized.
- Make code readable for yourself and for other programmers.
- Add functionality. (I talk about this topic later.)
- Help you debug your code because the code is understandable; if there's a problem, you can find it and solve it quickly.
- Make changes globally. If you change code in one class, it changes in all the places it's referenced.
- Make sharing code easy. (You could make a class for line drawing and put it on the internet for thousands of people to see and use.)
- Give you more great features, such as initializers and inheritability, that aren't available without classes. You learn about these features in this chapter.

Have some fun with classes

Ready to have some fun? I'm going to ask you some questions about some pictures—what are the things in rows A, B, C, and D of table 9.1?

Table 9.1 What are these things?

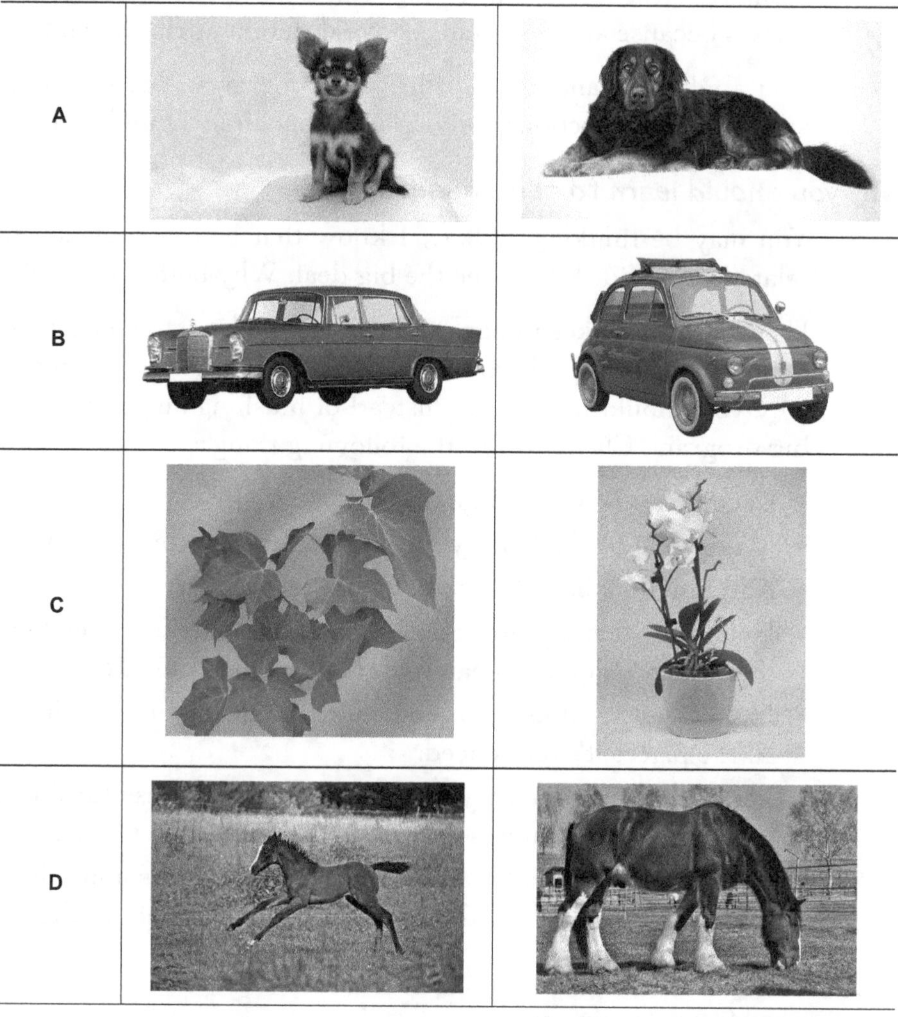

You probably got the answers right: A. dogs, B. cars, C. plants, and D. horses. That quiz was easy because you can identify classes of things, even if you don't know all the details (or properties, as you'll learn soon).

THINK How can your brain distinguish among a dog, a horse, a plant, and a car? Your brain knows that what it's looking at belongs to a class named `Dog`, for example. The specs of the object (`Dog` in this case) can be worked out by looking closely at it. Similarly, your brain works its way out for recognizing horses, plants and cars! This is how the concept of classes works in everyday life.

Classes are part of everyday life. Each car may be slightly different in size or shape from other cars, for example, but the basic idea is the same: "a structure with four wheels, a hood, a trunk, a steering wheel, and the ability to throttle its wheels when the gas pedal is pressed."

In a similar way, classes are used in programming. Classes are templates that can be filled out to create a final thing. (I'm using the word *thing* because the template can create anything of that kind.)

You can create a template for a `Dog` and use that template to create a specific `Dog`. Anything in class `Dog` performs the same actions (or functions), such as barking and tail-wagging, and has a good sense of smell. You can set attributes, or properties, such as name, color, breed, size, amount of fur, tail size, shape of mouth, and eye color in the template to make a final thing—in this case, a final dog. The final thing you create is called an *object* or *instance*. The actions that these objects are capable of performing are called *functions* or *methods*. Fur color, length of tail, eye color, and other qualities are called *variables* and *properties*.

If I'm talking about any dog, I'm talking about the actual template or class. If I'm talking about a specific dog, such as Amy's dog Ranger, that dog is an instance (or object) of the template (or class).

Table 9.2 may help you visualize classes better.

Table 9.2 Visualization of a simple `Dog` class and instance

Class	Properties	Values	Instance
`Dog`	`Name`	`Ranger`	`Ranger`
	`Color`	`Brown`	
	`Size of ears`	`3 inches`	
	Functions		
	`Bark`		
	`Wag tail`		
	`Fetch ball`		

Pop quiz

Write down 3 classes based on real-life things. Add attributes (what makes one of these things stand out from others in the same class) and functions (what this thing can do) to your classes.

One of the best things about classes is that they let you reuse your code and reduce the size of your programs.

How do classes reduce code?

The best way to see how classes reduce code is to try one for yourself and see what it can do with a few lines.

In this section, you create a class named `TestClass`, which starts off empty. Then you add a variable called `name` to the class. After that, you'll see how you can access the `name` variable that you declared in the class and even change its value.

I explain the rest with the flow as you go.

SNEAK PEEK You'll be learning about adding functions, initializing the class you made, and even making classes inherit from other classes. When you learn that much, you'll create a special Calculator app.

Create a class

Get started by creating a simple class in a new playground called classes_in_swift:

```
class TestClass {

}
```

Start the class with the class keyword, the class name (TestClass), and an opening brace.

End the class with a closing brace.

It's that easy to get started with a class. Keep in mind that this class is the simplest kind you can have, with no functions, variables, methods, or initializers inside it.

Add a variable

Now add a variable to the class. Between the braces, type this line of code:

```
var name: String = "Frank"
```

I have a variable called `name` inside a class, with the value set to `Frank`. What if I want to do something with it? How do I access this class's variable, called `name`, from the rest of the playground?

Before I answer, type the `name` variable in the playground outside the class. Go ahead; I'll wait.

Why didn't it work? What's happening?

You should be getting an error (`Use of unresolved identifier 'name'`) because the `name` variable is reserved for use inside the `TestClass` class. You won't be able to access this variable from any other scope (as you see later in this chapter). To access the `name` variable, you have to create an instance of the type `TestClass`.

Create Instances of your class

To create an instance, use

```
var testClassInstance = TestClass()
```

Try typing outside the class, in the playground area.

You've created your own type of variable. This variable isn't a data type like `Int` or `String`, but it's close because you can make a variable instance of it. Here, the variable you've created is called `testClassInstance`.

You may have noticed that you're not using a colon to declare a type of variable, as you sometimes do for other data types. The key is type inference, which you learned about in chapter 3.

Even though it's completely valid to say

```
var testClassInstance: TestClass = TestClass()
```

with type inference, you can avoid the type (and colon) and cut to the chase (or, in this case, the instance part):

```
var testClassInstance = TestClass()
```

Now that you know this much, how will it help you? Well, the variable `testClassInstance` is essentially a box, and not any box, but a box of type `TestClass`. You should recall that this box contains the variable, or a placeholder of `String` type, called `name`. You can do this in the playground:

```
testClassInstance.name
```

The code should print `"Frank"`.

This is how you access a variable inside a class. First, you create an instance of a class; then you type `<instanceName>.<variableName>` to get access to it and in this case to see it print.

NOTE Instances are also called objects of the class.

Change the value of a variable

Amazing, right? Well, there's more. You can change the value in the `name` variable (because it's not a constant) to something like this:

```
testClassInstance.name = "Tim Billy"
```

So you've also changed the value inside the box itself.

Pop quiz

Here's a tricky question for you. What do you think will happen if you create a new instance

```
var instance2 = TestClass()
```

and print its name

```
instance2.name
```

Will the ouput be `"Frank"` or `"Tim Billy"`?

If you guessed `"Frank"`, you're right! When you changed the name earlier, you changed only that specific box's (`testClassInstance`) name. You didn't change the variable stored in the class; only the variable that was inside the specific box instance (`testClassInstance`) changed, as illustrated in figure 9.1.

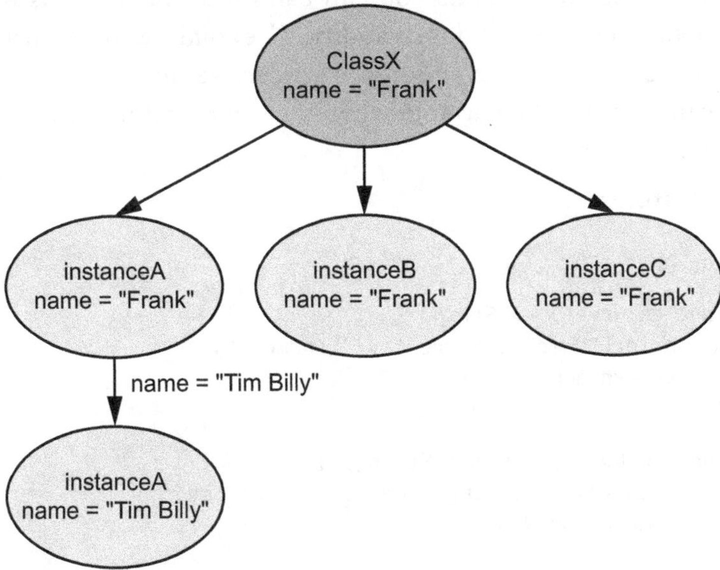

Figure 9.1 Instances of a class are independent.

Adding functionality to classes

Now that you know the bare-bones details of classes, add some functionality, or functions, to your class. You want to add some functions that let you get and set the value of the variable `name`:

```
class TestClass {

    var name = ""

    func getName() -> String {
        return name
    }

    func setName(yourName: String) {
        name = yourName
    }

}
```

You added the `getName() -> String` function and the `setName(yourName: String)` function because getting and setting the name in your code becomes easier for you, as you can call these functions as many times and include checks for data validity. (I explain another way of doing this in the Metric Conversion app-excercise later in this chapter.) If you want to print the variable when you set or get it, for example, enter this code:

```
class TestClass {

    var name = ""

    func getName() -> String {
        print("Name is currently: \(name) ")
        return name
    }

    func setName(yourName: String) {
        print("Now setting name to: \(yourName) ")
        name = yourName
    }

}
```

Table 9.3 takes a closer look at these two functions.

Table 9.3 Functions for the `TestClass` class

Function	Purpose
`getName() -> String`	This function gets (accesses) and returns the value of the variable called `name`.
`setName(yourName: String)`	This function sets (stores) the value of `yourName` in the variable called `name`.

If you were to create an instance, you'd use

```
var testClassInstance = TestClass()
```

And to access the `name` variable, use

```
testClassInstance.name
```

This still works but won't execute the code you asked it to in the function, which is the `print` statement, because you're accessing the variable directly instead of going through the `getName() -> String` function.

Quick review

To assign a value to the `name` variable that you created, use the `setName(yourName: String)` function, which prints the new value and then sets the new value.

Add an initializer that does something every time you create an instance

Next, you add an *initializer*—a function that's called automatically whenever the instance (object) of a class is created. This function can take parameters but can't return anything. There are a few types of initializers (*inits*, for short), but the three main ones are

- *Required*—This type of init must be called when you create an instance of the class.
- *Convenience*—This type of init is optional, and you can have many inits of this kind in a class.
- *Designated*—To create a designated init, you don't specify the type of init; Swift takes it as designated.

There are other initializers, but you don't need to worry about them at this point.

If initializers are like functions, why can't they return anything, even though they can take parameters?

It may not seem obvious at first, but you probably already know the answer. If an initializer returns an `Int`, how do you create an instance of the class it's initializing? You could say that initializers do return objects of type `<their_own_class>`.

To see why you need an initializer, try this code in a playground:

```
class TestClass {

    var name = ""

    // This is a required init, which means it has to run
    required init(yourName: String) {
        name = yourName
    }

    func getName() -> String {
        print(name)
        return name
    }

}
```

To create a new instance of this class, do this:

```
var testClassInstance = TestClass()
```

Oops—you got an error. You set your initializer to `required`, so you got an error because you didn't supply the argument for the required init to run! Here's that error:

```
"Missing argument for parameter 'yourName' in call"
```

To fix this problem, give the required `init` function a value, because it's expecting one. You can try this:

```
var testClassInstance = TestClass(yourName: "Amy Rizzo")
```

No more error.

To access the name, call the `getName()` function or print the variable:

```
testClassInstance.getName()
```

This prints the name you gave in the initializer: `"Amy Rizzo"`, in this case.

Now you know that to initialize this class, you have to give it a `name` argument.

What if the user wants to give only the first name and last name in separate arguments? How can you make the app handle the situation given?

That's a good question. Get ready, because here's your answer (the rest of this section, until you start the Inheritance section).

To solve this problem, you have to take a look at how to use convenience initializers. Look at the following code and make some guesses about what's going on. Then I'll explain.

```
class ConvenientClass {

    var name = ""

    init(yourName: String) {
        name = yourName
    }

    convenience init(fName: String) {
        self.init(yourName: fName)
    }

    convenience init(lName: String) {
        self.init(yourName: lName)
    }

    convenience init(fName: String, lName: String) {
        self.init(yourName: "\(fName) \(lName)")
    }

    func getName() -> String {
        print(name)
        return name
    }

}
```

NOTE Don't get rid of this code; you're going to need it in the next section!

You can initialize an instance of this class in several ways:

- Give the full name in `String` format in a single argument, `yourName`.
- Give the name in one argument, `fName`.
- Give the name in one argument, `lName`.
- Give the full name in two separate arguments, `fName` and `lName`.

When the designated `init` is called, you do the same thing that you did with the required `init`. When a convenience `init` is called, however, call the designated `init` with the values that you get from the convenience `init`.

NOTE When you work with convenience inits, they have to call another regular init (designated or required), not of type convenience, on their first line of code.

This is what each init does in `ConvenientClass`:

- `init(yourName: String)`—The designated init. It runs if you give a `"yourName"` parameter as a string. It sets the `name` variable to `"yourName"`.
- `convenience init(fName: String)`—A convenience init that runs if you give an `"fName"` parameter as a string. It calls the designated init with the `"yourName"` parameter as the `"fName"` that it gets from you.
- `convenience init(lName: String)`—A convenience init that runs if you give an `"lName"` parameter as a string. It calls the designated init with the `"yourName"` parameter as the `"lName"` that it gets from you.
- `convenience init(fName: String, lName: String)`—A convenience init that runs if you give an `"fName"` string and an `"lName"` string as separate parameters. It doesn't set the `name` variable to the parameters given; instead, it calls the designated init with the parameter `"yourName"`, as `fName` and `lName` concatenated with a space between.

Now you know the basics of classes. Here's the simple syntax of a class:

```
class <classname> {
    <variables>
    <initializers>
    <methods & functions>
}
```

Table 9.4 breaks down the syntax.

Table 9.4 Syntax definitions for the class

Syntax block	Definition
`<classname>`	The name of the class
`<initializers, methods, variables...>`	The place for all the code that can go in the class

I hope you got the answer to your question!

In the next section, you look at more-advanced class topics.

Like father, like son: Inheritance

In this section, you'll take some of the code you created and use it to learn what inheritance is. Try it out!

In the same playground with the `ConvenientClass` code, try typing this:

```
class sonOfConvClass: ConvenientClass {

}
```

Believe it or not, this class is complete. In this example, you're also telling the class called `sonOfConvClass` to inherit and act like `ConvenientClass`. If you were to take the code

```
var dad = ConvenientClass(yourName: "Robert Brooks")
dad.getName()                                        // Prints "Robert Brooks"
```

And modify it to look like

```
var son = sonOfConvClass(yourName: "Jim Brooks")
son.getName()                                        // Prints "Jim Brooks"
```

Figure 9.2 Representing the likeness of classes as in "dad" and "son"

it works exactly the same way. The reason is that `sonOfConvClass` (I'll call it sonny) is a duplicate, or clone, of `ConvenientClass` (I'll call it daddy), as represented by figure 9.2.

What if you wanted a clone of daddy but then changed a few things in sonny to make it smarter than daddy? How would you do that? You'd override whatever you needed to change from daddy's class in sonny's class.

You can't use words like daddy in code, of course. Use the word `super` in the code.

Furthermore, sonny doesn't have a name in daddy's code, because daddy is unaware of sonny's existence (the sad life of a daddy class). If you want to override the `getName()` function and make it return the name, along with an extra message, use this:

```
class sonOfConvClass: ConvenientClass {

    override func getName() -> String {
        return name + " from Convenient's son"
    }

}
```

If you try this

```
var son = sonOfConvClass(name: "Jim Brooks")
son.getName()
```

the code returns `"Jim Brooks from Convenient's son"`.

If you do this

```
var dad = ConvenientClass(name: "Robert Brooks")
dad.getName()
```

the code returns "Robert Brooks" because it doesn't contain the modified function.

IMPORTANT When a class inherits from another class, it automatically gets all the functions, initializers, and variables from the parent class. Then you can add a few more functions to the child class or rewrite some functions of the parent class with some modifications in the child class so that the child class is different from the parent.

All about scope

Scope is where in your code you can access certain variables, functions, or classes.

NOTE I'm not going to load you down with jargon such as public, private, and global scope. I'll give you enough knowledge to write intermediate-level apps. Anything more, you'll find when you need it in the rest of the book.

What is variable's scope?

In any playground exercise or app, you've seen that curly braces ({}) start and end blocks of code. These braces are always paired and can be nested in another pair (as in a function in a class). These braces divide your code into little blocks, which you can understand part by part. Keeping these braces in mind, here's the basic idea of *variable's scope*: anything declared inside a pair of braces isn't accessible outside the braces.

Try this code in the playground to understand how scope works:

```
var age = 20
if age >= 18 {
    let status = "Adult"
    status
}
status
```

This code works fine and prints the status Adult. (annotation on `status` inside the braces)

This line gives you an error because "status" was declared in the braces of the if block, so after that brace pair ends, it's inaccessible. (annotation on the final `status`)

Because you declared the variable `status` inside the braces, when you're outside the braces, you can't get to it. What happens if you try to access it before the `if` statement?

You also get an error. Your program doesn't know what status is until you've declared it (`let status`). Figure 9.3 explains scope visually.

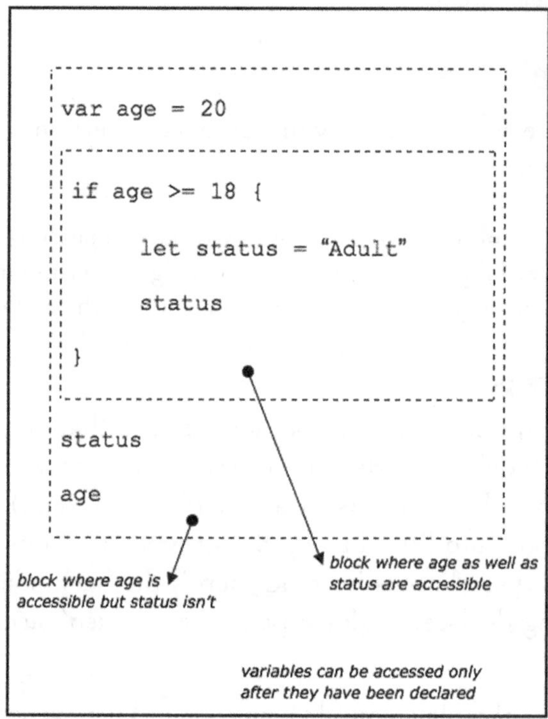

Figure 9.3 A diagram explaining the way scope works inside of code blocks

IMPORTANT I've been talking about declaring a variable. Don't get *declaring* confused with *defining*!

- To declare is to create the variable (var age: Int!)
- To define is to give the variable a value (age = 20)

Or you can declare and define at the same time:

```
(var age = 20 or var age: Int = 20)
```

What if I need to be able to access a variable outside the braces?

If you need to get the value of `status` to be used even after the brace pair ends, you could do this:

```
var age = 20
var status: String = "Child"
if age >= 18 {
    status = "Adult"
    print(status)
}
print(status)
```

This code works fine and prints Adult. (annotation on `print(status)` inside the braces)

This line works because the declaration of "status" was before the braces opened or closed, but it was defined in the brace (which doesn't matter in programming). So it was accessible in that scope and prints Adult here as well. (annotation on the final `print(status)`)

FIGURE IT OUT!

1. Create a function.
2. Now declare a variable in your function.
3. Try to define this variable inside and outside this function. What happened?
4. Next, declare a variable outside the function.
5. Try to define this variable inside and outside this function. What happened?

Are you ready to practice with classes and scope? In the next section, you build an app.

Calculator app

Now build the Calculator app to help you out with your math.

What does this app do?

NOTE You can find the code for this application in the Chapter09_Calculator folder inside the Hello-Swift-Code-master folder that you downloaded from GitHub. If you haven't downloaded the code from GitHub, go to: https://github.com/tanmayb123/Hello-Swift-Code/archive/master.zip. You should download the code only once for all chapters.

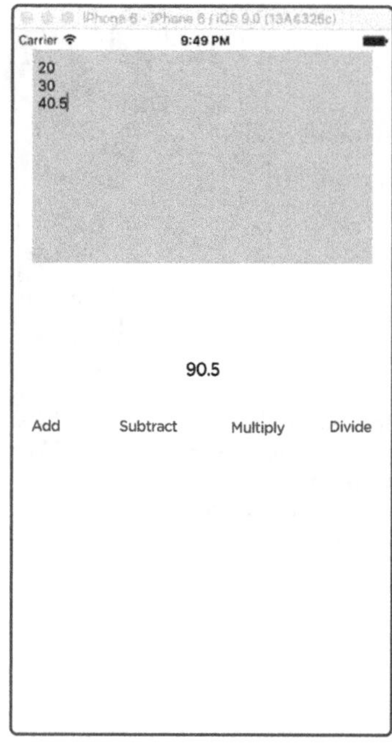

Figure 9.4 The final running app

In this section, you create an app that can add, subtract, multiply, or divide any number of values at the same time. Figure 9.4 shows what your app will look like when you're done.

Create the UI

Create the user interface (UI). Use the details in figure 9.5 to create your controls.

How does this app work?

This app takes lots of numbers in a text view, each number on a new line, without gaps. You create an array of these numbers. You write a `ListOfNumbers` class that contains an array of numbers called `numberList`. This class also has a required init that takes one parameter: `initWithNumberList: [Double]`. In the `init`, set the

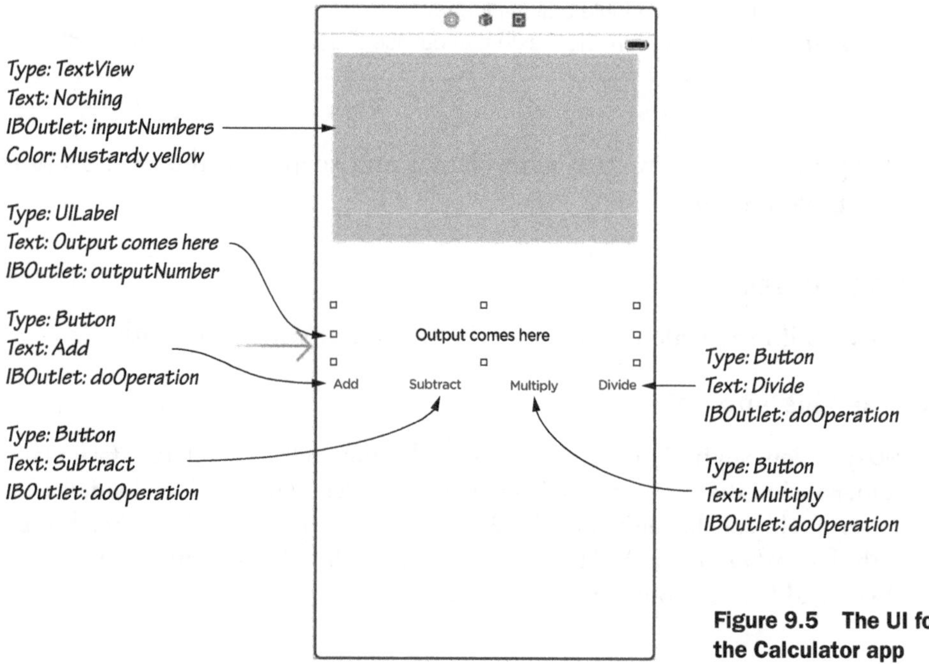

Figure 9.5 The UI for the Calculator app

numberList variable to the initWithNumberList parameter. Next, create a class called Calculator that inherits from the ListOfNumbers class. The Calculator class becomes a clone of the ListOfNumbers class. When that's done, add a few functions to the Calculator class:

```
addAllInNumberList() -> Double          ← Add all numbers in the list.
subtractAllInNumberList() -> Double     ← Subtract all numbers in the list.
multiplyAllInNumberList() -> Double     ← Multiply all numbers in the list.
divideAllInNumberList() -> Double       ← Divide all numbers in the list.
```

You don't need to understand the code inside these functions beyond the basic idea.

Code the app

Listing 9.1 contains the code for the Calculator app.

Listing 9.1 *Code for the Calculator app*

```
extension UIButton {
    var text: String {
        get {
            return self.titleLabel!.text!
        }
        set {
            self.setTitle(newValue, for: .normal)
        }
    }
}

class ListOfNumbers {
    var numberList: [Double] = []

    required init(initWithNumberList: [Double]) {
        numberList = initWithNumberList
    }
}

class Calculator: ListOfNumbers {

    func addAllInNumberList() -> Double {
        let temp = numberList
```

```
        var finalVal = numberList[0]
        numberList.remove(at: 0)
        _ = numberList.map({finalVal += $0})
        numberList = temp
        return finalVal
    }

    func subtractAllInNumberList() -> Double {
        let temp = numberList
        var finalVal = numberList[0]
        numberList.remove(at: 0)
        _ = numberList.map({finalVal -= $0})
        numberList = temp
        return finalVal
    }

    func multiplyAllInNumberList() -> Double {
        let temp = numberList
        var finalVal = numberList[0]
        numberList.remove(at: 0)
        _ = numberList.map({finalVal *= $0})
        numberList = temp
        return finalVal
    }

    func divideAllInNumberList() -> Double {
        let temp = numberList
        var finalVal = numberList[0]
        numberList.remove(at: 0)
        _ = numberList.map({finalVal /= $0})
        numberList = temp
        return finalVal
    }

}

class ViewController: UIViewController {

    @IBOutlet var inputNumbers: UITextView!

    @IBOutlet var outputNumber: UILabel!

    override func viewDidLoad() {
        super.viewDidLoad()
        // Do any additional setup after loading the view,
        ➥ typically from a nib.
```

```
}

@IBAction func doOperation(sender: UIButton) {
    var finalNumberlist: [Double] = []

    _ = inputNumbers.text
      ➥ .components(separatedBy: "\n")
      ➥ .map({finalNumberlist.append(Double($0)!)})

    let calculatorInstance = Calculator(
        initWithNumberList: finalNumberlist)

    if sender.text == "Add" {
        let shouldRemove =
        ➥ "\(calculatorInstance.addAllInNumberList())"
        ➥ .componenents(separatedBy: ".")[1] == "0" ? true : false
        let intVal =
        ➥ Int("\(calculatorInstance.addAllInNumberList())"
        ➥ .components(separatedBy: ".")[0])!
        outputNumber.text = shouldRemove ? "\(intVal)" :
        ➥ "\(calculatorInstance.addAllInNumberList())"
    } else if sender.text == "Subtract" {
        let shouldRemove =
        ➥ "\(calculatorInstance.subtractAllInNumberList())"
        ➥ .components(separatedBy: ".")[1] == "0" ? true : false
        let intVal =
        ➥ Int("\(calculatorInstance.subtractAllInNumberList())"
        ➥ .components(separatedBy: ".")[0])!
        outputNumber.text = shouldRemove ? "\(intVal)" :
        ➥ "\(calculatorInstance.subtractAllInNumberList())"
    } else if sender.text == "Multiply" {
        let shouldRemove =
        ➥ "\(calculatorInstance.multiplyAllInNumberList())"
        ➥ .components(separatedBy: ".")[1] == "0" ? true : false
        let intVal =
        ➥ Int("\(calculatorInstance.multiplyAllInNumberList())"
        ➥ .components(separatedBy: ".")[0])!
        outputNumber.text = shouldRemove ? "\(intVal)" :
        ➥ "\(calculatorInstance.multiplyAllInNumberList())"
    } else if sender.text == "Divide" {
        let shouldRemove =
        ➥ "\(calculatorInstance.divideAllInNumberList())"
        ➥ .components(separatedBy: ".")[1] == "0" ? true : false
        let intVal =
        ➥ Int("\(calculatorInstance.divideAllInNumberList())"
```

```
            ➥ .components(separatedBy: ".")[0])!
            outputNumber.text = shouldRemove ? "\(intVal)" :
            ➥ "\(calculatorInstance.divideAllInNumberList())"
        }
    }

    override func didReceiveMemoryWarning() {
        super.didReceiveMemoryWarning()
        // Dispose of any resources that can be recreated.
    }

}
```

NOTE When you've entered your number in the text view, please don't press the Return key on your keyboard! If you do, you'll cause the app to crash, because Swift doesn't know how to convert a newline to an integer; it's not a valid number. You can click the buttons at the bottom of the screen, however.

Why do I use an underscore (_) in the line of code "`_ = numberList.map({finalVal += $0})`"?

When you run the `map` function, remember that it returns a value. If a function returns a value and you don't use that value, Swift gives you a warning (meaning that it thinks you might be doing something wrong). If you set the underscore's value to the result of the function, however, Swift knows that it needs to trash the return value from the function; it understands that you don't need it.

Connect IBOutlets and IBActions

Now that you've coded the app, connect the `IBOutlets` and `IBActions`, as shown in tables 9.5 and 9.6.

Table 9.5 `IBOutlets` for the Calculator app

IBOutlet	Control
`inputNumbers`	`Yellow, TextView`
`outputNumber`	`"Output Comes Here", Label`

Table 9.6 `IBActions` for the Calculator app

`IBAction`	Buttons
`doOperation`	Add, Subtract, Multiply, and Divide

Run the app

Run the app, enter some numbers in the text view, and click a button like Add. You see something like figure 9.6.

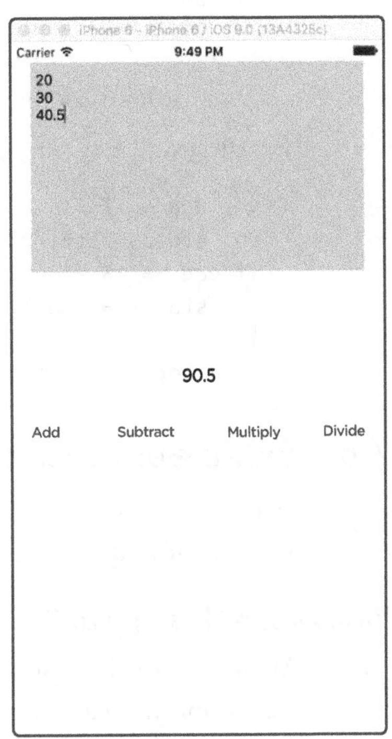

Figure 9.6 The running Calculator app

This special calculator helps you do data-management problems in math, such as finding the mean or average of some numbers.

That's it for this chapter except for checking your app knowledge and an app-exercise. I hope you enjoyed it! In chapter 10, you learn about managing files.

Check your app knowledge

1. What's the difference between declaring and defining?
2. What characters control the scope of a variable?
3. What are the different types of initializers, and what do they do?
4. What can classes in programming be compared to in real life?
5. What's wrong with the following code?

```
class somethingIsWrong {

    convenience init(name: String) {
        print(name)
    }

}
```

6 What is one thing you must do with convenience initializers?

7 What will the following code print?

```
var age = 20
var status: String = "Child"
if age >= 18 {
    status = "Adult"
}
"I am a(n) \(status) "
```

8 What will the following code print?

```
var age = 17
var status: String = "Child"
if age >= 18 {
    status = "Adult"
}
"I am a(n) \(status)"
```

App-Exercise: Metric Conversion

All right, it's time for the first exercise: building and running the Metric Conversion app to help you with your measurements!

What does this app do?

Welcome to the app-exercise that does metric-unit conversion. It converts one metric unit to another. It converts 2.5 kilometers to meters, for example, or 25 millimeters to centimeters. It doesn't convert meters to miles or yards.

NOTE You can find the code for this application in the Chapter09_MetricConversion folder inside the Hello-Swift-Code-master folder that you downloaded from GitHub. If you haven't downloaded the code from GitHub, go to: https://github.com/tanmayb123/Hello-Swift-Code/archive/master.zip. You should download the code only once for all chapters.

Math: Negative powers

Before you start, I need to talk about a little math that I haven't taught you how to do in Swift yet: negative powers. Do you remember powers from chapter 3?

10 to the power 2 = 10 x 10, which is 100

10 to the power 5 = 10 x 10 x 10 x 10 x 10, which is 100,000

There are also negative powers:

10 to the power -3 = (1 / 10) x (1 / 10) x (1 / 10), which is 0.001.

10 to the power -5 = (1 / 10) x (1 / 10) x (1 / 10) x (1 / 10) x (1 / 10), which is 0.00001

And even though it's not a negative power:

10 to the power 0 = 1

Got it? Okay, in the next section you create the UI.

Creating the UI

The details of the UI you need to create are in figure 9.7.

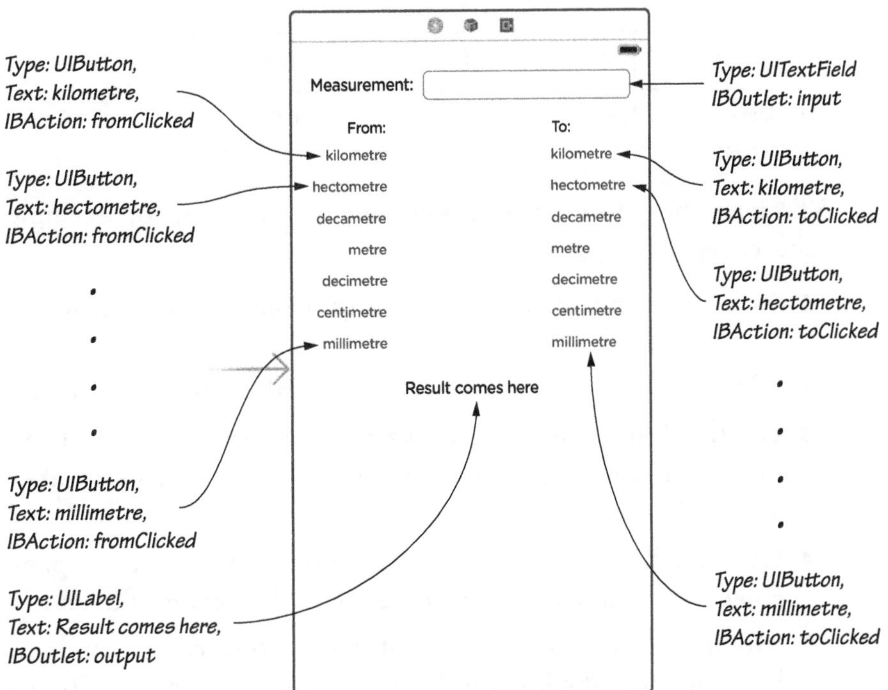

Figure 9.7 Metric Conversion UI

Code the app

First, look at how you convert from kilometers to meters so you can write the code.

Table 9.7 lists the units of the metric system in order. You'll use the rank to help figure out the conversion.

Table 9.7 Unit rankings for Metric Conversion

Unit	Abbreviation	Rank	Example value
kilometer	km	1	1
hectometer	hm	2	10
decameter	Dm	3	100
meter	m	4	1,000
decimeter	dm	5	10,000
centimeter	cm	6	100,000
millimeter	mm	7	1,000,000

To learn how to convert 5 kilometers to meters, for example, follow these steps:

1 Note the unit you're converting from—in this case, kilometer (ranked 1).
2 Note the unit you're converting to—in this case, meter (ranked 4).
3 Get the difference of the ranks from the To unit to the From unit—in this case, rank of meter to rank of kilometer. In numbers, that's 4 – 1 = 3.
4 Get 10 to the power of the number you got in the last step, even if it's a negative number—in this case, 10 to the power of 3, or 1000.
5 Multiply the amount of the unit you're converting from by the number you got in the last step —in this case, 5 × 1000, or 5000 m).

Done! You should have the right answer: 5 kilometers = 5000 meters.

You use these seven steps to convert 2.5 kilometers to meters and 348 millimeters to centimeters. You're going to work on these two examples: 2.5 km = ? m and 348 mm = ? cm (see table 9.8).

Table 9.8 Steps for Metric Conversion

Steps	Description of steps	How to convert: 2.5 kilometers to meters	How to convert: 348 millimeters to centimeters
1	Rank the units as shown in table 9.6.		
2	Note the rank of the unit you're converting from.	Rank is 1	Rank is 7
3	Note the rank of the unit you're converting to.	Rank is 4	Rank is 6
4	Get the difference of ranks of the To unit and the From unit as rank of unit to – rank of unit from.	4 – 1 = 3	6 – 7 = -1
5	Get 10 to the power of (the number you got in the last step).	10 to the power of 3 = 1,000	10 to the power of -1 = 0.1
6	Multiply the number of units you're converting from by the number you get in step 4.	2.5 x 1,000 = 2,500	348 x 0.1 = 34.8
7	Write your answer.	2.5 km = 2,500 m	348 mm = 34.8 cm

Now you have to code this in Swift, as shown in Listing 9.2. Create a class called `MetricConversionHandler`, which has a dictionary that ranks all the units; then you have variables that store the from unit, from amount, and to unit.

Listing 9.2 MetricConversion app

```
import UIKit
extension UIButton {
    var text: String {
        get {
            return self.titleLabel!.text!
```

```
            }
            set {
                self.setTitle(newValue, for: .normal)
            }
        }
}

class MetricConversionHandler {
    var from = ""
    var   to = ""
    var fromNumber: Double = 0.0

var value = ["kilometer": 1, "hectometer": 2, "decameter": 3, "meter": 4,
➥ "decimeter": 5, "centimeter": 6, "millimeter": 7]

    init(userFrom: String, userTo: String, fromNum: Double) {
        from = userFrom
        to = userTo
        fromNumber = fromNum
    }

    func convert() -> Double {
        let numberToUse = pow(10.0, Double(value[to]!) -
        ➥ Double(value[from]!))
        return Double("\(fromNumber * numberToUse)")!
    }
}

class ViewController: UIViewController {
    @IBOutlet var input: UITextField!
    @IBOutlet var output: UILabel!
    var from = ""
    @IBAction func fromClicked(sender: UIButton) {
        from = sender.text
    }

    @IBAction func toClicked(sender: UIButton) {
        let metricHandlerInst = MetricConversionHandler(userFrom: from,
        ➥ userTo: sender.text, fromNum: Double(input.text!)!)
        let converted = round(pow(10.0, 10.0) *
        ➥ metricHandlerInst.convert()) / pow(10.0, 10.0)
```

```
        if floor(converted) == converted {
            output.text = "\(input.text!) \(from)(s) = \(Int(converted))
            ➥ \(sender.text)(s)"
        } else {
            var convertedString = String(format: "%.10f", converted)
            while "\(convertedString.last!)" == "0" {
                convertedString.removeLast()
            }
            output.text = "\(input.text!) \(from)(s) =
            ➥ \(convertedString) \(sender.text)(s)"
        }
    }

    override func viewDidLoad() {
        super.viewDidLoad()
        // Do any additional setup after loading the view, typically
        ➥ from a nib.
    }
}
```

That's the code! And this time, you don't need to ignore the extension. An extension extends the code that's written in the class that it extends (its base class).

Why would you need an extension? The answer is simple. To see why you need an extension, see what your extension currently does. The current extension adds a computed property, called `text`, to the `UIButton` class. In case you're wondering what a computed property is, it's a variable with a getter and a setter.

NOTE Extensions don't allow you to add variables or constants, but computed properties are allowed.

You add a variable (I'm calling it a variable for the time being so that you aren't confused) called `text` to the class `UIButton`. The `UIButton` class is the class you use for buttons in your `IBOutlets`.

Why is it called a computed property?

Property is another word for *variable*. A *computed property* is a property that's computed whenever it's get or set. Here's an example. Suppose that you've got variables `A`, `B`, and `C`. When you get `C`, it's always equal to `A + B`. Whenever you set `C`, that value should go into `A` and `B`. Instead of always inserting the numbers into `A` and `B` manually, adding `A` and `B` manually, and inserting the result into `C`, you can make `C` a computed property to run a function to do these sorts of things whenever `C` is get or set.

Create a class called `MetricConversionHandler`, which does what the seven steps do.

If you are wondering why we have an if statement calling the floor function, and a while loop inside the else block, we do this to format the numbers displayed in output label. Using this code you'll be able to display "3 meter(s)" instead of "3.0 meter(s)", and "3.1 meter(s)" instead of "3.1000000000 meter(s)" in case that occurs.

Connect IBOutlets and IBActions

Table 9.9 lists all the `IBOutlets` and `IBActions` in the `ViewController` class.

Table 9.9 `IBOutlets` for Metric Conversion app

`IBOutlet`	Explanation
`input`	The text field that tells you the amount of the starting unit you need Example: 15 in the phrase `15 kilometers`
`output`	The label that tells the user how many of one type of unit will be equal to how many of another type of unit Example: 15 kilometer(s) = 15000 meter(s)

Table 9.10 lists the IBActions.

Table 9.10 IBActions for Metric Conversion app

IBAction	Explanation
`fromClicked(sender: UIButton)`	Called whenever one of the buttons from the From side is clicked
`toClicked(sender: UIButton)`	Called whenever one of the buttons from the To side is clicked

Run your app!

Run the app with a value of 30 in the measurement box, starting with meters and converting to kilometers. You should see the output as in figure 9.8.

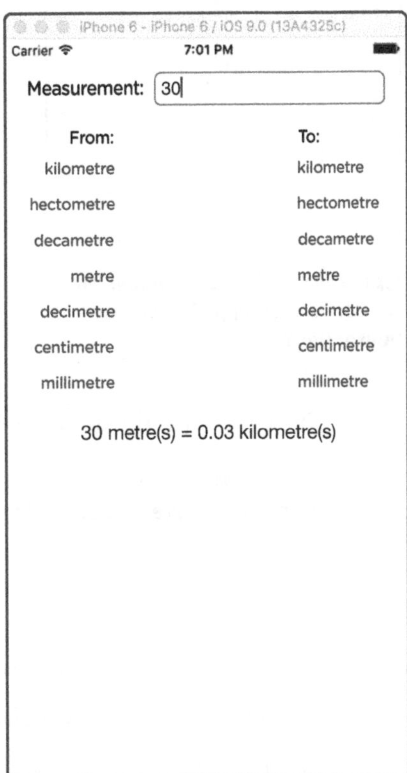

Figure 9.8 Metric Conversion app running.

Extra app-exercise: Metric Conversion app, Part 2

This section covers Part 2 of the Metric Conversion app.

What does this app do?

NOTE You can find the code for this application in the Chapter09_MetricConversionLined folder inside the Hello-Swift-Code-master folder that you downloaded from GitHub. If you haven't downloaded the code from GitHub, go to: https://github.com/tanmayb123/Hello-Swift-Code/archive/master.zip. You should downloaded the code only once for all chapters.

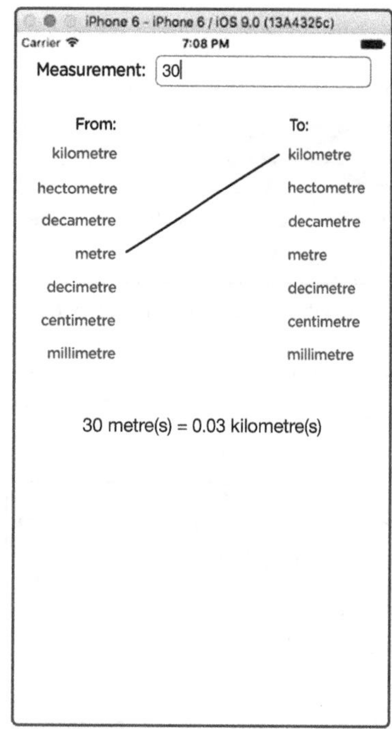

Figure 9.9 The new running Metric Conversion app. See the connector line?

You already have the UI created, so continue to what's new in this part. Figure 9.9 shows your new UI.

In this second part, you add a connecting line, making a line from the unit you're converting from to the unit you're converting to. This line graphically displays to the user the type of unit that is being converted from its left end to another at its right end.

Code the app

Instead of recoding the entire app, you can modify your existing code from the preceding app.

To start, insert the `Connector` class in your code. You can copy and paste the code after your extension to the `UIButton` class, or type it yourself after the `UIButton` extension.

Next, create these two variables:

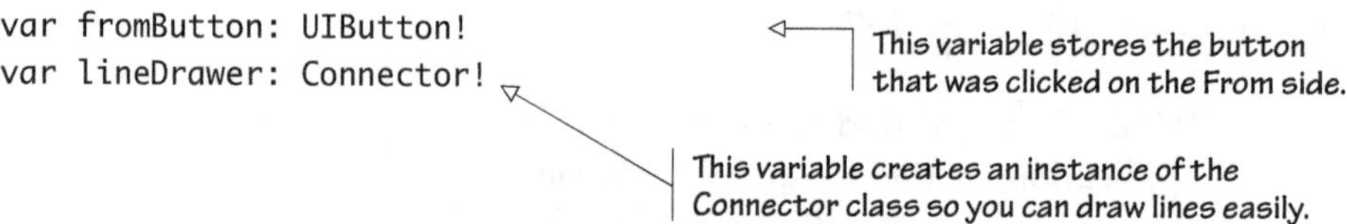

```
var fromButton: UIButton!
var lineDrawer: Connector!
```


Add the following line to your `viewDidLoad()` function:

```
lineDrawer = Connector(initWithView: self.view)
```

Add this line to your `fromClicked(sender: UIButton) IBAction`:

```
fromButton = sender
```

Finally, add these lines to the bottom of your `toClicked(sender: UIButton) IBAction`:

```
lineDrawer.clear()
lineDrawer.drawLineBetweenPoints(
    CGPoint(
        x: 110,
        y: fromButton.frame.origin.y + lineDrawer.thickness),
    CGPoint(
        x: 260,
        y: sender.frame.origin.y + lineDrawer.thickness))
```

You don't need to understand these lines of code yet. You're essentially clearing older connecting lines and then calculating and drawing a line from any of the From buttons to any of the To buttons.

You may be thinking, "Hey, Tanmay, that was pretty easy! I drew lines, but I didn't need to code the line-drawing part. How was that possible?" The secret is that I shared code with you through classes. Classes are great for sharing code, and there's one more thing you should know: classes hide functionality from the coder. I hid the code for drawing lines from you, for example, so you added that code in the form of a class that I already wrote. After that, you drew lines by creating an instance of the class `Connector` with the required parameters inside the initializer.

So all you need to know to draw the lines is how to use the class, not the functionality behind it. You may not be interested in knowing how the class works. If you are, though, you should look at the code in the class. (Nothing's stopping you. You can even modify or extend it to work differently and better!)

This is the final code:

Listing 9.3 Metric Conversion app, Part 2

```
import UIKit
extension UIButton {
    var text: String {
        get {
            return self.titleLabel!.text!
        }
        set {
            self.setTitle(newValue, for: .normal)
```

```
            }
        }
    }

    class Connector {
        var lines = [UIImageView]()
        var lineHeight = 3
        var lineWidth = 3
        var thickness: CGFloat {
            get {
                return CGFloat(((lineWidth + lineHeight))  + 10)
            }
        }
        var viewToEdit: UIView!
        var allFrames = [CGRect]()
        convenience init(initWithView view: UIView) {
            self.init()
            viewToEdit = view
        }
        func drawLineBetweenPoints(_ p1: CGPoint, _ p2: CGPoint) {
            if p1.x == p2.x && p1.y == p2.y {
                handleTouch(p1)
            }
            if p1.y == p2.y {
                if p2.x - p1.x > 1 {
                    var xVal = p1.x
                    for _ in 1...Int(p2.x - p1.x) {
                        xVal  += 1
                        handleTouch(CGPoint(x: xVal, y: p1.y))
                    }
                } else if p2.x - p1.x < -1 {
                    var xVal = p1.x
                    for _ in (Int(p2.x - p1.x)) * 2...Int(p2.x - p1.x) {
                        xVal -= 1
                        handleTouch(CGPoint(x: xVal, y: p1.y))
                    }
                } else {

                }
            }
            else if p1.x == p2.x {
                if p2.y - p1.y > 1 {
                    var yVal = p1.y
```

```
        for _ in 1...Int(p2.y - p1.y) {
            yVal += 1
            handleTouch(CGPoint(x: p1.x, y: yVal))
        }
    } else if p2.y - p1.y < -1 {
        var yVal = p1.y
        for _ in (Int(p2.y - p1.y)) * 2...Int(p2.y - p1.y) {
            yVal -= 1
            handleTouch(CGPoint(x: p1.x, y: yVal))
        }
    } else {

    }
}
else {
    let rise = p2.y - p1.y
    let run  = p2.x - p1.x
    let res: Double = Double(rise) / Double(run)
    var xVal = Double(p1.x)
    var yVal = Double(p1.y)
    if run > 1 {
        for _ in 1...Int(run) {
            yVal += res
            xVal += 1
            handleTouch(CGPoint(x: xVal, y: yVal))
        }
    } else if run < -1 {
        xVal = Double(p2.x)
        yVal = Double(p2.y)
        for _ in Int(run) * 2...Int(run) {
            yVal += res
            xVal += 1
            handleTouch(CGPoint(x: xVal, y: yVal))
        }
    } else if run == 1 {
        for _ in 0...Int(run * (rise > 0 ? rise : -rise)) {
            yVal += res / Double(rise > 0 ? rise : -rise)
            xVal += 1 / Double(rise > 0 ? rise : -rise)
            handleTouch(CGPoint(x: xVal, y: yVal))
        }
    } else if run == -1 {
        drawLineBetweenPoints(p2, p1)
        return
```

```
            }
        }
    }
    func handleTouch(_ location: CGPoint) {
        let newImage = UIImageView()
        newImage.backgroundColor = UIColor.black
        newImage.frame = CGRect(x: Int(location.x), y: Int(location.y),
        ➥ width: lineWidth, height: lineHeight)
        allFrames.append(newImage.frame)
        lines.append(newImage)
        drawLines()
    }
    func drawLines() {
        _ = viewToEdit.subviews.map({ if self.allFrames
        ➥ .contains($0.frame) { $0.removeFromSuperview() } })
        for i in lines {
            viewToEdit.addSubview(i)
        }
    }
    func clear() {
        lines = []
        drawLines()
    }
}

class MetricConversionHandler {
    var from = ""
    var   to = ""
    var fromNumber: Double = 0.0

    var value = ["kilometer": 1, "hectometer": 2, "decameter": 3,
    ➥ "meter": 4, "decimeter": 5, "centimeter": 6, "millimeter": 7]

    init(userFrom: String, userTo: String, fromNum: Double) {
               from = userFrom
                 to = userTo
        fromNumber = fromNum
    }
    func convert() -> Double {
        let numberToUse = pow(10.0, Double(value[to]!) -
        ➥ Double(value[from]!))
        return Double("\(fromNumber * numberToUse)")!
    }
```

```
}

class ViewController: UIViewController {
    @IBOutlet var input: UITextField!
    @IBOutlet var output: UILabel!
    var from = ""
    var fromButton: UIButton!
    var lineDrawer = Connector()

    @IBAction func fromClicked(sender: UIButton) {
        from = sender.text
        fromButton = sender
    }
    @IBAction func toClicked(sender: UIButton) {
        let metricHandlerInst = MetricConversionHandler(userFrom:
        ➥ from, userTo: sender.text, fromNum: Double(input.text!)!)
        let converted = round(pow(10.0, 10.0) * metricHandlerInst
        ➥ .convert()) / pow(10.0, 10.0)
        if floor(converted) == converted {
            output.text = "\(input.text!) \(from)(s) =
            ➥ \(Int(converted)) \(sender.text)(s)"
        } else {
            var convertedString = String(format: "%.10f", converted)
            while "\(convertedString.last!)" == "0" {
                convertedString.removeLast()
            }
            output.text = "\(input.text!) \(from)(s) =
            ➥ \(convertedString) \(sender.text)(s)"
        }
        lineDrawer.clear()
        lineDrawer.drawLineBetweenPoints(CGPoint(x: 110,
        ➥ y: fromButton.frame.origin.y + lineDrawer.thickness),
        ➥ CGPoint(x: 260, y: sender.frame.origin.y +
        ➥ lineDrawer.thickness))
    }
    override func viewDidLoad() {
        super.viewDidLoad()
        lineDrawer = Connector(initWithView: self.view)
        // Do any additional setup after loading the view,
        ➥ typically from a nib.
    }
}
```

Run the app

Figure 9.10 shows the output you see when you run the app.

It worked! Hooray!

Well done; you've finished your first intermediate-level Swift concept! See you in chapter 10, where you learn about reading and writing files.

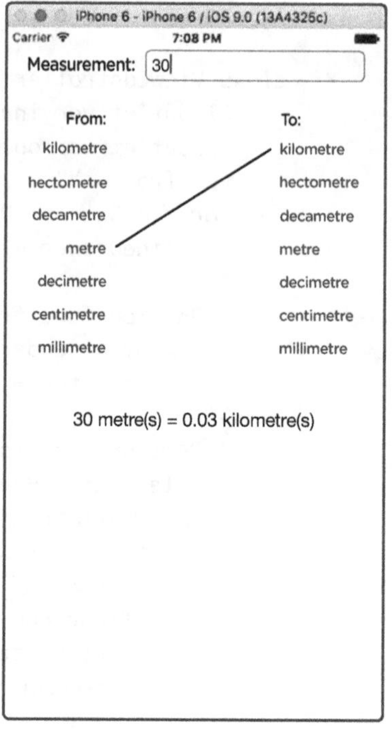

Figure 9.10 Metric Conversion app, Part 2, running

10

Reading and writing files

In this chapter, you'll start a new Swift topic: file content management, so that your data is preserved across sessions.

This chapter covers

- *What are files?*
- *Why do you need to read from and write to files?*
- *How do you read from and write to files?*
- *How do you download a file from the internet to use in an app?*
- *What are file management and file content management?*

You've reached Milestone 10: reading and writing files. Learning a new computer language isn't complete without learning to read and write files using code. Reading and writing files lets apps store data that they can access later in the app, in another session of the app, or even when the device restarts.

An example of this is a game score. In games like Temple Run, you'd like to keep the coins that you earn after a round, so if your game stores the scores in variables, you lose your scores every time you remove your app from memory or restart your device. If the score is stored in a file, however, it can be retrieved at any time. You can store many other pieces of information in files, such as user or personal information, user preferences, volume settings, and where someone left off reading an e-book or watching a movie.

What's in a file?

A *file* is a place to store information you'd like to use again and again, such as music, homework, and your apps. Files allow you to store data and retrieve it later, even if the RAM (random-access memory) has been reset by restarting the app or even restarting your iDevice.

Here's an example: if you're reading this book on a computer, you're reading it from a file, possibly a .pdf file (or maybe a .mobi or .ipub).

Or if you downloaded some new music, it's stored in a file on your computer that can be opened with special apps that understand how to use that type of file. If you try to peek into a .mp3 file with a text editor, you'll see some weird characters that won't make any sense. If you play this file by using an MP3 player, however, you'll be able to listen to the sounds it contains. You can see some more examples in figure 10.1.

Every file has a format. Formats tell you what type a file is. Depending on the type, a file may need some special software that's capable of understanding what it contains.

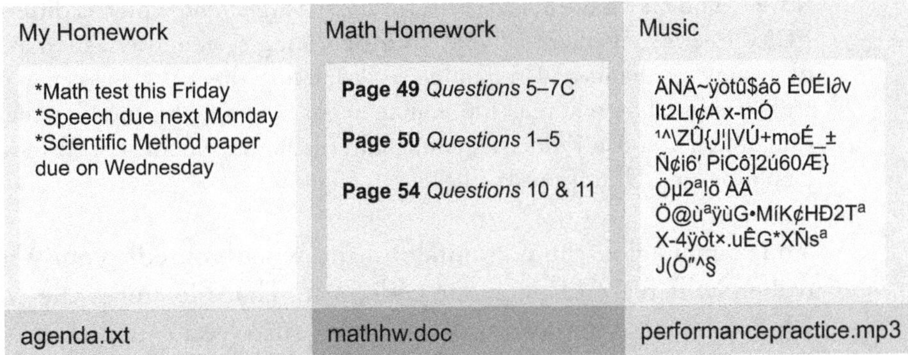

My Homework
*Math test this Friday
*Speech due next Monday
*Scientific Method paper due on Wednesday
agenda.txt
Math Homework
Page 49 Questions 5–7C
Page 50 Questions 1–5
Page 54 Questions 10 & 11
mathhw.doc
Music
ÄNÄ~ÿòtû$áõ Ê0ÉI∂v
It2LI¢A x-mÓ
¹^\ZÛ{J¦|VÚ+moÉ_±
Ñ¢i6' PiCô]2ú60/Æ}
Öµ2ª!õ ÀÄ
Ö@ùªÿùG•MíK¢HÐ2Tª
X-4ÿòt×.uÊG*XÑsª
J(Ó"^§
performancepractice.mp3

Figure 10.1 Examples of file types

Your music file, for example, probably has the format .mp3. This book, read on a computer, might be .pdf, and the Xcode projects you've been writing are stored in the .xcodeproj file format. Furthermore, the playgrounds that you've been creating for many chapters are stored in a special file format: .playground.

There are thousands of file formats. I've listed only a few here.

Pop quiz

Name a couple of other file formats you sometimes work with. (Hint: Images you see online can be in a couple of formats, and if you use Microsoft Word, you may know another format.)

One common file type is .txt. This particular file format holds nothing but plain text. You'll be using this file format in this chapter for your file content management apps.

What is file content management?

File content management (FCM) is keeping control of what's inside a file so you can store, view, and edit it.

NOTE You may have heard the term *file management*, which is different from FCM. File management is what your operating system does, such as copying files, moving them, and renaming and deleting them. FCM is managing the stuff inside a file, whereas file management is managing the files themselves. On a Mac, you use Finder as your main file management tool. Windows uses Explorer, and Ubuntu uses Files.

You're managing the contents of a file when you edit your ViewController.swift file and put your code in it. That file stores the code that you type so that you can create an app. Also, you usually use Xcode to view, edit, and save your .swift files.

Go back and take a look at figure 10.1, with the agenda.txt file that saves My Homework content. Suppose that you have a scary-looking math test this Friday, but the test gets postponed to next Tuesday. You want to reflect that change in your file. To do so, you open that file, type `next Tuesday` in place of `this Friday`, and then save the file. This is a simple example of FCM.

File Content Manager app

The best way to see how FCM works is with a simple app.

NOTE You can find the code for this application in the Chapter10_FCMApp file inside Hello-Swift-Code-master folder that you downloaded from GitHub. If you haven't downloaded the code from GitHub, go to: https://github.com/tanmayb123/Hello-Swift-Code/archive/master.zip. You should download the code only once for all chapters.

What does this app do?

This app stores text that a user types in a file. Then the user can retrieve the info whenever he wants with a tap of a button. This app is capable of handling a lot of text. How much text, or information, it can store depends on your iDevice's memory.

Set up the project, and create the UI

The user interface (UI) for your app is shown in figure 10.2.

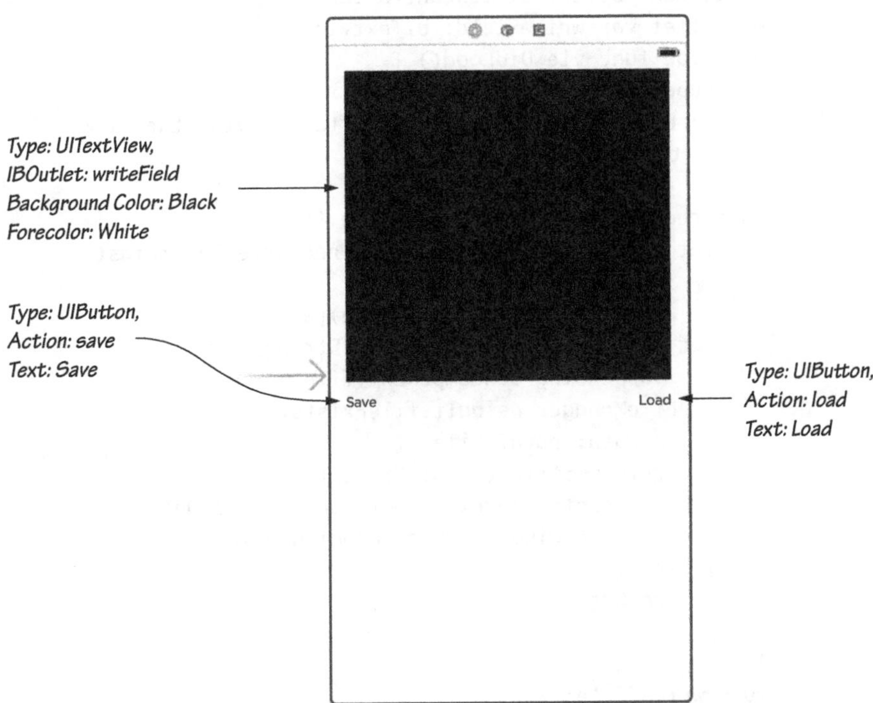

Figure 10.2 The UI for the simple FCM app

Code the app

Next, create a few file manipulation functions that you can use to read from and write to files (listing 10.1).

Listing 10.1 The code for the simple FCM app

```
import UIKit

class ViewController: UIViewController {
    @IBOutlet var writeField: UITextView!
    override func viewDidLoad() {
        super.viewDidLoad()
        // Do any additional setup after loading the view,
        ➥ typically from a nib.
    }
    func read(file: String) -> String {
        let paths = NSSearchPathForDirectoriesInDomains(
                .documentDirectory,
                .userDomainMask, true)[0]
        let pathToFile = (paths as NSString)
            .appendingPathComponent(file)
        if FileManager.default.fileExists(
            atPath: pathToFile) {
            return String(data: NSData(
                contentsOfFile: pathToFile)! as Data,
                encoding: String.Encoding.utf8)!
        } else {
            return ""
        }
    }
    func write(file: String,
               value: String,
               newline: Bool,
               overwrite: Bool) {
        var paths = NSSearchPathForDirectoriesInDomains(
            .documentDirectory, .userDomainMask, true)
        let documentsDirectory: String = paths[0]
        let filePath = "\(documentsDirectory)/\(file)"
        if !overwrite {
            if newline {
                try! (read(file: file) + "\n" + value)
                    .write(toFile: filePath,
                           atomically: true,
                           encoding: .utf8)
            } else {
                try! (read(file: file) + value)
```

```
                    .write(toFile: filePath,
                           atomically: true,
                           encoding: .utf8)
            }
        } else {
            try! value.write(to: URL(
                fileURLWithPath: filePath),
                atomically: true, encoding: .utf8)
        }
    }
    @IBAction func save() {
        write(file: "infoSave.txt",
              value: writeField.text!,
              newline: false, overwrite: true)
    }
    @IBAction func load() {
        writeField.text = read(file: "infoSave.txt")
    }
}
```

Learn how the code works

Now I'll talk about the code.

THE SAVE IBACTION

You're taking the input that the user gave you in the TextView and putting it in a file named infoSave.txt. You're overwriting any text that was already in the file so that the file always contains the user's latest data. In other words, you're writing your new text to a file.

THE LOAD IBACTION

You're taking the information from the infoSave.txt file and displaying it in your TextView. Then the user can edit and save the info or choose to read it. So you're reading text from a file.

THE WRITE FUNCTION

The `write()` function

write(file: "infoSave.txt", value: writeField.text!, newline: false, overwrite: true) writes files for you with the content you provide. This function is capable of creating a new file if the file doesn't exist, overwriting an existing file, and even appending to an existing file.

Table 10.1 describes the parameters in this function.

Table 10.1 Parameters for the `write` function

Parameter	Description
`file`	The name of the file that you're going to save (write to)
`value`	The value that will be stored in the file: the content
`newline`	If the file isn't to be overwritten (next parameter), tells you whether the value should be appended on a new line or continued on the same line
`overwrite`	Tells the system whether it should overwrite the file if it exists. If the file doesn't exist, it's created.

Now I'll talk about the code. The first line uses the built-in function `NSSearchPathForDirectoriesInDomains` and finds the path to the Documents directory:

```
let paths = NSSearchPathForDirectoriesInDomains(
    .documentDirectory, .userDomainMask, true)[0]
```

Wait—I'm confused. What is the Documents directory?

The Documents directory is one of the few places where an iOS app can store its files and data. Any time you want to write or read a file, you need to figure out the location, or path, to the Documents directory.

NOTE All iOS apps have their own separate Document directories. This is called sandboxing. Each app has its own private sandbox to do things such as modify files and create variables. One app can't change or even access another app's sandbox.

When the code finds the path to the Documents directory, the following things have to happen:

1 The path is stored in a variable named `documentsDirectory`.
2 You figure out the complete path to the file that you want to create by appending a slash (/) and then the filename your app is using to the `documentsDirectory` variable.
3 Put this complete path and filename in the `filePath` variable.

Suppose that you're creating a file called scores.txt. The path and filename documentsDirectory/scores.txt are finally stored in a variable called `filePath`.

Next, check whether you want to overwrite the file, if it exists. If you don't, check whether you want to append the contents to a new line (after the old text). If you do, concatenate the earlier contents of the file, a newline code, and the new value into one big string and write it into that file.

EXTRA When you append, the code does overwrite the file; because it keeps the old contents as well as the new, you can't tell. It looks like the old file with the new information added. Tricky, right?

If you don't want a newline, the code concatenates the old contents in the file and the new contents and then writes to the file. Again, you're overwriting the old file but keeping the old contents as well.

If you do want to overwrite the contents of the file, the code writes to the file with the new contents you gave to the function. In this case, anything that was in the file is overwritten with the new contents.

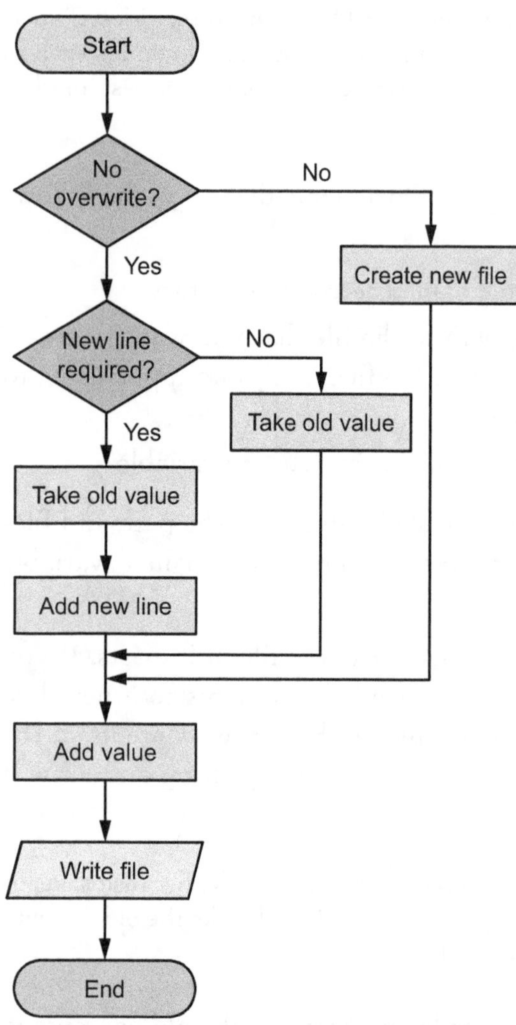

Figure 10.3 The `write` function as a flow chart

The flow chart in figure 10.3 may make this concept clearer.

THE READ FUNCTION

The read() function

```
read(file: file)
```

is much simpler than the write function. This function takes one parameter: `file`, which is the name of the file you want to read from. Then this function returns a string value with the contents of that file.

In the first two lines of code, you find the path to the file that you want to read.

Then, in conditional #1, you check whether the file exists. Please refer to the first if-statement in read-function, in code listing 10.2. If it does, you return the string value of the NSData of the file. (You don't know what NSData is, but don't worry; you don't need to care about it yet. For now, all you need to know is that it stores data.) If the app code file doesn't exist, the app code returns an empty string.

Run your app

To see for yourself that the app saves your text, do this:

1. Open the app.
2. Type something in the field.
3. Tap Save.
4. Exit the app.

5 Do anything on your device (such as remove an app from memory or reboot).
6 Open the app again.
7 Tap Load.

   The text you typed in step 2 reappears.

This app allows you to edit the text and save again.

Now that you know how all this works, you can move on to more advanced and interesting topics.

Hangman app

You're finally ready to build a game. Not a game with complex animation or anything close to Surgeon Simulator, but a game of Hangman.

But FCM is too hard!

If you think FCM is a bit too hard to code in every time, well, so did I when I was beginning iOS development. In chapter 11, however, you learn how to create a framework or library for FCM. (Spoiler: It's named Swifto'File.) That should make things much easier for you!

What does this app do?

In this game, there are no graphics. Instead, you tell the user how many tries he has left. This app lets you learn the code without having to learn the graphics yet.

NOTE You can find the code for this application in the Chapter10_Hangman file inside the Hello-Swift-Code-master folder that you downloaded from GitHub. If you haven't downloaded the code from GitHub, go to: https://github.com/tanmayb123/Hello-Swift-Code/archive/master.zip. You should download the code only once for all chapters.

If you've come from Mars (greetings, alien!), you may not know what Hangman is. Here's a description:

1 The computer picks a random word that a player has to guess and shows a set of underlines, one for each character in the word, in a label. (Example: *Swift* displays as _ _ _ _ _.)

2 The player is given at least ten chances to guess all the letters in the word.

   Suppose that the word is *objective*, and the user guesses *e*. The computer fills out the template with all the *e*s as follows: _ _ _ e _ _ _ _ e. Because the letter is in the word, the player still has ten chances left.

   If the user guesses g, however, he's used up one of his chances. Now he has nine chances left.

3 The game goes on until the player guesses the entire word (player wins) or runs out of tries (app wins).

Set up the project, and create the UI

First, create a UI that looks like figure 10.4.

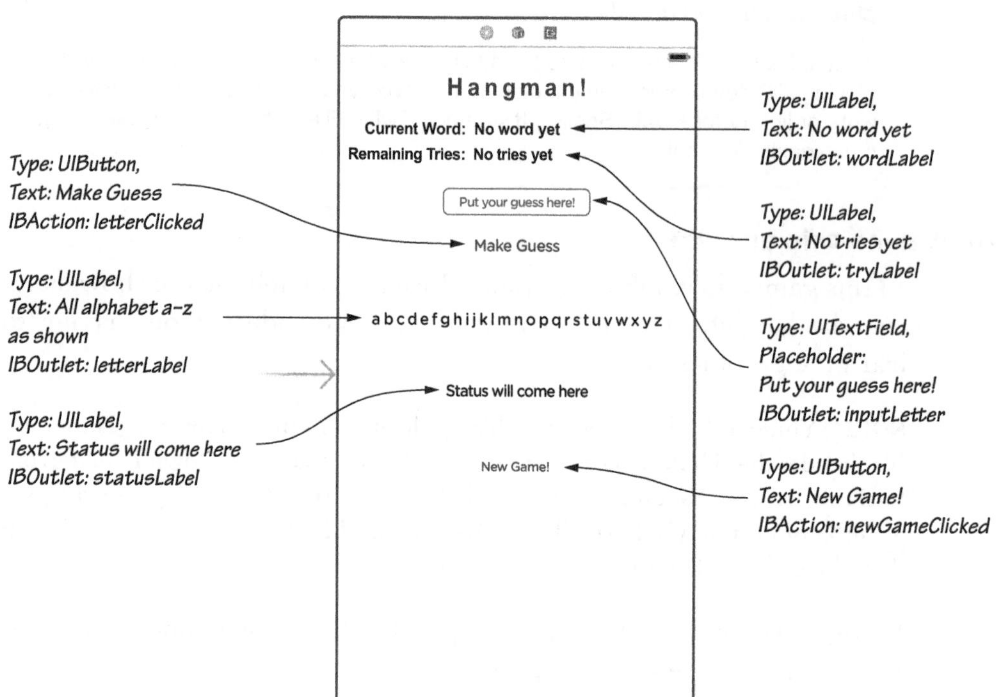

Figure 10.4 The UI for the Hangman app

Code the app

When you've created the UI, it's time to add the code. Listing 10.2 is the code you need to add. The code creates a few simple starter functions that make the Hangman game work; I'll explain them after the listing.

Listing 10.2 The code for the Hangman app

```
import UIKit

extension Array {

    func randomElement() -> String {
        return self[Int(arc4random_uniform(UInt32(
            self.count-1)))] as! String
    }
}

class ViewController: UIViewController {

    @IBOutlet var wordLabel: UILabel!
    @IBOutlet var triesLeft: UILabel!
    @IBOutlet var inputLetter: UITextField!
    @IBOutlet var lettersLabel: UILabel!
    @IBOutlet var statusLabel: UILabel!

    let maximumTries = 10
    var currentTries = 0

    var currentWord = ""
    var wordArray: [String] = []
    var tryArray: [String] = []
    var usedLetters: [String] = []

    override func viewDidLoad() {
        super.viewDidLoad()
        newGame()
        // Do any additional setup after loading the view,
        ➥ typically from a nib.
    }

    func possibleWords() -> [String] {
        let stringVal = String(data: try! Data(
            contentsOf: URL(string: "https://github.com/
            ➥ tanmayb123/english-words/raw/master/words.txt")!),
              encoding: .utf8)
```

```
        return stringVal!.replacingOccurrences(
        of: "\r", with: "").components(separatedBy: "\n")
}

@objc func read(file: String) -> String {
    let paths = NSSearchPathForDirectoriesInDomains(
        .documentDirectory, .userDomainMask, true
    )[0] as String
    let pathToFile = (paths as NSString)
        .appendingPathComponent(file)
    if FileManager.default.fileExists(atPath: pathToFile) {
        return String(data: NSData(
            contentsOfFile: pathToFile
            )! as Data, encoding: .utf8)!
    } else {
        return ""
    }
}

@objc func write(file: String, value: String,
                 newline: Bool, overwrite: Bool) {
    var paths: [AnyObject] =
    NSSearchPathForDirectoriesInDomains(
        .documentDirectory, .userDomainMask, true
    ) as [AnyObject]
    let documentsDirectory = paths[0] as! String
    let filePath: String = "\(documentsDirectory)/\(file)"
    if !overwrite {
        if newline {
            try! (read(file: file) + "\n" + value)
                .write(toFile: filePath, atomically:
                    true, encoding: String.Encoding.utf8)
        } else {
            try! (read(file: file) + value).write(
                toFile: filePath, atomically: true,
                encoding: String.Encoding.utf8)
        }
    } else {
        try! value.write(toFile: filePath,
                         atomically: true,
                         encoding: .utf8)
    }
}

func getHighscoreStatus() -> String {
    var finalValue = ""
```

```
    if read(file: "highscore.txt") == "" && read(
         file: "lastscore.txt") == "" {
        finalValue = "No saved scores."
    } else {
        let lastScore = read(file: "lastscore.txt")
        let highScore = read(file: "highscore.txt")
        finalValue = "Last score: \(lastScore)"
        finalValue += "\n | Highest score: \(highScore)"
    }
    return finalValue
}

func writeScore() {
    var highscore = 0
    if read(file: "highscore.txt") != "" {
        highscore = Int(read(file: "highscore.txt"))!
    }
    if currentTries > highscore {
        highscore = currentTries
    }
    write(file: "highscore.txt",
          value: "\(highscore)", newline: false,
          overwrite: true)
    write(file: "lastscore.txt",
          value: "\(currentTries)", newline: false,
          overwrite: true)
}

func newWord() {
    wordLabel.text = possibleWords().randomElement()
    currentWord = wordLabel.text!
    wordArray = []
    tryArray = []
    for i in currentWord.characters {
        wordArray.append("\(i)")
        tryArray.append("_")
    }
}

func newGame() {
    currentTries = maximumTries
    newWord()
    updateWordLabel()
    updateTryLabel()
    usedLetters = []
    updateLetterLabel()
```

```
        inputLetter.text = ""
        statusLabel.text = getHighscoreStatus()
    }

    @IBAction func newGameClicked() {
        newGame()
    }

    func gameover() {
        writeScore()
        statusLabel.text = getHighscoreStatus()
        tryArray = wordArray
        updateWordLabel()
    }

    @IBAction func letterClicked() {
        if currentTries != 0 && !usedLetters.contains(
            inputLetter.text!) && inputLetter.text! != "" {
            ➥ // Conditional #1
            var wasUseful = false
            for (ind, val) in wordArray.enumerated() {
                if val == inputLetter.text! {
                    tryArray[ind] = val
                    wasUseful = true
                }
            }
            if !wasUseful {
                currentTries -= 1
            }
            usedLetters.append(inputLetter.text!)
            updateTryLabel()
            updateWordLabel()
            updateLetterLabel()
        }
        if tryArray == wordArray {              // Conditional #2
            triesLeft.text! = "YOU WON!"
            gameover()
        }
        if currentTries == 0 {                  // Conditional #3
            triesLeft.text = "You lost."
            gameover()
        }
        inputLetter.text = ""
    }
```

```
    func updateTryLabel() {
        triesLeft.text = "\(currentTries)"
    }

    func updateWordLabel() {
        wordLabel.text = ""
        for i in tryArray {
            wordLabel.text! += "\(i)  "
        }
    }

    func updateLetterLabel() {
        lettersLabel.text =
        "a b c d e f g h i j k l m n o p q r s t u v w x y z"
        for i in usedLetters {
            lettersLabel.text = lettersLabel.text!.
            replacingOccurrences(of: i, with: " ")
        }
    }

    override func didReceiveMemoryWarning() {
        super.didReceiveMemoryWarning()
        // Dispose of any resources that can be recreated.
    }
}
```

Usually, you see a lot of code annotation after a listing. I tried that but thought this listing would be easier to read without it.

Connect the variables, IBOutlets, and IBActions

Table 10.2 shows what the variables in the program do.

Table 10.2 Variables for the Hangman app

Variable	Description
`maximumTries`	Allows you to set the maximum number of tries that the user has
`currentTries`	Allows you to keep track of the number of tries the user has taken
`currentWord`	Current word that the user is trying to guess
`wordArray`	Array of letters in the word the user is guessing

Table 10.2 Variables for the Hangman app *(continued)*

Variable	Description

`tryArray`	Array of letters that the user correctly guessed. This array has the same number of elements as `wordArray`. When a user gets a letter correct, it pops up in this array.
	Examples:
	Word the user is trying to guess: *Swift*
	`wordArray = [s, w, i, f, t]`
	`tryArray = [_, _, _, _, _]`
	Suppose that the user guesses the letter *f*:
	`wordArray = [s, w, i, f, t]`
	`tryArray = [_, _, _, f, _]`

`usedLetters`	Letters that the user has already guessed, right or wrong

Table 10.3 shows the `IBOutlets`.

Table 10.3 `IBOutlets` for the Hangman app

IBOutlet	Description
`wordLabel`	The word that the user is trying to guess
`triesLeft`	How many tries the user has left
`inputLetter`	The letter that the user is guessing
`lettersLabel`	The label that shows the user which letters she has left to use
`statusLabel`	The user's last game score and her highest score

Table 10.4 shows the functions.

Table 10.4 Functions for the Hangman app

Function	Description
`possibleWords`	This function downloads and returns all the possible words from a word list on my website. The address is https://raw.githubusercontent.com/tanmayb123/Hangman/master/wordlist.txt.

Table 10.4 Functions for the Hangman app *(continued)*

Function	Description
newWord	This function sets the text of wordLabel to a randomElement from the array that the possibleWords function returns. Then it sets the currentWord to the text you put in the wordLabel. Finally, it loops through the characters of the currentWord. For every character in currentWord, you append the character to the wordArray and an underscore to the tryArray.
newGame	This function starts a game by setting currentTries to maximumTries so that the user has ten tries when he starts. It also calls the newWord, updateWordLabel, updateTryLabel, and updateLetterLabel functions. It sets usedLetters to nothing and sets inputLetter's text to nothing as well. Last, it puts the value of a function, getHighscoreStatus, in the statusLabel.
updateTryLabel	This function puts currentTries in tryLabel.
updateWordLabel	This function puts tryArray in wordLabel.
updateLetterLabel	This function updates the letterLabel so that users know what letters they have used and have left.
getHighscoreStatus	This function displays the status of the user, meaning the last game's score and the high score. First, create a variable called finalValue. This variable holds the final result until you can return it. Next, read highscore.txt and lastscore.txt, and if both of the values from the files are nothing, you know that the user has never played a game and therefore doesn't have a high score. So you set finalValue to No saved scores. If those two files had values, however, set finalValue to Last score: <THE USER'S LAST SCORE> | Highest score: <THE USER'S HIGH SCORE>.
writeScore	If you're wondering how the values get into the file in the first place, this function takes care of that process. First, this function creates a highscore integer, which is 0 by default. Then it checks whether highscore.txt has something in it. If so, it sets the highscore variable to the contents of the file. Next, it checks whether currentTries is higher than the last highscore. If so, it sets the highscore variable to currentTries. Finally, it writes the value of the highscore variable in highscore.txt and the value of currentTries in lastscore.txt.
gameover	When this function is called, call writeScore; set the statusLabel's text to the value returned by getHighscoreStatus(); set the tryArray to wordArray; and update the word label.

Table 10.5 shows the final `IBActions`.

Table 10.5 `IBActions` for the Hangman app

IBAction	Description
`letterClicked`	**1** This `IBAction` checks if `currentTries` is not `0`, and the letter that the user is guessing hasn't been used, and the user typed a letter. **2** If all those conditions are `true`, do the following: **3** Create a Boolean named `wasUseful`, with a default value of `false`. **4** Loop through the enumerated `wordArray`. **5** Check whether the `val` you were on is equal to the input letter. If so, set the `tryArray`'s `ind` element to `val`, and set `wasUseful` to `true`. **6** After the loop, check whether `wasUseful` is false. If it is, subtract 1 from `currentTries`. **7** Append the input letter to the `usedLetter` array. **8** Call all your update functions. **9** Clear the `inputLetter` TextField. **10** In conditional #2, check whether the `tryArray` is equal to the `wordArray`. If so, the user has won. In this case, set the `triesLeft` label's text to `YOU WON!` and then call `gameover`. **11** In conditional #3, check whether `currentTries` is equal to `0`. If so, the user lost, so set `triesLeft`'s text to `You lost` and then call `gameover`. **12** Finally, return to the caller of this function or the button.
`newGameClicked`	When this `IBAction` function executes, it calls the newGame function.

Run your app

When you run the app, you should see an interface similar to figure 10.4. To see an example of what it looks like when someone wins, take a look at figure 10.5.

Check your app knowledge

1 Which function from the `String` class allows you to write to files? Give an example.

2 What does `newline: true` do in this code?

```
write(file: "test.txt", value: writeField.text!, newline: true,
overwrite: false)
```

3 What happens when you append new data to an existing file?

4 What parameter does the `read()` function take?

5 Create an app that allows you to write your first name to a file, read it later, and display it on a label. The app should have Load and Save buttons.

Figure 10.5 The running Hangman application.

App-Activity: Store your name and birth date

Create an app that takes the user's name and date of birth in two separate text fields and stores them in separate files. Later, whenever the user wants to, he should be able to read the values back from the files and see what he stored. When the Load button is clicked, the app should display the contents of the two files in two labels.

11

Frameworks: Bookshelves of classes

You've made it through ten chapters, and you've finished most of your iOS developer education. Now it's time to move on to some special topics of interest, starting with frameworks.

This chapter covers

- *What a framework is and how to use it*
- *How to build frameworks for simulators and iDevices*
- *How to use a framework in an Xcode project*
- *What UIKit is*

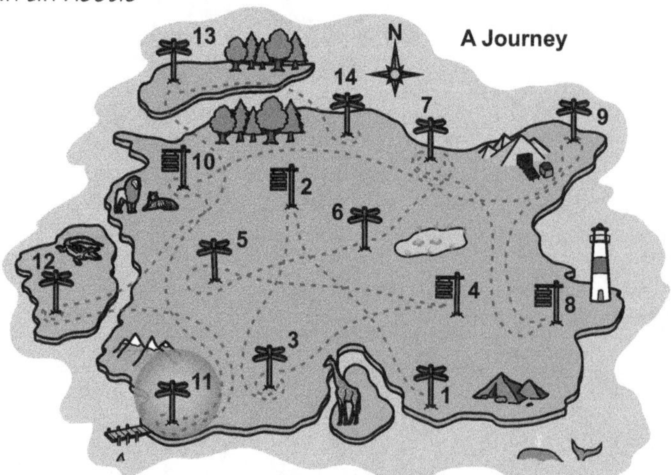

Milestone 11 is frameworks. This chapter is for people who plan to help others code, not by teaching them, but by uploading sets of code for people to use on sites such as GitHub, BitBucket, and GitLab. You can also create local repositories so that you can keep track of your learning and use older code as building blocks for your newer, full-fledged apps!

How can I be almost done learning iOS development if I still have more chapters to go?

What you learn in the final chapters, including this one, covers topics you use for specific purposes instead of the general-purpose code you've used so far. At the beginning of each chapter, I explain what that chapter is most useful for.

What is a framework?

I'll start with a simple question: what is a framework? A *framework* is a set of classes, functions, code, and even other frameworks that can be easily reused.

The easiest way to understand frameworks is to look at what contains what.

You must start organizing your code in functions when your code starts to grow. You can group a collection of related functions into a class, and then create frameworks by using a group of related classes. This group of classes, called a framework, can be given to others in an integrated way.

So a function is a set of code and other functions. (A function can even contain another function.) A class is a set of functions and other classes. (A class can contain another class.) Finally, a framework is a set of classes and even other frameworks. (Yes, a framework can contain another framework.)

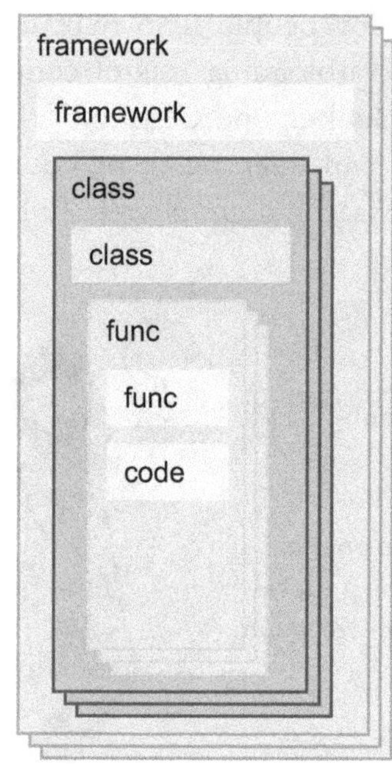

Figure 11.1 The "What-contains-what?" diagram

This hierarchy is described in figure 11.1.

Here's another example that you're already familiar with. You may recall file content management (FCM) from chapter 10. If you're creating a new app and want it to use the FCM functions, you have to create the `read` and `write` functions every time you want to manage files.

Now imagine that you want to create 20 apps with FCM incorporated into them. You could copy and paste the same functions into each app, but that would make the code messy, bulky, and unorganized.

Also, suppose that you find a bug in your code or a change you want to make. If you were to change the function, you'd still have to copy it to all of your apps manually.

Frameworks help you further clean up your code and solve both of those problems.

Frameworks offer you a better option than having repeated functions and classes in each app. You create or download a framework with the FCM classes in it and drag that file into your project, and your project instantly gets code for reading and writing files. You can do this for each app in which you want to implement FCM. All you need to do is import the framework into your code (which takes only one line of code).

Without further ado, get straight to it!

Create a framework

To start, create a framework called Swifto'File. To realize the power of frameworks, you're going to re-create the FCM app from chapter 10, with these differences: all the classes reside in a framework, and the code for the app is one line of code using the framework. In the following sections, you see how.

What does this app do?

You're creating a new project, but this project won't be a single-view application. In fact, this app will have no view at all!

NOTE You can find the code for this application in the Chapter11_SwiftoFile file inside the Hello-Swift-Code-master folder that you downloaded from GitHub. If you haven't downloaded the code from GitHub, go to: https://github.com/tanmayb123/Hello-Swift-Code/archive/master.zip. You should download the code only once for all chapters.

Create the project

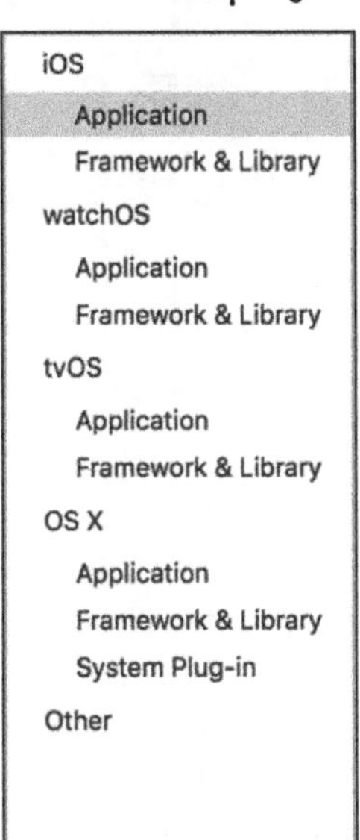

Figure 11.2 The Project Template pane.

To select the right setting, choose iOS > Framework & Library (instead of Application, as you did in the preceding chapters), as shown in figure 11.2.

Next, click the Cocoa Touch Framework button, as shown in figure 11.3; then click Next again.

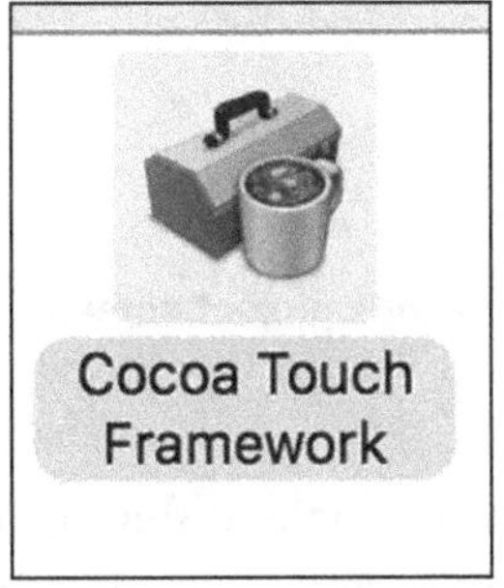

Figure 11.3 Cocoa Touch Framework is the template you should choose.

Now you can fill out this page as you would for any other project.

NOTE Make sure that you don't include apostrophes (') in the project name. Apostrophes are invalid characters for an Xcode project's name, and they may interfere with the building part of the process. Don't write Swift'o'File; write SwiftoFile.

When you've done that, you should see a screen like the one in figure 11.4.

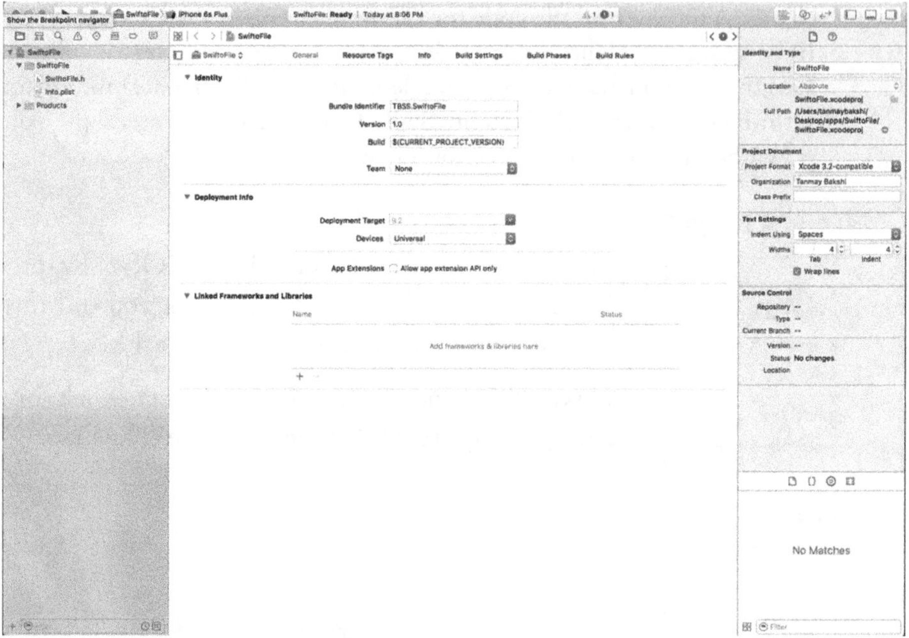

Figure 11.4 The Xcode project screen

This screen looks different from normal. Why don't I see ViewController.swift and Main.storyboard in the file navigator?

You don't see them because you don't need them. You won't be developing a user interface (UI) for this project, so you don't need those files. Xcode knows that and didn't automatically generate them for you this time.

Okay, but how am I going to code the app without a Swift file?

That's a good question! Instead of having Xcode autogenerate those files for you, you create the files manually. Xcode doesn't know what to name the files, so it leaves that job to you.

Get started by pressing Command-N. This key combination tells Xcode to create a new file. You should see a screen like figure 11.5.

Double-click Swift File, and you see the dialog box shown in figure 11.6.

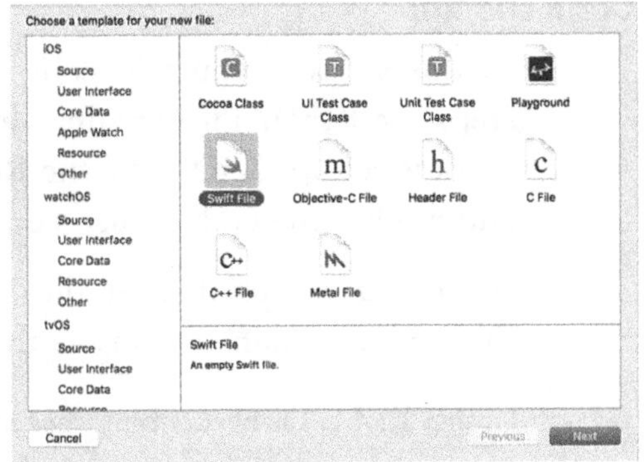

Figure 11.5 New File Template screen

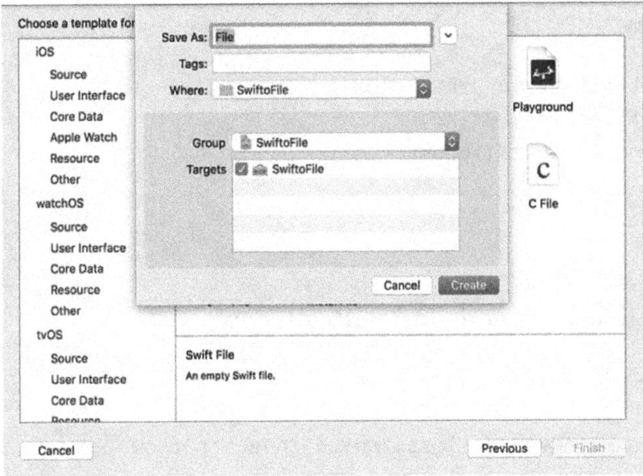

Figure 11.6 Giving the file a name

Type a name for the file (in this case, FileContentManager) in the Save As field; then press the Return key or click the Create button. A new file appears in the file navigator pane, and the file opens in the main area.

Now do the same thing to create three more files: FileReader, FileWriter, and SwiftoFile.

Code the app

In this section, you add code to your new files. Follow the next few steps, and then I'll explain what all the code does. When the framework is set up, you'll take the Read and Write example from chapter 10 and modify the code to use your new SwiftoFile framework.

After you create all four files, click FileContentManager.swift in the file navigator pane, and type the following code:

Listing 11.1 The FileContentManager class

```
class FileContentManager {

    // This variable will contain the name of the file to read or write,
➥ coming from the FileReader and FileWriter classes, respectively.
    var filename = ""

    // The initializer for this class.
    init(inputfilename: String) {
        filename = inputfilename
    }

}
```

Then type the following code in FileReader.swift.

Listing 11.2 The FileReader class

```
// Defining the FileReader class, which inherits from
  FileContentManager.
class FileReader: FileContentManager {

    func returnContents() -> String {
        let paths = NSSearchPathForDirectoriesInDomains(
            .documentDirectory, .userDomainMask, true)[0]
        let filePath = paths.last! == "/" ?
            paths + filename : paths + "/" + filename
        if FileManager.default.fileExists(atPath: filePath) {
            return try! String(contentsOfFile: filePath)
        }
        return ""
    }
}
```

Type the code in listing 11.3 in FileWriter.swift.

Listing 11.3 The FileWriter class

```
import Foundation

class FileWriter: FileContentManager {

    var towrite = ""
    var overwrite = false
    var newline = false

    func writeToFile() {
        let paths = NSSearchPathForDirectoriesInDomains(
          .documentDirectory, .userDomainMask, true)[0] as String
        let filePath = paths.characters.
            last! == "/" ? paths + filename :
            paths + "/" + filename
        if newline {
            towrite = "\n" + towrite
        }
        if !overwrite {
            if FileManager.default.fileExists(
                atPath: filePath) {
                towrite = FileReader(inputfilename: filename)
                    .returnContents() + towrite
            }
        }
        try! towrite.write(toFile: filePath,
                           atomically: true,
                           encoding: .utf8)
    }

}
```

Type the code in listing 11.4 in SwiftoFile.swift.

Listing 11.4 The SwiftoFile class

```
import Foundation

public class SwiftoFile {
```

```
    var reader: FileReader!
    var writer: FileWriter!

    var canOperate = false

    public init() {
        canOperate = false
    }

    public init(userfilename: String) {
        canOperate = true
        reader = FileReader(inputfilename: userfilename)
        writer = FileWriter(inputfilename: userfilename)
    }

    public func write(content: String,
                      overwriteFile: Bool,
                      appendNewline: Bool) {
        if canOperate {
            writer.towrite = content
            writer.overwrite = overwriteFile
            writer.newline = appendNewline
            writer.writeToFile()
        } else {
            print("Not able to operate. " +
                  "You probably missed out the file name.")
        }
    }

    public func read() -> String {
        if canOperate {
            return reader.returnContents()
        } else {
            print("Not able to operate. " +
                  "You probably missed out the file name.")
        }
        return ""
    }
}
```

Why did I put the word `public` in so many places inside SwiftoFile.swift?

These places are the only places you want developers (users of the framework) to be able to access from outside the framework. I'll explain further after I explain FileContentManager, FileReader, and FileWriter.

Learn how the code works

Now take a look at what each of these chunks of code is doing.

FILECONTENTMANAGER

FileContentManager doesn't do anything; it's a base class that both FileReader and FileWriter inherit from. (If you want to know more about inheritance, refer to chapter 9.)

Figure 11.7 should help you understand inheritance (hierarchy) a bit better.

In FileContentManager, you define `filename` as a `String`, and you make an initializer that takes `inputfilename` and puts its value in `filename`. This

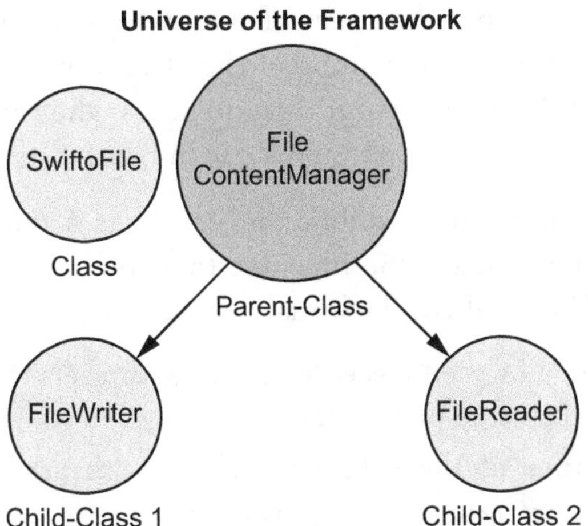

Figure 11.7 Universe of the Framework, an Inheritance diagram

initializer is required, even though you don't specify it because it's the only initializer.

FILEREADER

As I mention earlier, this class inherits from FileContentManager, so it has the initializer and filename variable that were created there.

Here, however, you define a function called `returnContents` that returns the contents of the file. In case you were wondering where you got the filename from, you have it in `filename`. If you don't remember, `filename` was set from the value that we gave FileContentManager's initializer as `inputfilename`.

FILEWRITER

Again, FileWriter inherits from the `FileContentManager` class. Here, however, you also define the variables `toWrite`, which contains the contents of the file; `overwrite`, which tells you whether to overwrite the file (the default value is `false`); and `newline`, which tells you whether to append `toWrite` to a new line (the default value is `false`).

Then you have a `writeToFile()` function that writes to the file that was passed through `FileContentManager`'s intializer, using the preceding variables.

SWIFTOFILE

SwiftoFile is the main class that the users of the framework will use! That's why you put `public` at the beginning of the class; you want people to be able to access it. You don't want them to access the `reader` and writer `variables`, however, so you don't put `public` in front of them.

Next, you have an initializer that's public and that has a parameter: `userfilename`. This parameter takes the filename that the user wants to read from or write to. When called, the initializer sets

- `reader` to a new instance of the `FileReader` class, with `userfilename` as the value for the `inputfilename` parameter
- `writer` to a new instance of the `FileWriter` class, with `userfilename` again as the value for the `inputfilename` parameter

Build the framework

You've created this framework in this chapter and partly in chapter 10. Before you can use one, however, you must build one.

Wait a minute—I already coded the framework! Why am I building it again?

In this sense, `build` doesn't mean to create or code files. Building means that you're compiling the files you've already coded to translate them into a language that the machine can understand and run.

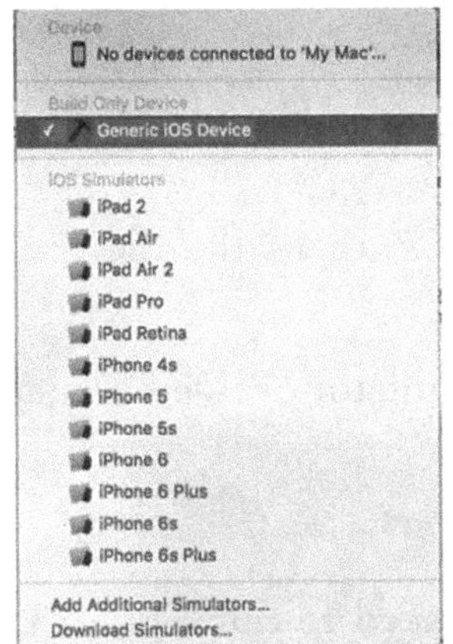

Figure 11.8 Device menu, with Generic iOS Device selected

This step is important: from the device menu (you learned about it in chapter 2), choose Generic iOS Device (figure 11.8).

Then press Command-B. To Xcode, this key combination means *build,* and it creates your framework.

Next, click the little arrow beside Products at the bottom of the file navigator pane (figure 11.9.

Figure 11.9 The Products folder in the file navigator

Finally, right-click the framework file and choose Show in Finder from the contextual menu. You should see a Finder window pop up, and if you have a .framework file selected, you're ready to use this framework. If your project name is SwiftoFile, for example, you should see SwiftoFile.framework here.

But there's a catch: this framework works only on a real iOS device. If you'd like this framework to work with the simulator, you need to follow these additional steps to build the framework differently:

1. Click the Finder window so that it gets the focus.
2. Press Command-Up arrow, which tells Finder to go up a directory.
3. Double-click the debug-iphonesimulator folder.

   You may not see a file, but don't worry. Even if you do, continue following the steps.
4. Go back to Xcode without closing the Finder window.
5. From the device menu, choose any random simulator—preferably the simulator for the device that you normally use (such as the iPhone 7 Plus).
6. Press Command-B again to create the .framework file that's compatible with the simulator only.

   The missing file should now appear in Finder.
7. Go back to the Finder window, and you can now see the file with the .framework extension.

   Whenever I refer to the *framework file*, that's the file I'm talking about.

You're ready to create your app with a simulator or iDevice, depending on whichever one you chose.

Use the framework

To use the framework you created, you need to think of an example. What better example is there than implementing this framework into the app you created in chapter 10?

In the next section, I teach you how to take the Read and Write example from chapter 10's file content management (FCM) app and modify the code to use the new SwiftoFile framework you created.

App: Load Save, Part 2, using frameworks

Now you can build the second part of the Read and Write app, using the new SwiftoFile framework you've created.

What will you do to this app?

NOTE You can find the code for this application in the Chapter11_Load-SaveChp10 folder inside the Hello-Swift-Code-master folder that you downloaded from GitHub. If you haven't downloaded the code from GitHub, go to: https://github.com/tanmayb123/Hello-Swift-Code/archive/master.zip. You should download the code only once for all chapters.

You'll be following this set of steps:

1 Remove the `read` and `write` functions, which are now contained in the framework you created.
2 Add the SwiftoFile framework to the Xcode project.
3 Import the framework and change some code in the project.

Removing the read and write functions

The process is about as simple as it sounds: You need to remove the `read` and `write` functions.

But when you do, you get two errors, as shown in figure 11.10. You may wonder why you're getting these errors in the `IBActions`.

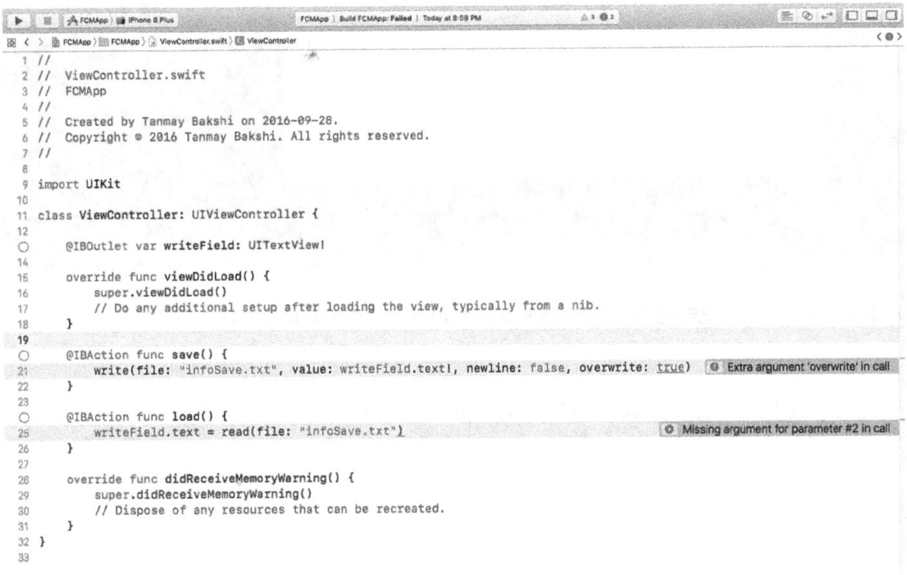

```
//
//  ViewController.swift
//  FCMApp
//
//  Created by Tanmay Bakshi on 2016-09-28.
//  Copyright © 2016 Tanmay Bakshi. All rights reserved.
//

import UIKit

class ViewController: UIViewController {

    @IBOutlet var writeField: UITextView!

    override func viewDidLoad() {
        super.viewDidLoad()
        // Do any additional setup after loading the view, typically from a nib.
    }

    @IBAction func save() {
        write(file: "infoSave.txt", value: writeField.text!, newline: false, overwrite: true)   ❗ Extra argument 'overwrite' in call
    }

    @IBAction func load() {
        writeField.text = read(file: "infoSave.txt")   ❗ Missing argument for parameter #2 in call
    }

    override func didReceiveMemoryWarning() {
        super.didReceiveMemoryWarning()
        // Dispose of any resources that can be recreated.
    }
}
```

Figure 11.10 The errors you get on removing the `read` and `write` functions

The `IBActions` are trying to refer to the `read` and `write` functions that don't exist anymore, because you've removed them, and the Swift compiler is telling you that you've made a mistake. Don't worry; you'll be fixing it later.

Creating the framework reference in Xcode

Next, you add the framework.

To do this, simply drag the framework file into the Xcode file pane (figure 11.11).

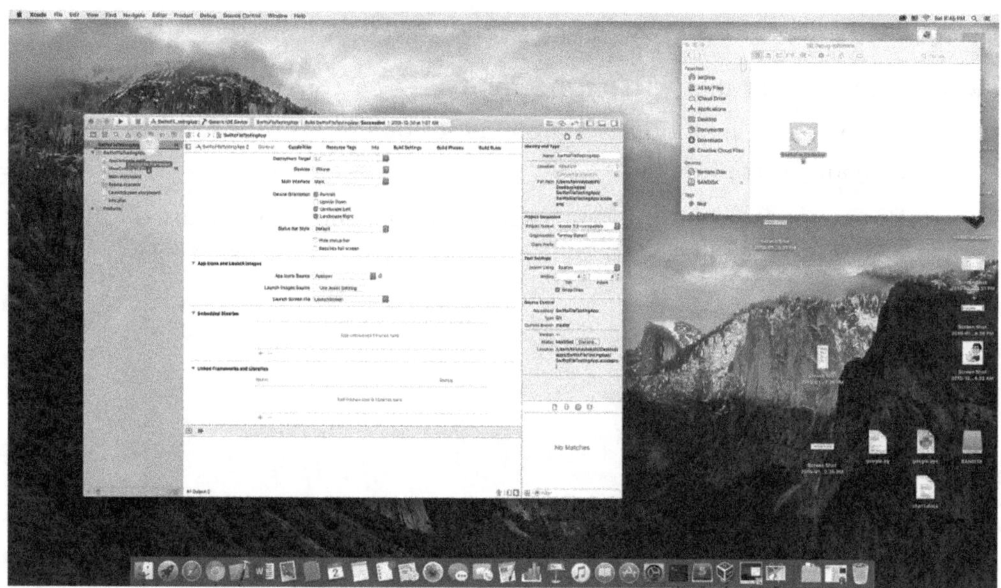

Figure 11.11 Dragging the framework file into an Xcode project

When you release the mouse button, you see a screen like figure 11.12.

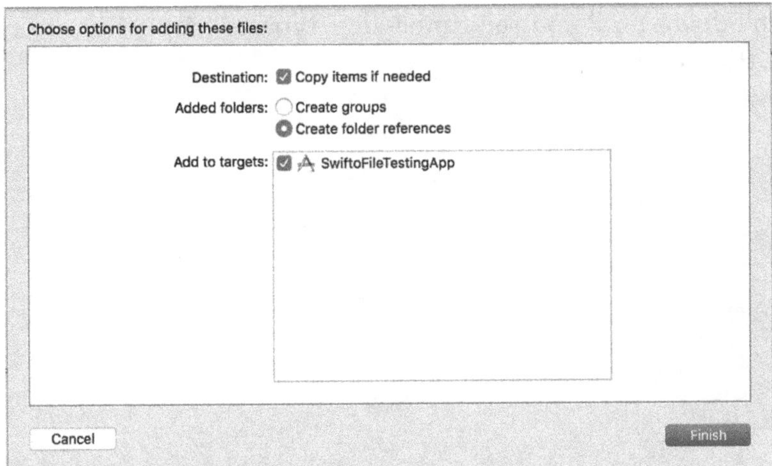

Figure 11.12 Putting the framework file into the Xcode project

On this screen, make sure that the Copy items if needed check box is checked; then click Finish.

Next, click the Xcode project in the file navigator pane (figure 11.13).

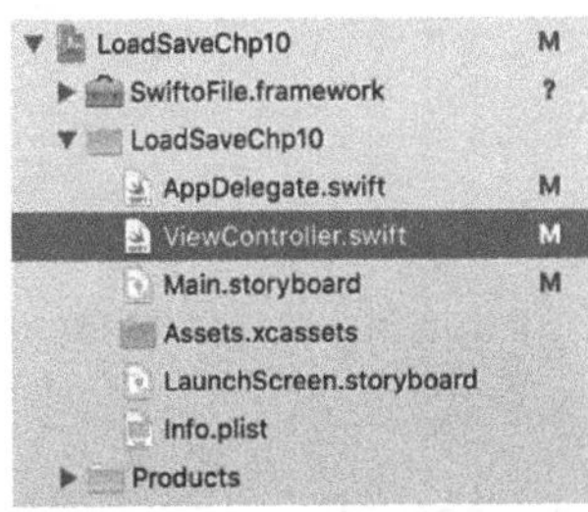

Figure 11.13 File navigator pane in Xcode

Specifically, click the file shown in figure 11.14.

Figure 11.14 The LoadSaveChp10 Xcode project

Scroll down until you see Embedded Binaries, and click the plus sign (+), (figure 11.15).

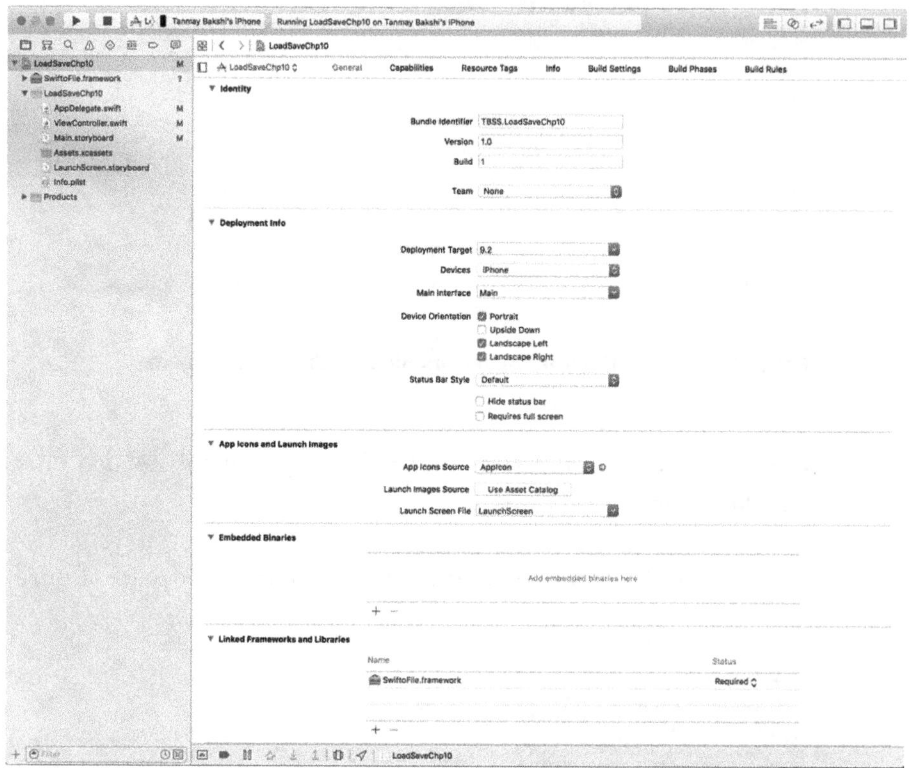

Figure 11.15 The Xcode project screen

Figure 11.16 shows the embedded binaries section.

Embedded Binaries

Add embedded binaries here

\+ −

Figure 11.16 Embedded Binaries section in the Xcode project

Finally, double-click your new framework file (in this case, SwiftoFile.framework) in the window that pops up (figure 11.17).

You're done creating the reference. Next, you'll code it.

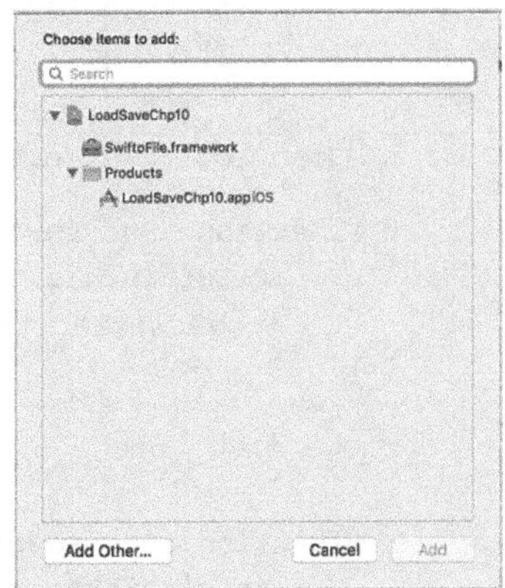

Figure 11.17 Embedded Binaries add page

Coding the framework in the LoadSave app

It's time to code. First, you need to import your framework.

You may remember that in chapter 1, I told you to ignore the line `import UIKit` in your playgrounds and apps? Well, don't do that anymore. UIKit is a framework that contains many classes and functions that Apple has put together for developers.

EXTRA, EXTRA! UIKit is the foundation framework with more classes related to UI development with Cocoa Touch, and the foundation framework is the Darwin (the open-source kernel that macOS is based on) framework with more developer-oriented classes.

To import, scroll in your ViewController.swift file to `import UIKit`, and add this new line after it:

```
import <FRAMEWORK_NAME_HERE>
```

If your framework is named SwiftoFile, for example, type

```
import SwiftoFile
```

Go to `load @IBAction`, and change

```
@IBAction func load() {
    writeField.text = read("infoSave.txt")
}
```

to

```
@IBAction func load() {
   let fileContentManaging = SwiftoFile(userfilename: "infoSave.txt")
```

```
    writeField.text = fileContentManaging.read()
}
```

Then go to the save IBAction, and change

```
@IBAction func save() {
    write("infoSave.txt", value: writeField.text!, newline: false,
    ➥ overwrite: true)
}
```

to

```
@IBAction func save() {
    let fileContentManaging = SwiftoFile(userfilename: "infoSave.txt")
    fileContentManaging.write(content: writeField.text!,
    ➥ overwriteFile: true, appendNewline: false)
}
```

Listing 11.5 shows how the code looks after all your modifications.

Listing 11.5 The final code for the Load Save app, Part 2

```
import UIKit
import SwiftoFile

class ViewController: UIViewController {

    @IBOutlet var writeField: UITextView!

    override func viewDidLoad() {
        super.viewDidLoad()
        // Do any additional setup after loading the view,
        ➥ typically from a nib.
    }

    @IBAction func save() {
        let fileContentManaging = SwiftoFile("infoSave.txt")
        fileContentManaging.write(content: writeField.text!,
            overwriteFile: true, appendNewline: false)
    }

    @IBAction func load() {
        let fileContentManaging = SwiftoFile("infoSave.txt")
        writeField.text = fileContentManaging.read()
    }
```

```
    override func didReceiveMemoryWarning() {
        super.didReceiveMemoryWarning()
        // Dispose of any resources that can be re-created.
    }

}
```

You're done!

Run your app

Make sure to note which framework type you chose. If you chose simulator, make sure to run or test only on a simulator. If you chose a real iDevice, make sure to run or test only on an iDevice. If you mix up the two platforms, you get an error. In case you want to get really technical, this error occurs because real iDevices run on ARM chips, whereas Macs, which run iOS simulators, run on Intel chips. The architectures are different, and Xcode needs to know what to build the app for to build it. In simpler terms, the simulator and iDevice speak different languages and need differently translated code to use the framework.

Therefore, choose simulator if you want to run the app on a simulator, or choose your iDevice if you want to run the app on an iDevice.

You've used a framework in Swift! In chapter 12, you move on to (drumroll, please) SpriteKit—or, as I like to think of it, animation and games.

Check your app knowledge

1. Why do you have to build for simulators and iDevices differently when you make a framework?
2. What's the advantage of using a framework instead of functions and classes?
3. Why do you use the keyword `public` in some classes when creating a framework?
4. Why don't you see files like Main.storyboard when you create a framework project in Xcode?
5. Describe two situations in which creating a new framework could be useful.

12

SpriteKit: Fun animation time

This chapter will help you build your confidence by getting your first simple graphics-based app up and running!

This chapter covers

- *What is SpriteKit?*
- *What is a pixel?*
- *How does the coordinate system work in SpriteKit?*
- *What are the differences between SpriteKit and UIKit?*
- *How can you use SpriteKit to create a simple app?*

In this chapter, you're going to get your toes wet with SpriteKit. It'll help you build your confidence, as you'll see your first simple graphics-based app up and running.

This chapter is for patient typists. I can assure you that you know what all this code means—or will understand it easily—even though the actual code listings are lengthier than you've seen so far.

Please don't hate me, but this chapter is math-intensive. It's not calculus-level math, but it's relatively more complex than in the other chapters.

In this book, however, I won't be going into too much detail with SpriteKit; you either get your toes wet or you dive into the pool. I may cover the more-complicated applications later in the online version of this book as an extension to this chapter.

This chapter is a starter for those who want to learn simple 2D animation for iOS apps.

Meet SpriteKit

SpriteKit is a framework designed by Apple for intense 2D graphics. By *intense*, I mean not only the type of graphics that allow you to show rectangular buttons onscreen, but also the type of graphics that enable you to simulate a ball that bounces as it hits a wall or a comic character flying across the screen.

UIKit also allows me to put graphics onscreen and in 2D. What's special about SpriteKit?

SpriteKit gives you tools in the code to create advanced graphics, and it lets you get closer to game development. One down side is that SpriteKit gives you no graphical way to create the user interface (UI). You won't be able to drag buttons or other widgets to the screen from a storyboard file, for example; you have to add buttons by specifying coordinates, size, color, and everything else your buttons need through your code. You won't be able to design the UI through a graphic interface by dragging and dropping elements.

If you like, however, you can create your own graphics for a game (fish, Christmas-tree ornaments, logos, and so on) by using a graphic design tool. I recommend Sketch or Adobe Photoshop for this purpose.

Now, without any further ado, get straight to some SpriteKit coding.

How does SpriteKit work?

You need to learn about pixels and the coordinate system to understand the concepts that come up in your journey of coding with SpriteKit.

Pixels

Before I can talk about SpriteKit, I have to talk about the basics, down to the hardware level.

To start, every screen or display you see uses lots and lots of tiny squares called *pixels*. Here, I'd like to remind you that the standard colors of light are red, green, and blue (RGB), which are different from the primary colors red, yellow, and blue. When you mix RGB in different proportions, you can create any color.

Look at the image in figure 12.1.

This image is a bunch of RGB values that control how much red, green, and blue should be displayed in every pixel to create a particular color.

Figure 12.2 shows what 1 pixel looks like, but it's magnified in the figure because a single pixel is so tiny that it's practically invisible to the naked eye.

Figure 12.1 Some colorful pencils

Figure 12.2 A magnified pixel

To see the images in color, refer to the eBook that comes free with the purchase of a print copy of this book.

Did you know that *pixel* is an acronym for *picture cell*? In fact, screens are made up of pixels. Now you know!

This information seems really nitpicky. Why do I need to know about pixels?

You need to learn about pixels for two reasons:

- You'll be able to appreciate the resolution of the screen.
- You'll use these pixels to draw shapes and position them onscreen.

A pixel can display almost any color imaginable by specifying how much red, green, and blue to mix together, as shown in table 12.1. RGB values can range from 0 to 255.

Table 12.1 How different proportions of RGB result in different colors

Amount of R	Amount of G	Amount of B	Resulting color
255	0	0	Red
0	255	0	Green
0	0	255	Blue
255	0	255	Purple
255	255	0	Yellow

When you have hundreds of thousands of pixels in a 2D array (which you can picture as a grid or matrix), you have a display that's capable of showing images.

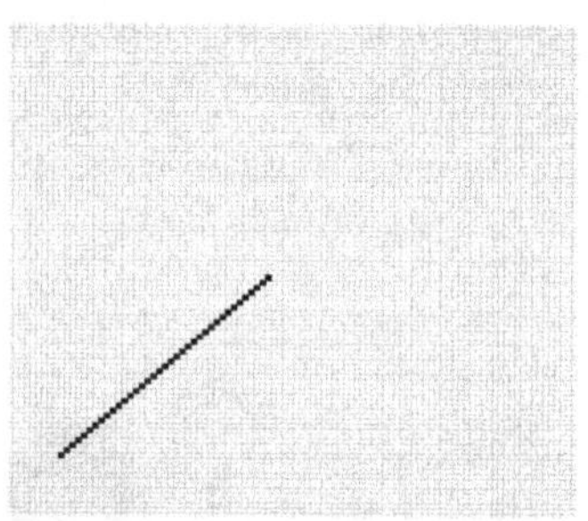

Figure 12.3 A 100 x 100 grid depicting pixels that have been illuminated in a way that represents a straight line

Suppose that you want to create a line from point A to point B in a 100 x 100 grid of pixels. Because a line is a set of points placed closely to one another, you light up all the pixels as points between A and B to create a line (figure 12.3).

You create any other shape or image similarly.

To conclude, an image is a bunch of RGB values at specific positions, reconstructed by the operating system to be displayed on a screen. Now, the more pixels you have packed together in a smaller space, the more HD (high-definition) that screen is, so in the same amount of space, you can show more pixels distinctly.

Apple and Dell have released 5K monitors, for example, which means that these monitors have an enormous amount of pixels: 5120 x 2880, which represents 14,745,600 individual pixels onscreen!

More pixels equal more detail in images, text, and the like because your eyes can perceive the image more easily; hence, your brain can pick out more details.

Coordinate system

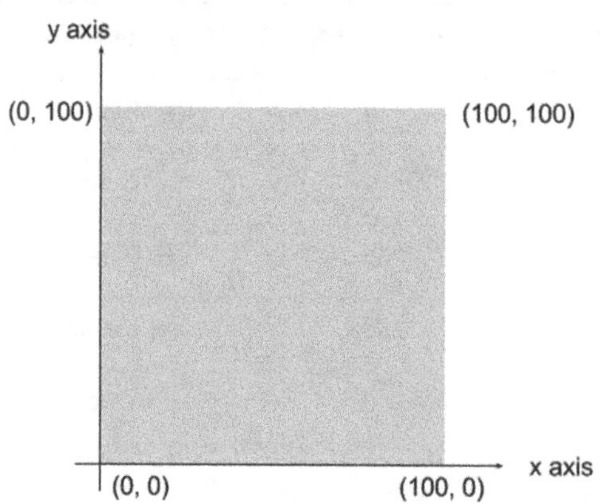

Figure 12.4 A square to explain the coordinate system, starting at bottom left and increasing to the right and to the top

In this section, you apply your new understanding of pixels to basic graph concepts. Learning this concept will help you understand how to locate a point or place an object on the iPhone's screen.

To start, draw a 100 x 100 pixel square (figure 12.4).

The bottom-left corner has (0, 0) beside it, which means that the computer takes this point as x: 0, y: 0.

NOTE The size of the square in the figure isn't really 100 x 100 pixels; it's represented that way to teach you the concept.

As you go up from that corner, the y value starts to increase. Eventually, in the top-left corner, you get to (0, 100), which means x: 0, y: 100.

Also, as you go toward the right from the bottom-left corner, the x value starts to increase. Eventually, in the bottom-right corner, you get to (100, 0), which means x: 100, y: 0.

So the top-right corner is (100, 100).

This square is 100 x 100 pixels. As you can well imagine, however, that grid would be way too small for an iPhone. Table 12.2 lists the dimensions of iPhones starting with the iPhone 5S.

Table 12.2 Screen sizes for iPhone 5S and later

iPhone Model	Pixels onscreen
iPhone XR	1792 x 828
iPhone XS Max	2688 x 1242
X/XS	2436 x 1125
6+/6S+/7+/8+	1920 x 1080
6/6S/7/8	1334 x 750
5S/SE	1136 x 640

As you can see, those dimensions are a lot of pixels, so you can fit a lot of stuff onscreen.

In the next section, you get into the apps.

Drag the Square (DTS) app

NOTE You can find the code for this application in the Chapter12_DragTheSquare folder inside the Hello-Swift-Code-master folder that you downloaded from GitHub. If you haven't downloaded the code from GitHub, go to: https://github.com/tanmayb123/Hello-Swift-Code/archive/master.zip. You should download the code only once for all chapters.

What does this app do?

Figure 12.5 The starting screen of the Drag the Square app

This app is simple: you put a square in the center of your screen and then drag it around by tapping it. You can tap anywhere on the screen, and as you tap, the square jumps to your finger's position. As you move your finger across the screen, the square follows. When you lift your finger, the square stays where it is.

Figure 12.5 shows you how the application starts.

With SpriteKit, you don't have a graphical method of creating the UI because there's no storyboard file.

Create the project

There are a few differences between creating a SpriteKit project and creating a UIKit project.

When you create a SpriteKit project in Xcode, Xcode fills your project with a small application automatically. The application is supposed to display `Hello World!` on your screen, along with some more functionality, but I don't want to confuse you with all that functionality yet.

To make your life a lot easier, in the blank project I created for you, I removed the example code and interface from the GameScene.swift and GameScene.sks files, and also reset the coordinate system. So download those code files before you begin.

NOTE You can find the code for this application in the Chapter12_SpriteKit-BlankTemplate folder inside the Hello-Swift-Code-master folder that you downloaded from GitHub. If you haven't downloaded the code from GitHub, go to: https://github.com/tanmayb123/Hello-Swift-Code/archive/master.zip. You should download the code only once for all chapters.

Alternatively, you can create a new default SpriteKit application and modify the template so that it's a blank application.

I'm assuming that you downloaded the project, however, so in the next section, you start coding.

Code the app

Here's an overview of the logic you'll code:

1 Create the square.
2 Set the position of the square to the center of the screen.
3 Make the square red.
4 Make the square appear onscreen.

Start by opening the Xcode project that you downloaded by double-clicking DragTheSquare.xcodeproj in Finder.

PUTTING THE SQUARE ONSCREEN

Every time you code an application by using UIKit (every app you've coded before this one), you have a `viewDidLoad` function, in which you can enter the code that you want to execute at the beginning of the application. Well, that function doesn't exist in SpriteKit applications. Instead, you have a `didMove(to: UIView)` function, so you have to enter your application-start code there.

There's one more difference between SpriteKit and UIKit: you usually code in your ViewController.swift file when you use UIKit, but that file doesn't exist in SpriteKit applications either. You have to use the GameScene.swift file instead (figure 12.6).

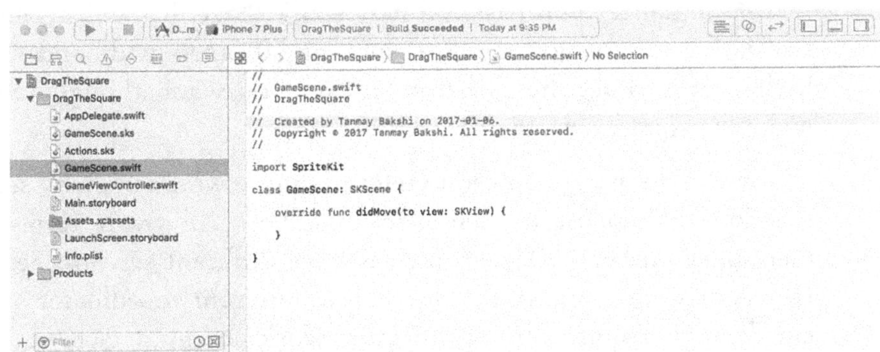

Figure 12.6 The GameScene.swift file

Head over to the GameScene.swift file on the left side of the file navigator pane. You'll see the `didMove()` function. Inside that function, insert the following code:

```
square = SKShapeNode(rectOf: CGSize(width: 60, height: 60))
square.position = CGPoint(x: self.frame.midX, y: self.frame.midY)
square.fillColor = UIColor.red
self.addChild(square)
```

By the way, this code corresponds to the four steps I mentioned at the beginning of this "Code the app" section.

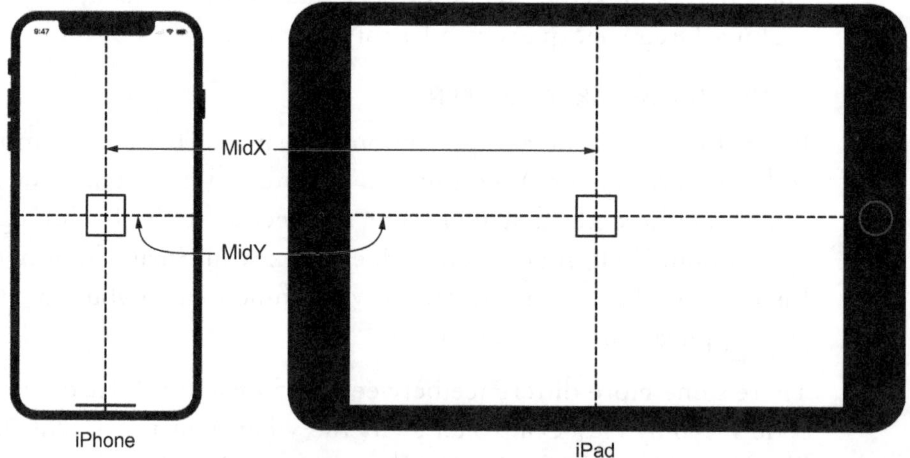

The first line initializes a new shape of class `SKShapeNode`. You use the `rectOf:` initializer and pass it a new size (`CGSize`, in Swift terms). This size is the size of your square, such as 60 pixels wide and 60 pixels high. You can set the size to whatever you want, though (and even make the square a rectangle).

When you do that, you need to tell the square where to go by setting its position to a point on the screen (`CGPoint`, in Swift terms). As I mentioned earlier, different devices have different screen sizes, which means that the center of the screen is at different coordinates on different devices. To make this application work on any device, you tell the square to go directly to the center of the screen, no matter where that is.

Find the `frame` of `self` and get the `midX` variable from it. This variable is your `middleX` coordinate. You get the `middleY` coordinate the same way.

Next, set the square's color to red.

Finally, when the square is created in memory, add it as a child to `self` so that it's visible onscreen. `self` refers to the `GameScene` class (an SKScene object). After you've initialized the object and specified its attributes (steps 1-3), you're ready to draw the object onscreen (step 4).

You still have to add a little more functionality to make the square move around the screen, and you do that in the next section.

MOVING THE SQUARE

The code file has two more functions: `touchesBegan` and `touchesMoved`. Those functions are responsible for telling the code what to do when the user touches the screen or moves a finger across the screen.

To move the square along with the user's finger, you need to use these functions. In table 12.3, I explain the `touches` functions.

Table 12.3 Functions in the Drag the Square app

Function	What it does
`touchesBegan`	This function is called right as the user puts a finger anywhere on the screen.
`touchesMoved`	This function is called when the user moves a finger across the screen, even if by only a pixel.
`touchesEnded`	This function is called when the user removes a finger from the screen. You won't be using this function in this application yet.

Now that you know what these functions do, continue with the code.

In the `touchesBegan` and `touchesMoved` functions, add this code (the same for both functions):

```
let touchLocation = touches.first!.location(in: self)
square.position = touchLocation
```

You need to find out where the user touched the screen—that is, the *coordinates* of the pixel that the user touched. Create a new constant called `touchLocation`, and set it to the location in `self` of the first finger that touched the screen. (You must unwrap the location of the first finger forcefully.)

Then, when you've extracted that location, set the square's position to that location.

The job is that simple. You're done. Here's the app's full code:

Listing 12.1 The final code for the Drag The Square app

```
import SpriteKit
import GameplayKit

class GameScene: SKScene {

    var square: SKShapeNode!

    override func didMove(to view: SKView) {
        square = SKShapeNode(rectOf: CGSize(width: 60, height: 60))
        square.position = CGPoint(x: self.frame.midX, y:
➥ self.frame.midY)
        square.fillColor = UIColor.red
        self.addChild(square)
    }

    override func touchesBegan(_ touches: Set<UITouch>, with event:
➥ UIEvent?) {
        let touchLocation = touches.first!.location(in: self)
        square.position = touchLocation
    }

    override func touchesMoved(_ touches: Set<UITouch>, with event:
➥ UIEvent?) {

        let touchLocation = touches.first!.location(in: self)
        square.position = touchLocation
    }

}
```

Here, you initialize the square.

This code allows you to set the position of the square to the middle of the screen.

This code makes the square red.

This code puts the square onscreen.

This code finds the location of the first finger that the user puts onscreen.

Here, you set the location of the square to the user's first finger.

Now if you run the application, you should see a red square in the middle of your phone's screen, and you should be able to move it around. Figure 12.7 shows the working app.

Figure 12.7 Moving the square across the screen

Run the app

As the app starts, you see a red square in the center of the screen. Place your finger anywhere on the screen, and the square jumps right under your finger. Now you can move your finger across the screen, and the square follows along right under your fingertip. When you lift your finger, the square stays at the point where you lifted your finger.

This app is the humble beginning of your journey to SpriteKit development!

A Christmas Tree app to try on your own

I'm sure that many of you want to try something more challenging and fun. If you'd like to, download a full explanation of, and code for, another SpriteKit app, called My Christmas Tree.

NOTE You can find the code for this application in the Chapter12_ChristmasTree folder inside the Hello-Swift-Code-master folder that you downloaded from GitHub. If you haven't downloaded the code from GitHub, go to: https://github.com/tanmayb123/Hello-Swift-Code/archive/master.zip. You should download the code only once for all chapters.

Figure 12.8 gives you a sneak peek at this app.

This application gives you a Christmas tree and some ornament options so that you can decorate your tree. With the help of this application, you learn how to do math to place objects on the screen.

And with that, you've finished your journey in SpriteKit.

Figure 12.8 The My Christmas Tree app with an ornament on the tree

Check your app knowledge

1 What is a pixel, and how does it create a particular color onscreen?

2 Where is the (0, 0) point of an `SKSpriteNode`, and where is the (0, 0) point of an `SKScene`?

3 How can you create a 20 x 20 pixel square?

4 Suppose that you have three squares. How can you center one square and put a square 20 pixels to the left of it and another 20 pixels to the right of it? (When you build this application, download the blank template as explained in subsection "Create the project" under section "Drag the Square app.")

5 In the Drag the Square app, you put the same code in two places: in the `touchesBegan` function and in the `touchesMoved` function. Reason out why the same code was put in two places. If you want to know what that code was, here it is:

```
let touchLocation = touches.first!.location(in: self)
square.position = touchLocation
```

6 Modify the Drag the Square app so that when a user drags the square (while her finger is onscreen), the square is yellow, but when she lifts her finger, the square snaps back to the center position and becomes red.

7 If you're not allowed to use `midX` and `midY`, how would you create an app that creates a 60 x 60 pixel square (your choice of color) in the middle of your device's screen?

13

Time to watch your WatchKit code

Welcome to Chapter 13, where you'll be introduced to Apple Watch application coding.

This chapter covers

- *How to create an interface for an Apple Watch app*
- *How to code a Watch app*
- *How to run the Watch app*
- *How WatchKit development is different from iOS development*

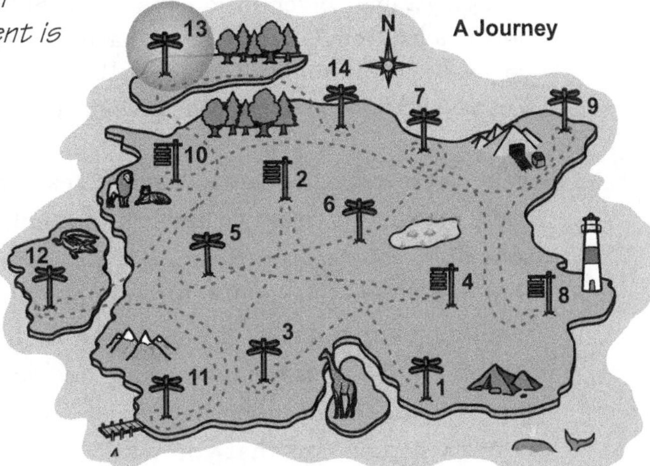

Time to watch your WatchKit code is stop 13 on your journey. The Apple Watch is like a mini iPhone that works with the iPhone in your pocket via Bluetooth, but with some obvious restrictions. If you get a text, you'll see it on your Watch. The Watch lets you know when you receive a call. It can also keep track of your calendar and alarms you've set. Finally, the Watch has a few special apps, such as activity trackers that can tell you how much exercise, or sleep, you've gotten.

Get ready to dive right into the topic of this chapter: Apple Watch development. You're going to code a Number Guessing Game app. Along the way, I show you how Watch development is different from standard iOS development.

NOTE The application you code in this chapter provides an introduction to Apple Watch development. I won't be taking you on a deep dive into Watch development; instead, you go knee-deep.

Number Guessing Game app

Get ready to dive right into creating the first app for this chapter: the Number Guessing Game app!

What does this app do?

NOTE You can find the code for this application in the Chapter13_Number-GuessingGame folder inside the Hello-Swift-Code-master folder that you downloaded from GitHub. If you haven't downloaded the code from GitHub, go to: https://github.com/tanmayb123/Hello-Swift-Code/archive/master.zip. You should download the code only once for all chapters.

When you start this game, it generates a random number from 1 to 120, and your goal is to try to guess it. To make a guess, tap the + and - buttons until you reach the number you want to submit as your guess, and then tap Make Guess. Each time you submit a guess, the app tells you whether your guess is greater than or less than the random number. Based on the message, you can decide your next guess. Rinse and repeat until the number you guess and the app's random number are equal, which means that you win!

The final running application looks like figure 13.1 on your Watch.

Before you begin developing WatchKit apps, keep in mind the fact that WatchKit applications are dependent on iOS applications. You have to create an iOS application to create a Watch application because the Watch is too small to perform massive computations; it needs the iPhone to do the heavy lifting for it (such as internet access). Watch apps are meant to be second and instant displays for the iPhone, as shown in figure 13.2.

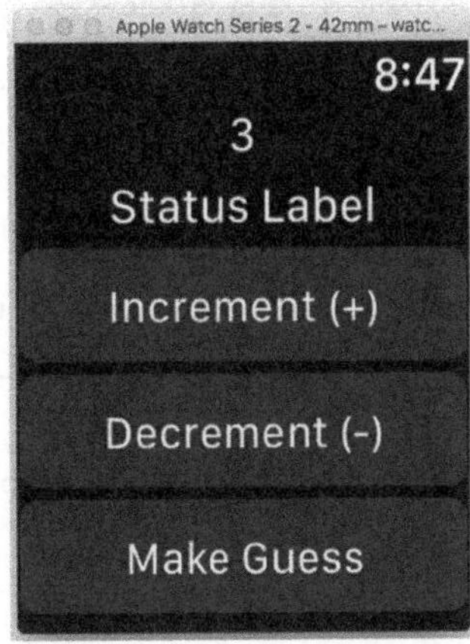

Figure 13.1 The Number Guessing Game app in action

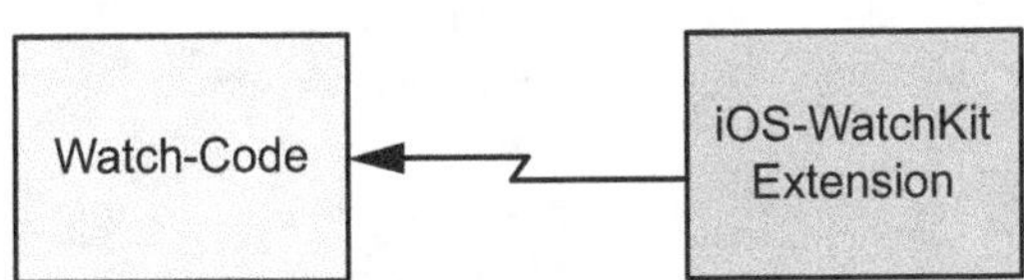

Figure 13.2 The relationship between iOS and watchOS apps

To start developing a Watch app, create a new project in Xcode, but instead of choosing iOS > Single View Application, choose watchOS > iOS App with WatchKit App. Then continue as usual.

You won't give the iOS app any user interface (UI) or code in this example; you're focusing on the Watch.

NOTE Apple requires a Watch app to have its own iOS app with it. In practice, you'd have an iOS app and an Apple Watch extension. Skype on your iPhone, for example, could be extended to Skype calls on your Apple Watch.

To code the Watch part, however, you can't code in ViewController.swift, as you've been doing for all your iOS apps thus far.

Instead, in your Xcode view, expand the NumberGuessingGame WatchKit Extension folder, and then click InterfaceController.swift, which is where you code the app.

Create the UI

Before you can code the app, you need to create the Watch UI, as you've been doing for all your iOS apps, so you can see the labels and buttons that are in the final UI. Open the NumberGuessingGame WatchKit App folder, and then click Interface.storyboard, as shown in figure 13.3.

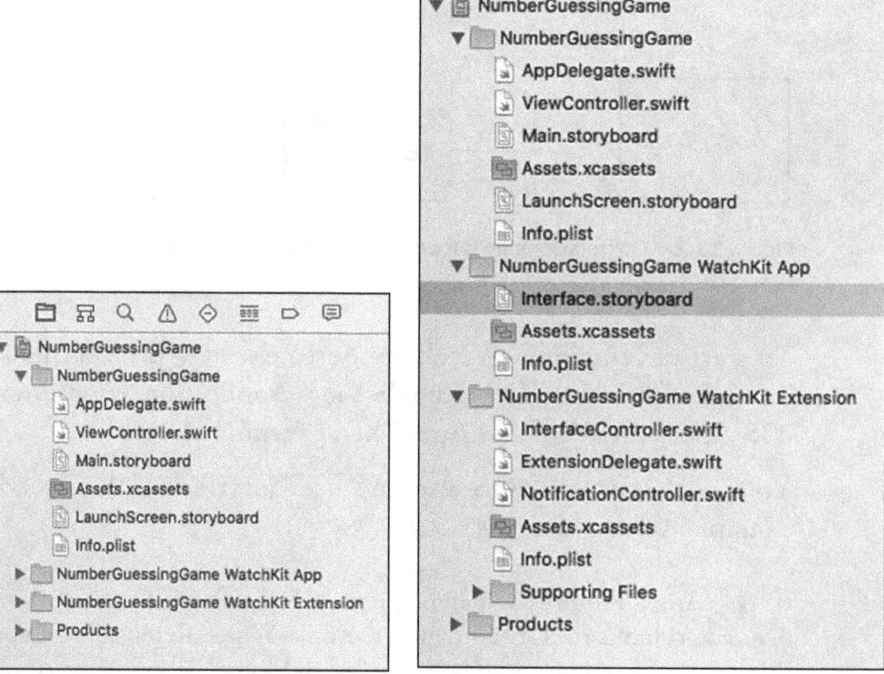

Figure 13.3 Showing your WatchKit development files

You see three views (sized as Apple Watches), as shown in figure 13.4. You develop your UI in the blank one.

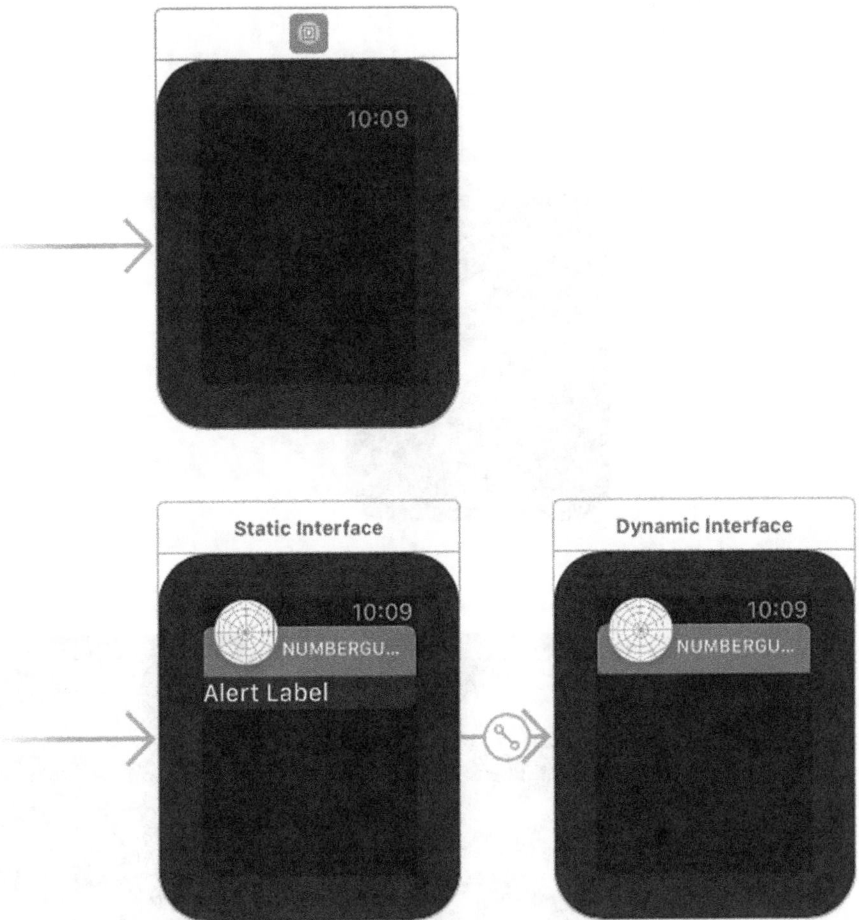

Figure 13.4 The three views in the Interface.storyboard file

Before you continue, be aware that Apple Watch comes in two sizes: 38mm and 42mm. Because the 42mm Watch is easier to work with, I show you how to develop for that screen size, but you can develop for the screen size of the Watch you have. To choose, go to the bottom-left corner of the Xcode window. By default, you should see a message saying `View As: Apple Watch 38mm`. Click that message, and you should see two Apple Watch graphics. The bigger one is 42mm, and the smaller one is 38mm, as shown in figure 13.5. Choose the one that suits your needs.

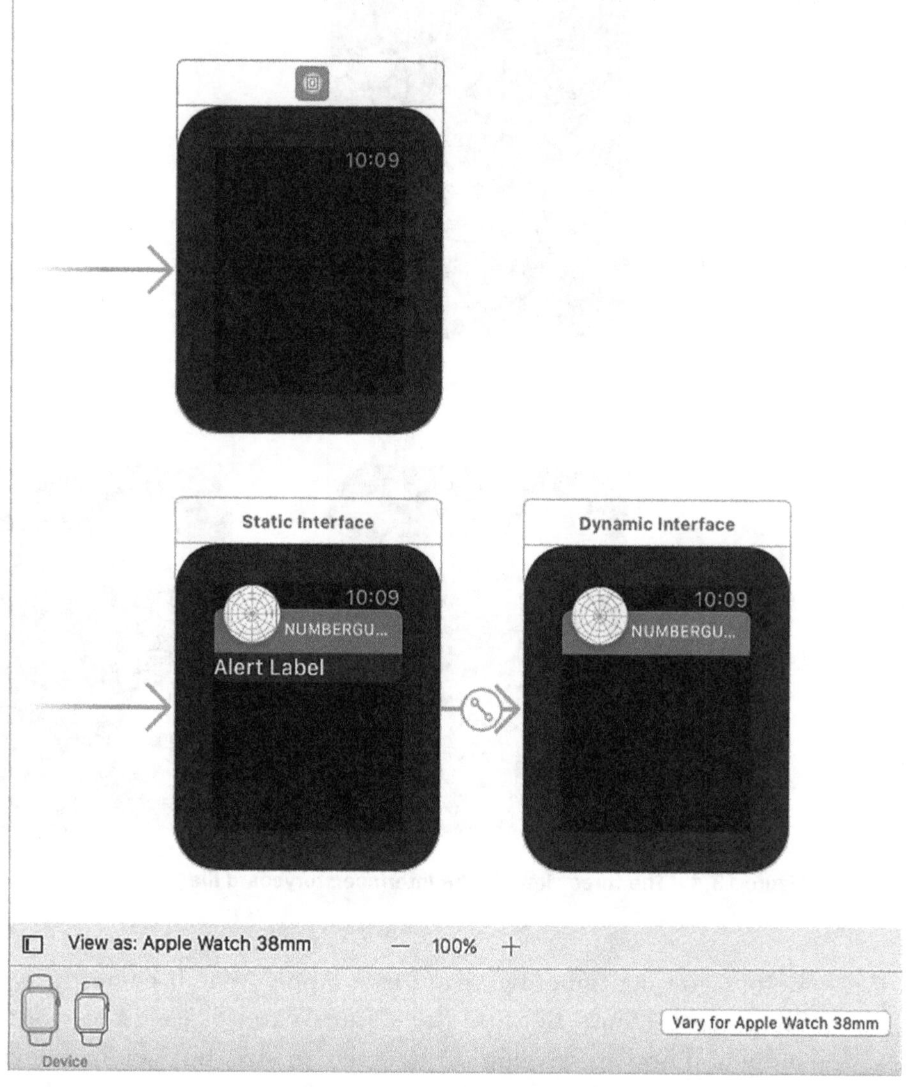

Figure 13.5 The two screen sizes of the Apple Watch. 38mm is the default size.

Back to the interface! Drag two labels and three buttons to your Watch view (figure 13.6).

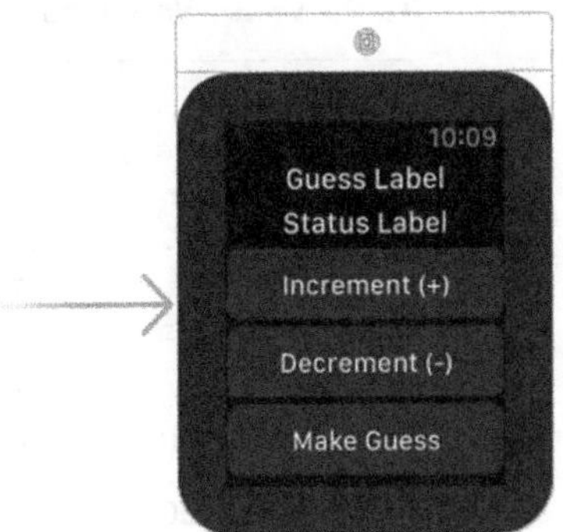

Figure 13.6 The final UI for the Number Guessing Game app

Table 13.1 explains these elements.

Table 13.1 Interface elements of the Number Guessing Game app

Interface element	Purpose
`Guess Label` label	Shows the user's current guess of the random number
`Status Label` label	Tells the user the status of the current guess: `Too Much!`, `Too Little!`, or `Correct!`
+ button	Increments the current guess by 1
– button	Decrements the current guess by 1
`Make Guess` button	Takes the number in the `Guess Label`, calculates the new status based on it, and puts that status in the `Status Label`

Coding the application

Now it's time to get to the fun part: coding your first Watch app, the Number Guessing Game (and then playing it)!

DECLARE VARIABLES, IBOutlets, AND IBActions

To begin, declare the variables shown in table 13.2 in the `InterfaceController` class.

Table 13.2 Variables of the Number Guessing Game app

Variable name	Type	Purpose
`tryingToGuess`	`Int`	Target number that the user is trying to get to
`currentGuess`	`Int`	User's current guess

Here's the code for declaring these variables:

```
var tryingToGuess: Int = 0
var currentGuess: Int = 0
```

Next, declare the `IBOutlets` shown in table 13.3.

Table 13.3 `IBOutlets` of the Number Guessing Game app

`IBOutlet`	Type	Purpose
`guessLabel`	`WKInterfaceLabel`	`IBOutlet` for the `Guess Label`
`statusLabel`	`WKInterfaceLabel`	`IBOutlet` for the `Status Label`

Here's the code for declaring these `IBOutlets`:

```
@IBOutlet var guessLabel: WKInterfaceLabel!
@IBOutlet var statusLabel: WKInterfaceLabel!
```

NOTE For WatchKit development, use `WKInterfaceLabel` instead of `UILabel`.

All right, now that you've done the `IBOutlet` and variable declarations, I'll talk about the real code.

Once again, there are quite a few differences between this type of development and iOS development. One of those differences is the fact that there's no `viewDidLoad` function. Instead, there's an `awake` function, the equivalent of `viewDidLoad` for watchOS. Type the following code in that function:

```
tryingToGuess = Int(arc4random_uniform(UInt32(120)) + 1)
guessLabel.setText("\(currentGuess)")
```

The first line sets the `tryingToGuess` variable's value to a random number from 1 to 120, using the `arc4random_uniform` function. Although this function returns a random number from 0 to 119, if you specify `120` as a parameter, when you add 1 to the result, the range shifts to 1 to 120. The second line, however, sets the text of the `Guess Label` to the `currentGuess` the user has made (which is 0 by default).

When you finish that part, you're done initializing the app. Next, see what happens when the user clicks one of the three buttons.

Create the three `IBActions` shown in table 13.4.

Table 13.4 `IBActions` of the Number Guessing Game app

IBAction	Purpose
`increment`	Called when the + button is tapped
`decrement`	Called when the - button is tapped
`makeGuess`	Called when the Make Guess button is tapped

Here's the code for those `IBActions`:

```
@IBAction func increment() {
    currentGuess = currentGuess + 1
    guessLabel.setText("\(currentGuess)")
}

@IBAction func decrement() {
    currentGuess = currentGuess - 1
    guessLabel.setText("\(currentGuess)")
}

@IBAction func makeGuess() {
    if currentGuess == tryingToGuess {
        statusLabel.setText("Correct!")
    } else if currentGuess < tryingToGuess {
        statusLabel.setText("Too Little!")
    } else if currentGuess > tryingToGuess {
        statusLabel.setText("Too Much!")
    }
  }
```

In the following sections, I explain this code.

INCREMENT AND DECREMENT IBActions

In the `increment` `IBAction`, you begin by incrementing the `currentGuess` variable by 1, and in the `decrement` `IBAction`, you decrement the `currentGuess` variable by 1. Each `IBAction` is followed by another line of code, which displays the value of the modified `currentGuess` variable to the `guessLabel`.

MAKEGUESS IBAction

This function is simple: it checks whether the value of the `currentGuess` variable is smaller than, greater than, or equal to the value of the `tryingToGuess` variable, and it sets the text of the `statusLabel` accordingly, as shown in table 13.5.

Table 13.5 The logic for the `statusLabel`

Condition	Text
`currentGuess == tryingToGuess`	`Correct!`
`currentGuess < tryingToGuess`	`Too Little!`
`currentGuess > tryingToGuess`	`Too Much!`

COMPLETE CODE

Finally, here's the complete code listing:

Listing 13.1 Complete code for the Number Guessing Game app

```
import WatchKit
import Foundation

class InterfaceController: WKInterfaceController {

    var tryingToGuess: Int = 0
    var currentGuess: Int = 0

    @IBOutlet var guessLabel: WKInterfaceLabel!
    @IBOutlet var statusLabel: WKInterfaceLabel!
```

```
    override func awake(withContext context: Any?) {
        super.awake(withContext: context)
        // Configure interface objects here.
        tryingToGuess = Int(arc4random_uniform(UInt32(120)) + 1)
        guessLabel.setText("\(currentGuess)")
    }

    @IBAction func increment() {
        currentGuess = currentGuess + 1
        guessLabel.setText("\(currentGuess)")
    }

    @IBAction func decrement() {
        currentGuess = currentGuess - 1
        guessLabel.setText("\(currentGuess)")
    }

    @IBAction func makeGuess() {
        if currentGuess == tryingToGuess {
            statusLabel.setText("Correct!")
        } else if currentGuess < tryingToGuess {
            statusLabel.setText("Too Little!")
        } else if currentGuess > tryingToGuess {
            statusLabel.setText("Too Much!")
        }
    }

    override func willActivate() {
        // This method is called when watch view controller is about
➥ to be visible to user
        super.willActivate()
    }

    override func didDeactivate() {
        // This method is called when watch view controller is no
➥ longer visible
        super.didDeactivate()
    }

}
```

CONNECTING THE IBACTIONS AND IBOUTLETS

One thing hasn't changed throughout the transition from iPhone to Apple Watch development (phew): connecting your `IBActions` and `IBOutlets`. You can do those jobs now.

Run your application

Unfortunately, one key element of iOS development changes in Apple Watch development: running your app. Getting your Apple Watch app running on your Watch is quite a process, so you need to watch my video tutorial at http://www.tanmaybakshi.com/runWatchApp to find out how. Please note that "runWatchApp" is case sensitive.

Running your Watch app in the Apple Watch simulator is much, much easier, however. To begin, change the target to run in Xcode: which target of your application Xcode must run when you click the Run or Play button. To do this, click NumberGuessingGame before the arrow that points to your device name (figure 13.7).

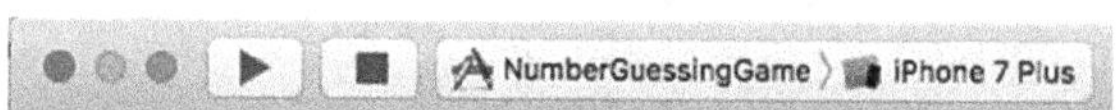

Figure 13.7 Changing the run target (part 1)

A drop-down menu appears, displaying a list of options. Choose the NumberGuessingGame WatchKit App option (figure 13.8).

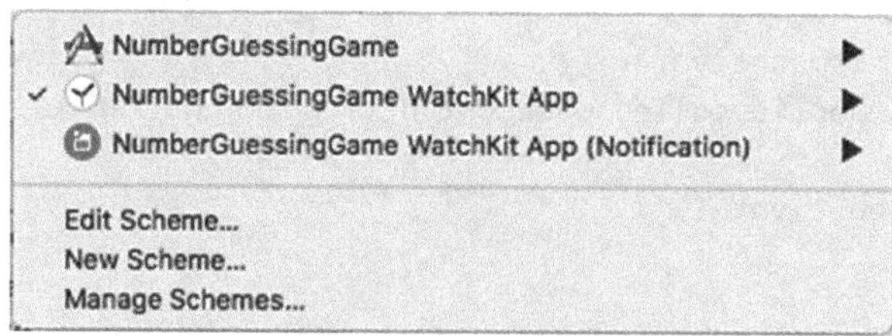

Figure 13.8 Changing the run target (part 2)

Next, where you usually select your simulator or device, choose the Apple Watch screen size you'd like to use (figure 13.9).

Figure 13.9 Choosing the Apple Watch simulator

Finally, run as normal. You should see your application in a Watch simulator (figure 13.10).

You should have a fun application to play with on the go!

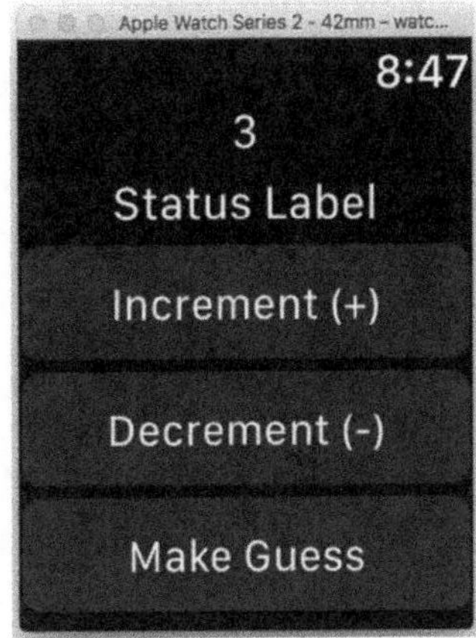

Figure 13.10 The final, running application

Check your app knowledge

1. Now that you've coded iOS and WatchKit apps, list some of the similarities and differences of the two kinds of developments that you've noticed along the way.
2. How can you modify this app so that when you guess correctly, it shows how many tries it took you to win?
3. Suppose that you want to teach someone how to play this game and come to the right guess in the minimum number of tries every time. How can you do this?
4. What's the equivalent of the watchOS `awake` function in iOS, and what does it do?
5. How can you modify the code to prevent the user's guess from going below 0 or above 120? (Note: Currently, the code doesn't handle this situation.)

14

Continuing your journey with Swift

You've successfully completed your journey of learning the fundamentals of iOS development with Swift. Great job! Now you may be wondering what comes next.

This chapter covers

- *What to do to continue your journey*
- *Which resources to use to continue learning*
- *What to learn next*

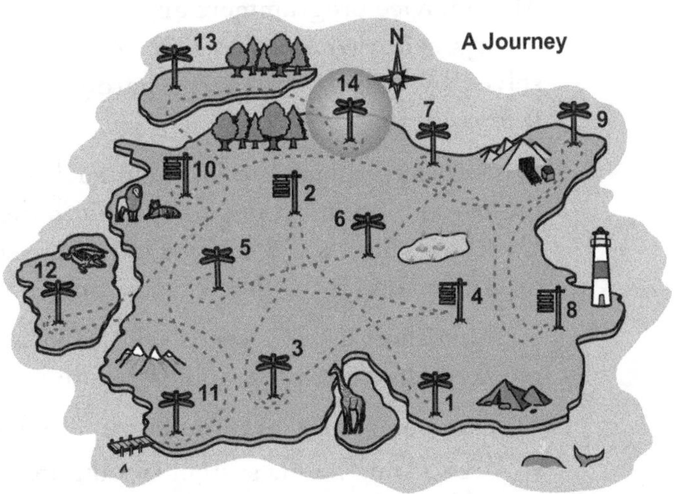

Your last milestone is continuing your journey with Swift. Before you go further, you need to learn one more topic: what you should do to continue your journey from here. To make your journey ahead smoother, I'm breaking this chapter into two main parts: the resources available for you to learn from and what you should learn next using those resources.

Resources

Programmers in need of help can turn to lots of resources, both online and physical. I take a look at a few of those resources in the following sections.

liveBook Discussion Forum

On the liveBook Discussion Forum, I'll try to answer any of the questions you may have that are directly or indirectly related to the content of this book. I'll also post new updates as Swift and Xcode evolve, as well as some tips and tricks to make your learning easier. I believe that this forum will help answer the questions that all readers have in common, and the questions can also be answered and read by other readers.

To access the forum, go to https://livebook.manning.com/#!/book/hello-swift/discussion.

Stack Overflow

Many novice programmers are confused about where to get the quick, quality help they need to solve problems. These problems have been solved by others, but there's hardly any documentation available for those solutions.

When programmers are stuck in such situations, forum sites come to the rescue! The most popular site with the biggest community is Stack Overflow (SO), a Q&A StackExchange site with more than 10 million programmers (at the time I wrote this book).

Here's a short list of reasons why SO is such a great place to give and receive help in the programming field:

- Great community of programmers in various fields.
- A rewarding points system (reputation) that encourages users to ask good questions and provide good answers.

- A solution to almost every problem in iOS development.
- Community and industry acceptance. SO can help you with employment when you need it (if you're still a kid, like me). You'll be viewed with respect if you're active and have a good reputation in SO.

You can become a member of the growing SO community by signing up at https://stackoverflow.com. As you gain membership, go through the Dos and Don'ts lists, which discuss the ethics and etiquette of SO. Figure 14.1 shows an example of a user asking a question and getting an answer from fellow users.

NOTE Make sure you're at least 13 years old before you sign up for Stack Overflow. If you're younger than 13, ask a parent or another guardian to sign up on your behalf.

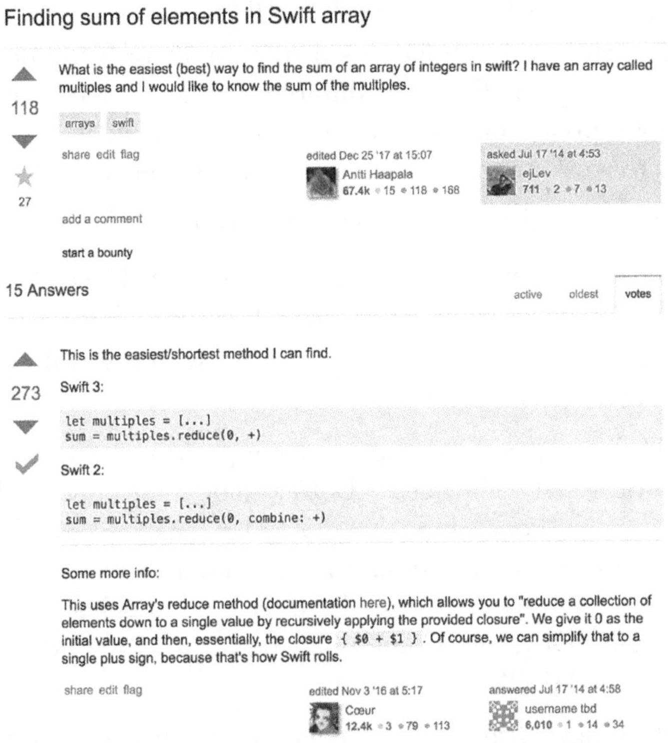

Finding sum of elements in Swift array

118

What is the easiest (best) way to find the sum of an array of integers in swift? I have an array called multiples and I would like to know the sum of the multiples.

arrays swift

27

share edit flag

edited Dec 25 '17 at 15:07 Antti Haapala 67.4k 15 118 168

asked Jul 17 '14 at 4:53 ejLev 711 2 7 13

add a comment

start a bounty

15 Answers

active oldest votes

273

This is the easiest/shortest method I can find.

Swift 3:

```
let multiples = [...]
sum = multiples.reduce(0, +)
```

Swift 2:

```
let multiples = [...]
sum = multiples.reduce(0, combine: +)
```

Some more info:

This uses Array's reduce method (documentation here), which allows you to "reduce a collection of elements down to a single value by recursively applying the provided closure". We give it 0 as the initial value, and then, essentially, the closure `{ $0 + $1 }`. Of course, we can simplify that to a single plus sign, because that's how Swift rolls.

share edit flag

edited Nov 3 '16 at 5:17 Cœur 12.4k 3 79 113

answered Jul 17 '14 at 4:58 username tbd 6,010 1 14 34

Figure 14.1 Example question and answer on Stack Overflow

GitHub

Nothing beats learning from examples, which is also true in the world of programming.

Learning to program from the code that other people write is a great way to learn, because you get to see everything (such as programming style, logic, and structure) that you can't get from regular documentation. Also, by understanding the way that others solved a particular problem, you not only learn, but also tend to come up with your own style, logic, and structure. Then you can share your knowledge with others, and the knowledge growth cycle continues. That cycle helps the programming community grow and improve every second.

This cycle is where GitHub comes in. GitHub is a code-sharing and open-sourcing platform for coders around the globe. It has a great Git backend for version control and code sharing.

On GitHub, you can see hundreds of thousands of iOS applications contributed to by millions of different programmers worldwide. GitHub allows programmers to do more than share code; it allows the community to work on the code, improve it, and contribute to it.

Here are two main advantages of using GitHub:

- You're learning from examples created by others. The code has been worked on by lots of people who made it better with each iteration.
- It has a great community of programmers who are willing to help and contribute to lots of projects.

I used GitHub to open-source some of my projects, such as AskTanmay, the world's first web-based NLQA system to be powered by IBM Watson. (If you're wondering what *NLQA* means, it stands for *Natural Language Question Answering*.) I created it in November 2015 and open-sourced it to share it with the developers during my keynote address at IBM DeveloperConnect 2016 (https://www.youtube.com/watch?v=xryTC-M7SWY).

If you're interested in learning how to use Git (the backend for GitHub) and GitHub, you can search online; you can find many great resources to learn from. You can also read *Learn Git in a Month of Lunches*, by

Rick Umali, as shown in figure 14.2 (https://www.manning.com/books/learn-git-in-a-month-of-lunches).

Figure 14.2 ***Learn Git In a Month of Lunches*, by Rick Umali, helps you become an expert in Git and GitHub.**

YouTube and books

Then again, sometimes you have to go back to the classics: YouTube and books.

I'm putting YouTube and books in the same category because they have the same basic advantages:

- Learning from the examples of others who created the content
- Learning from others who are coding live

The only real advantage of a video over a book is that . . . well, it's a video. You can watch all the cursor movements, screen navigation, and keystrokes to get a better idea of what's happening.

On YouTube, it's easy to find videos related to your topic, which can complement your learning; search for them. I also have the YouTube channel Tanmay Teaches, where I like to teach Swift and many other topics. Here's the address: https://www.youtube.com/c/tanmaybakshiteaches.

In terms of books, I recommend Manning's *iOS Development with Swift*, by Craig Grummitt, as a further reading resource (figure 14.3).

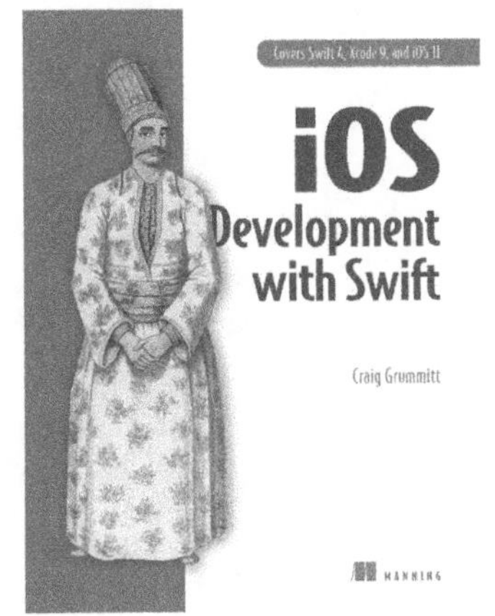

Figure 14.3 ***iOS Development with Swift*, by Craig Grummitt, for your further reading**

What's next?

As a final topic, I'd like to tell you what I believe you should be pursuing next by using the resources listed in this chapter:

- *Debugging*—Learn how to debug your code when there's an exception or your app doesn't work the way you intended, using breakpoints, inspection, dry runs, and more. Debugging will help you methodically solve the problem and create better code quickly.
- *Protocols*—Learn how to implement protocols in your applications. This skill will help you create apps with more-complex objects, such as Table Views and Picker Views.
- *Structures*—Learn how to implement structures in your apps to make apps that use and work better with complex data of specific types.
- *UITableView*—Learn how to implement lists in your apps so that you can list an unknown amount of data dynamically.
- *UIPickerView*—Learn how to implement scroll-pickers in your apps to help your users pick data from a few options.
- *Auto Layout*—Learn how to use Auto Layout to make your apps work on all different devices automatically, to eliminate the process of creating separate screens for each device manually.

I recommend learning those six topics in order as you continue your journey to becoming an advanced iOS developer.

Appendices

Preface

Congratulations for completing your journey of iOS app programming through Swift. You're now entering the appendices section of this book. Here, you'll learn the concepts and see how to create apps related to your studies. This section not only gives you an opportunity to learn technology, but also makes these mathematical concepts easy and fun to understand (and at the same time may improve your grades in school). Don't worry—you'll be learning these concepts by creating apps, so you'll have a different learning experience. This won't be like your everyday math class—you're going to build iOS Apps with Swift that will help you learn mathematical concepts like prime numbers, fractions, calculating a triangle's area, and more—but you'll have fun on the way!

Here's a sneak peek at what's in each appendix:

- *A*—Prime
- *B*—Mean and median
- *C*—Factors
- *D*—Area of triangles
- *E*—Fractions
- F—Installation

NOTE As I mention in the "About the Book" section at the front of this book, make sure that you've gone through the first 14 chapters before you attempt to try the appendixes. You need to build a sound foundation to understand the relatively advanced concepts in the appendices. However, you've already gone through Appendix F to install your developer tools and set up your software environment.

- What about building games? Well, you're now in a position to pick up an intermediate- to advanced-level book on game development, refer to online tutorials, watch YouTube videos, and even attend college to specialize in game development. Soon, you'll be able to build your own games that use animations, audio, video, gestures, augmented reality, and many more features. The game idea you're interested in developing may or may not involve some mathematical or scientific concepts such as gravity, speed or velocity, reflection, and energy. If they do, you should be knowledgeable about those concepts. If you don't have that knowledge, you can always go to online forums or to a library, or ask others who know about these concepts. It's not difficult to learn these concepts so you can develop great apps.

Without further ado, it's time to get to the appendices!

Appendix A

Check whether I'm prime

In this appendix, you learn how to build an app to check whether a number is prime.

What does this app do?

Because you've already read this entire book, I won't be providing an in-depth explanation of the concepts or code, but I'll walk you through the steps involved in building this app.

NOTE You can find the code for this application in the Appendix A file inside the Hello-Swift-Code-master folder that you downloaded from GitHub. If you haven't downloaded the code from GitHub, go to: https://github.com/tanmayb123/Hello-Swift-Code/archive/master.zip. You should download the code only once for all chapters.

You'll end up with an app that looks like figure A.1.

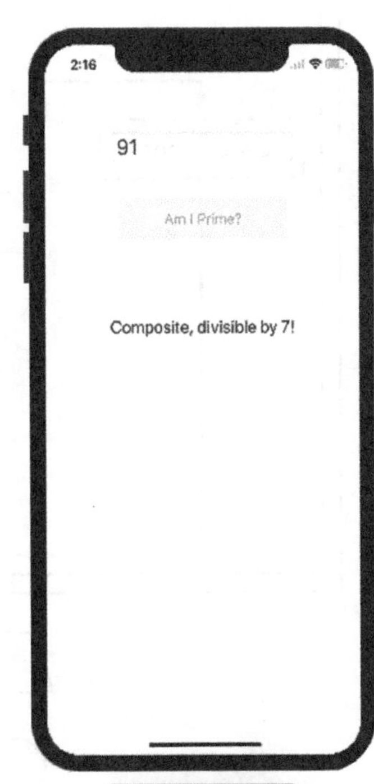

Figure A.1 The finished app

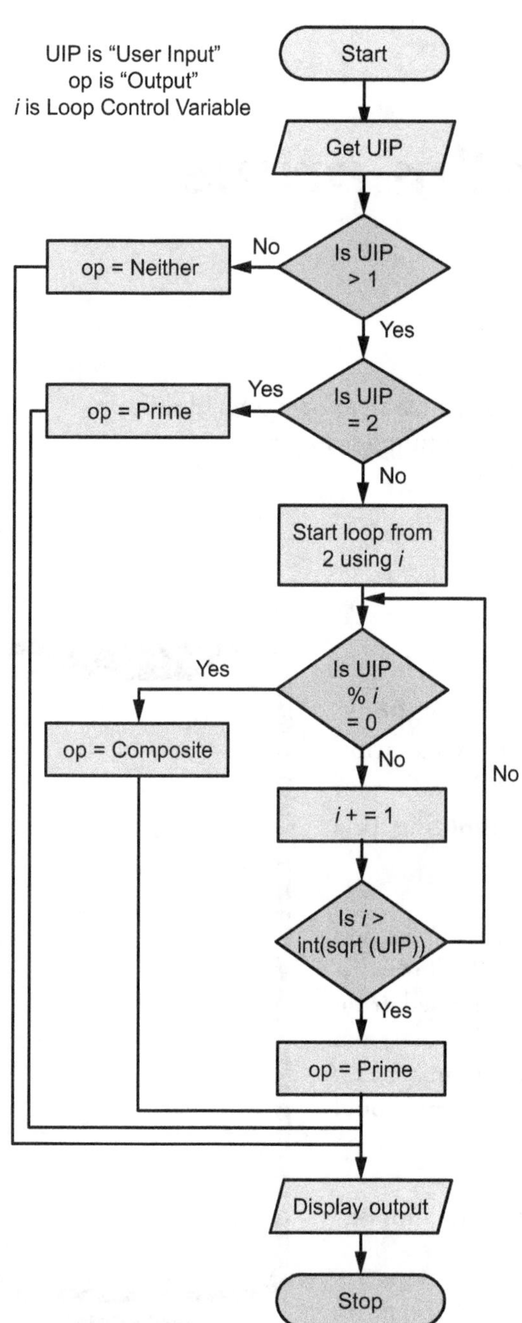

When you've made a similar user interface (UI) in your application, you can start coding. To begin, find out how you can check whether a number is prime.

A whole number is considered to be prime if it's divisible only by 1 and itself. Examples of such numbers are 2, 3, 5, 7, 11, and 13. The smallest prime number is 2. Also remember that the whole numbers are 0, 1, 2, 3, 4, and so on into infinity. As the name suggests, whole numbers are non-negative integers without a decimal or fraction part.

A simple way to check whether a number is prime is to loop from 2 to the square root of that number. If the input is divisible by a number in that loop, the number isn't prime, and you can end the loop. However, if the number is not divisible by any value of *i*, then it is a prime. The flow chart in figure A.2 describes this concept.

Figure A.2 How to figure out whether a number is prime

Set up the project, and create the UI

To start, create a user interface like the one in figure A.3.

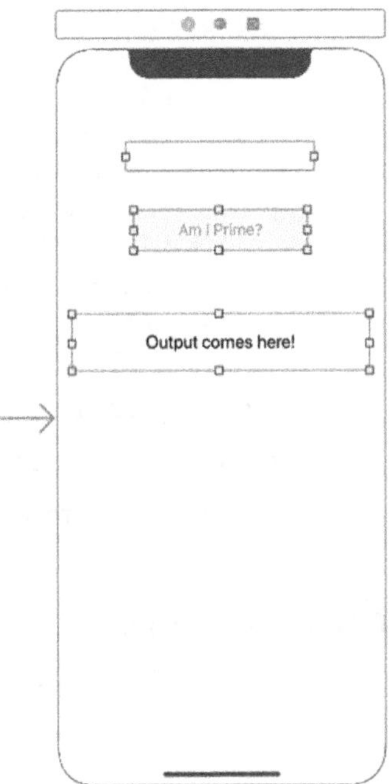

Figure A.3 Build this UI

The UI's three main elements are

- *Input TextField*—This `UITextField` at the top of the view takes the number that the user wants to check for being prime.
- *Am I Prime?*—This `UIButton` runs a function to check whether the number in Input Here is prime.
- *Output Comes Here!*—This `UILabel` displays the final output.

Code the app

Now that you know how the algorithm works and what the UI elements are, start coding the application.

Create IBOutlets

To start, add the `IBOutlets`:

```
@IBOutlet var inputField: UITextField!
@IBOutlet var outputField: UILabel!
```

Create IBActions

Next, add your `IBActions`:

```
@IBAction func processInput() {
    let userInput = Int(inputField.text!)!
    var output = "Prime!"
    if userInput > 1 {
        if userInput == 2 {
            outputField.text = "Prime!"
        } else {
            for i in 2...Int(sqrt(Double(userInput))) {
```

```
                    if userInput % i == 0 {
                        output = "Composite, divisible by \(i)!"
                        break
                    }
                }
            }
        } else {
            output = "Neither prime, nor composite."
        }
        outputField.text = output
    }
```

There you go! You've successfully implemented a prime-number checker in Swift. Now connect your `IBActions` and `IBOutlets` to your text field, button, and label, and you should be good to go!

Run your app

Figure A.4 is a screenshot of the app running on the simulator.

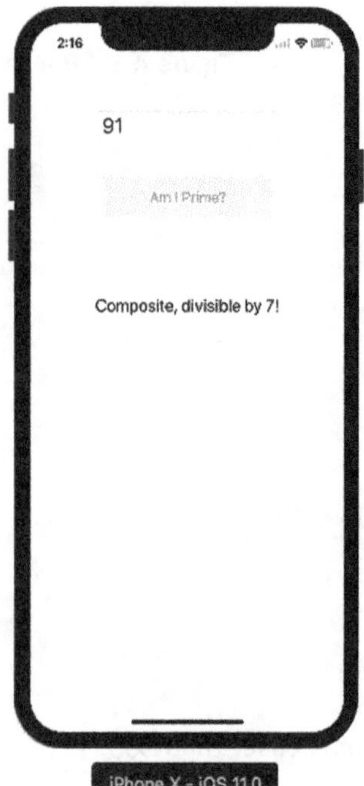

Figure A.4 The app running on the simulator

Appendix B

Mean Median Detective

The Mean Median Detective application teaches you how to build an app that finds the mean and median of a set of numbers.

What does this app do?

NOTE You can find the code for this application in the Appendix B folder inside the Hello-Swift-Code-master folder that you downloaded from GitHub. If you haven't downloaded the code from GitHub, go to: https://github.com/tanmayb123/Hello-Swift-Code/archive/master.zip. You should download the code only once for all chapters.

Figure B.1 is a screenshot of the running app.

Before you can start, though, you need to understand what the mean and median are. The *mean* and *median* are numbers that represent the center of a set of numbers. You may remember other numbers

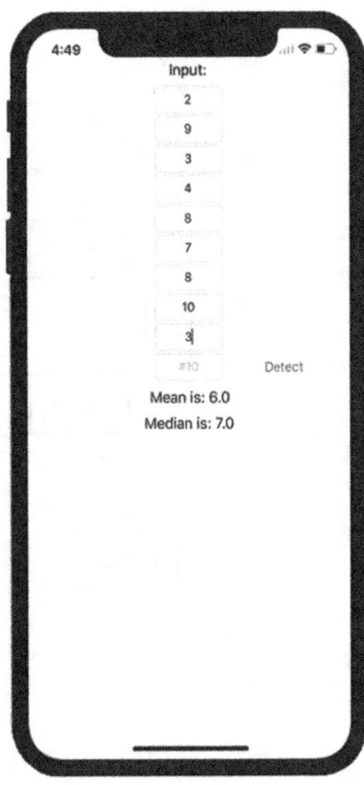

Figure B.1 The final running Mean Median Detective app

from math class, such as the mode, that also represent the central number in different ways, but I go through only the mean and median in this appendix.

Here's how you can find the mean of a set of numbers:

Mean is a fancier way to say *average*, and the formula for calculating it is simple. Suppose that you want to find the average of a set of six numbers:

[1, 6, 7, 4, 2, 10]

First, add the numbers together to find the sum. In this case, the sum is 30.

Then divide the sum (30) by the number of items in the list of numbers (6). For this example, the answer is 5.0.

This process is illustrated in figure B.2.

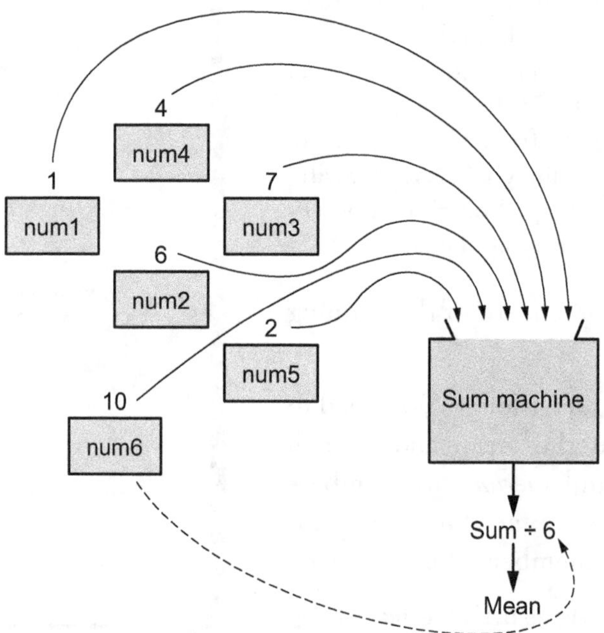

Figure B.1 How to find the mean of a set of numbers

But wait—what is the median? The *median* is the number in the middle of the list.

Suppose that you want to find the median of a list of seven numbers. The calculation is simple. You start with the list, or array:

[1, 9, 4, 5, 3, 7, 6]

You sort the array from smallest to largest. It's OK if numbers repeat, even though they don't in this list.

[1, 3, 4, 5, 6, 7, 9]

Subtract 1 from the lengh of the array—in this case, 6. You're doing this because an array's index starts at 0. Then divide the length by 2. For this example, the answer is 3.

Next, locate the element at index 3 of the array. (Remember to start counting at zero!) That element is your median—in this array, 5. This number is in the middle of the array, with an equal number of elements before and after it.

You may have thought of a problem: what if the length of the array is even, with no middle number?

Because you already know how to find the mean (average), there's a simple solution: find the average of the two elements in the middle of the array.

Suppose that your list is these eight elements:

[1, 9, 4, 5, 3, 2, 8, 7]

The sorted version is

[1, 2, 3, 4, 5, 7, 8, 9]

The two middle elements are

[4, 5]

The mean of those 2 elements is

(4+5)/2 = 4.5

Figure B.3 clarifies the process of finding the median.

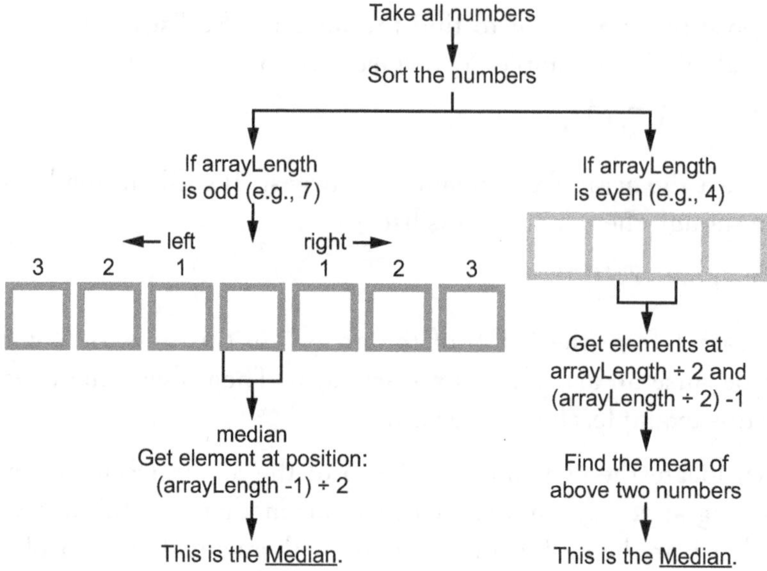

Figure B.2 How to find the median of a set of numbers

Set up the project, and create the UI

To start, create a user interface (UI) like the one in figure B.4.

The UI has 13 main elements:

- *#1–#10*—These 10 `UITextFields` allow the user to enter up to 10 numbers as input.
- *Detect*—This `UIButton` runs a function to find the mean and median of the set of numbers.

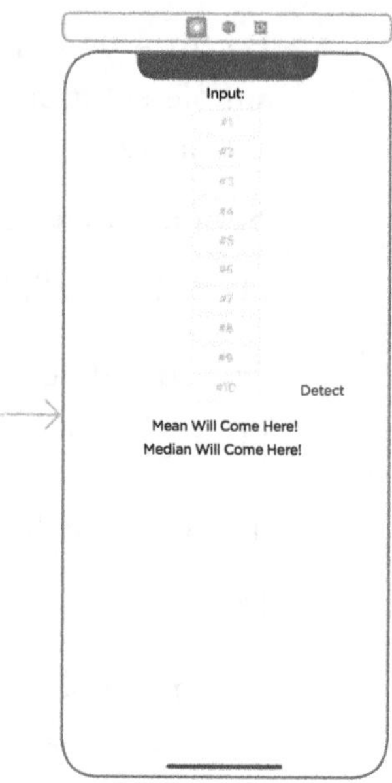

Figure B.3 The UI for the Mean Median Detective app

- *Mean Will Come Here!*—This `UILabel` displays the mean.
- *Median Will Come Here!*—This `UILabel` displays the median.

When you've made a similar UI in your application, you can start coding.

Code the app

To begin, add this extension before your `ViewController` class:

```
extension UITextField {
    var decimalValue: Double? {
        return Double(self.text!)
    }
}
```

This computed property in the `UITextField` class allows you to get the text in the `TextField` as a `Double` without converting it to a `Double` manually each time.

Create the IBOutlets, functions, and IBAction

To start, add the `IBOutlets`:

```
    @IBOutlet var input1: UITextField!
    @IBOutlet var input2: UITextField!
    @IBOutlet var input3: UITextField!
    @IBOutlet var input4: UITextField!
    @IBOutlet var input5: UITextField!
    @IBOutlet var input6: UITextField!
    @IBOutlet var input7: UITextField!
    @IBOutlet var input8: UITextField!
    @IBOutlet var input9: UITextField!
    @IBOutlet var input10: UITextField!

    @IBOutlet var medianLabel: UILabel!
    @IBOutlet var meanLabel: UILabel!
```

Next, add the functions:

```
    func median(arr: [Double]) -> Double {
        let sortedArr = arr.sorted()
        if sortedArr.count % 2 == 0 {
            return mean(arr: [sortedArr[sortedArr.count / 2],
➥ sortedArr[sortedArr.count / 2 - 1]])
```

```
        }
        return sortedArr[sortedArr.count / 2]
    }

    func mean(arr: [Double]) -> Double {
        var totalValue = 0.0
        for i in arr {
            totalValue += i
        }
        return totalValue / Double(arr.count)
    }
```

Finally, add your `IBAction`:

```
    @IBAction func meanMedianCalculator() {
        let inputTextfields = [input1, input2, input3, input4, input5,
➥ input6, input7, input8, input9, input10]
        var input: [Double] = []
        for i in inputTextfields {
            if i!.decimalValue != nil {
                input.append(i!.decimalValue!)
            }
        }
        if input.count == 0 {
            medianLabel.text = "Enter Values for Median"
            meanLabel.text = "Enter Values for Mean"
            return
        }
        meanLabel.text = "Mean is: \(mean(arr: input))"
        medianLabel.text = "Median is: \(median(arr: input))"
    }
```

There you go! You've successfully implemented the Mean Median Detective in Swift! Now connect your `IBActions` and `IBOutlets` to your text fields, button, and labels, and you should be good to go.

Extra challenge

For a challenge, extend this app to allow the user to find the mode of the numbers as well. The mode is the most frequently occurring number in a list, but there can be multiple numbers in a tie of occurrences. Go for it!

Appendix C

Factoring factory

The Factoring Factory teaches you how to build an app that finds the first ten factors of any number. I've chosen the Factoring Factory app because it helps you learn concepts such as LCM (least common multiple), GCF (greatest common factor), fractions, prime and composite numbers, and (later) factoring polynomials.

What does this app do?

NOTE You can find the code for this application in the Appendix C folder inside the Hello-Swift-Code-master folder that you downloaded from GitHub. If you haven't downloaded the code from GitHub, go to: https://github.com/tanmayb123/Hello-Swift-Code/archive/master.zip. You should download the code only once for all chapters.

Figure C.1 is how the running app will look.

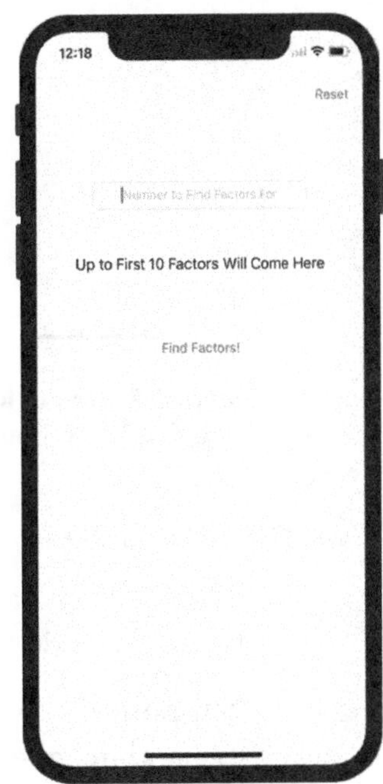

Figure C.1 The final running Factoring Factory app

Before you build this app, I'd like you to have a good understanding of factors. Suppose that you have to find all the factors of 10. Factors of 10 are any whole numbers that can divide it fully. The factors of 10 are 1, 2, 5, and 10 because when you divide 10 by any of these numbers, you get a remainder of 0.

The factors of 20, similarly, are 1, 2, 4, 5, 10, and 20. You have to be able to evenly divide a factor into the target with no remainder. So 3, for example, wouldn't be a factor of either 10 or 20.

Set up the project, and create the UI

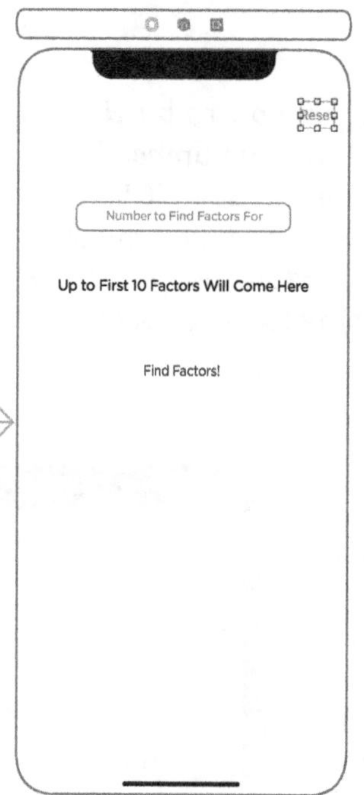

Figure C.2 The UI for the Factoring Factory app

To start building your app, create a user interface (UI) like figure C.2.

Table C.1 describes the UI.

Table C.1 UI main elements

Element	Description
`Number To Find Factors For`	This `UITextField` accepts the user's input.
`Find Factors!`	This `UIButton` finds up to the first ten factors of the user's input number.
`Up to First 10 Factors Will Come Here`	This `UILabel` displays the final output.
`Reset`	This `UIButton` resets the input and output fields.

When you've made a similar UI in your application, you can start coding.

Code the app

You know what a factor is, but now you need to understand how to write the code to find factors of a number.

Suppose that you have an input number of 9. Loop from 1 to 9, and every time, check whether the input number is divisible by the number in the loop. If so, append it to a new array and also keep a count of factors you found. Keep doing this while the length of this array is less than or equal to 10. You do this so that you're able to find the first ten factors of the number. If there are more, only the first ten are displayed; if there are fewer, all factors are displayed. This process is illustrated in figure C.3.

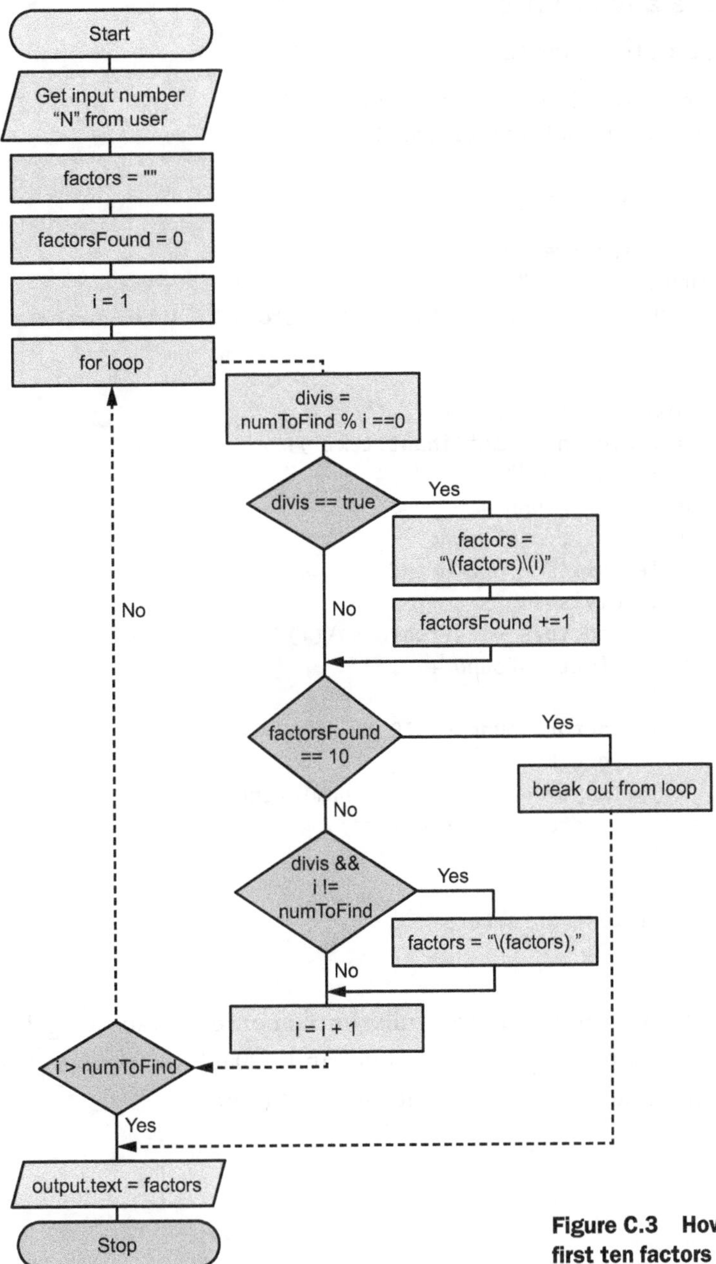

Figure C.3 How to find up to the first ten factors of a number

Now that you know how the algorithm works, you're reading to start coding the application itself.

Create IBOutlets and IBActions

To start, add the `IBOutlets`:

```
@IBOutlet var input: UITextField!
@IBOutlet var output: UILabel!
```

Finally, add your `IBActions`:

```
@IBAction func reset() {
    input.text = ""
    output.text = "Up to First 10 Factors Will Come Here"
}

@IBAction func findFactors() {
    let numToFind = Int(input.text!)!
    var factors = ""
    var factorsFound = 0
    for i in 1...numToFind {
        let divis = numToFind % i == 0
        if divis {
            factors = "\(factors)\(i)"
            factorsFound += 1
        }
        if factorsFound == 10 {
            break
        } else if divis && i != numToFind {
            factors = "\(factors), "
        }
    }
    output.text = factors
}
```

There you go! You've successfully implemented a factoring factory in Swift! Now connect your `IBActions` and `IBOutlets` to your text field, button, and label, and you should be good to go.

Appendix D

How big is a triangle?

This app finds the area of a triangle for you if you have either the height and base length or the lengths of the three sides.

What does this app do?

NOTE You can find the code for this application in the Appendix D folder inside the Hello-Swift-Code-master folder that you downloaded from GitHub. If you haven't downloaded the code from GitHub, go to: https://github.com/tanmayb123/Hello-Swift-Code/archive/master.zip. You should download the code only once for all chapters.

Figure D.1 is a screenshot of the running app.

Figure D.1 The final running How Big is a Triangle? app

Do you remember how to find the area of a triangle? Suppose that you have a triangle like the one in figure D.2. The base of the triangle is 9; the height is 4.

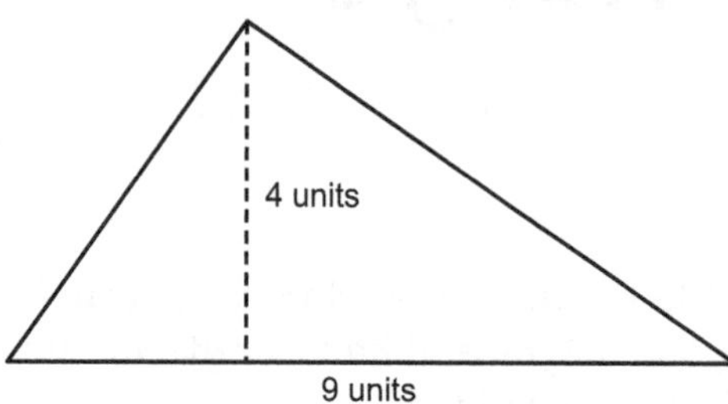

Figure D.2 A triangle with a base length of 9 units and a height of 4 units. Its area is 18 square units.

To find the area of a triangle, you need its height and the length of its base. When you have those values, multiply the height (h) by the base (b) and then divide them by 2:

(b * h)/2

Using this formula, you can see that the area is 18:

(9 * 4)/2 = 18

But what if you don't have the height and do have the length of all three sides? This problem is a little more complicated, but you can still figure it out. In the triangle in figure D.3, you have sides with the lengths of 5, 7, and 9. You don't know the angles of any of the corners.

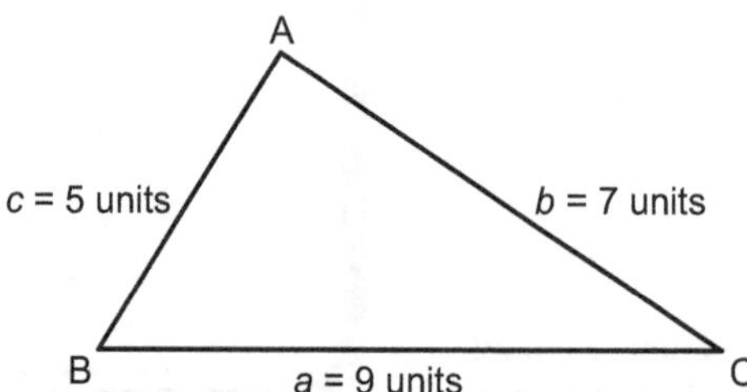

Figure D.3 A triangle with side lengths of 9, 7, and 5 units

If you'd like to find the area of the triangle in this case, you can use *Heron's formula,* which is

$$\sqrt{sp * (sp - a) * (sp - b) * (sp - c)}$$

Here, the symbols a, b, and c, are the side lengths of the triangle, and sp is *semi-perimeter,* which you can find by dividing the perimeter of a triangle by 2.

You must be wondering how in the world to find sp, which is the perimeter of the triangle divided by 2. Here's how you find it:

sp = (a + b + c) / 2

In this specific case, the semi-perimeter of the triangle is

sp = (9 + 7 + 5) / 2
sp = 21 / 2

So sp is 10.5 units.

Wow! Right? That process looks long, but it's simple. You don't have to figure out how to code it, but I do want to tell you how it works.

TIP This explanation may be a little more math than you were hoping to see right now. If it's too complicated for you today, go ahead and create the app anyway, because I'll show you how. One day, this formula may come in handy, and maybe you'll remember that you saw it here first!

Work through your triangle so you can see this formula in action. The variables that you need values for are a, b, c, and sp:

a = 5
b = 7
c = 9
sp = (5 + 7 + 9) / 2 = 10.5

Plug those values into Heron's formula:

Area = SQRT(10.5 * (10.5 - 5) * (10.5 - 7) * (10.5 - 9))
Area = SQRT(10.5 * (5.5) * (3.5) * (1.5))

Area = SQRT(10.5 * (28.875))
Area = SQRT(303.188)
Area = 17.41 square units

I'm sure that this formula will prove to be useful to you in some situations!

Set up the project, and create the UI

To start, create a user interface (UI) like figure D.4. More information about the elements is in table D.1.

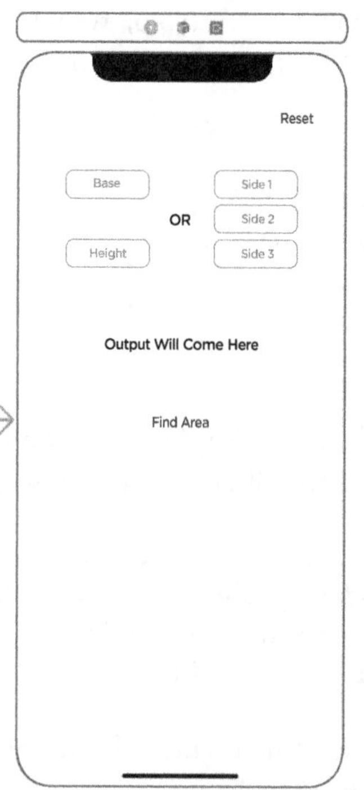

Figure D.4 The UI for the How Big Is a Triangle? app

Table D.1 UI main elements

Element	Description
`Base Length of Triangle`	This `UITextField` takes in the triangle's base length.
`Height of Triangle`	This `UITextField` takes in the triangle's height to the base.
`Output Will Come Here`	This `UILabel` stores the area of the triangle once it has been calculated.

Table D.1 UI main elements *(continued)*

Element	Description
`Side 1, Side 2, Side 3`	These three `UITextFields` take in the triangle's side lengths if the height is unavailable.
`Find Area`	This `UIButton` finds the area of the triangle.
`Reset`	This `UIButton` resets the application's `UITextField` and `UILabel`.

When you've made a similar UI in your application, you can start coding.

Code the app

Now it's time to code the application so that you and your friends can find the area of a triangle with ease (and maybe check your homework as well)!

Add the IBOutlets and IBActions

To start, add the `IBOutlets`:

```
@IBOutlet var triangleHeight: UITextField!
@IBOutlet var triangleBase: UITextField!
@IBOutlet var triangleSide1: UITextField!
@IBOutlet var triangleSide2: UITextField!
@IBOutlet var triangleSide3: UITextField!
@IBOutlet var triangleArea: UILabel!
```

Finally, add your `IBActions`:

```
@IBAction func reset() {
    triangleSide1.text = ""
    triangleSide2.text = ""
    triangleSide3.text = ""
    triangleHeight.text = ""
    triangleBase.text = ""
    triangleArea.text = "Output Will Come Here"
}

@IBAction func getArea() {
    if Double(triangleHeight.text!) != nil &&
    ➥ Double(triangleBase.text!) != nil {
```

```
            triangleArea.text = "\(Double(triangleHeight.text!)! *
        ➥ Double(triangleBase.text!)! / 2) sq units"
        } else if Double(triangleSide1.text!) != nil &&
        ➥ Double(triangleSide2.text!) != nil &&
        ➥ Double(triangleSide3.text!) != nil {
            let perim = Double(triangleSide1.text!)! +
            ➥ Double(triangleSide2.text!)! +
            ➥ Double(triangleSide3.text!)!
            let semiperim = Double(perim / 2)
            let heron = sqrt(Double(semiperim * (semiperim -
            ➥ Double(triangleSide1.text!)!) * (semiperim -
            ➥ Double(triangleSide2.text!)!) * (semiperim -
            ➥ Double(triangleSide3.text!)!)))
            triangleArea.text = "\(heron) sq units"
        }
    }
```

There you go! You've successfully implemented a calculator for a triangle's area in Swift! Now connect your `IBActions` and `IBOutlets` to your text fields, labels, and buttons, and you should be good to go.

Learn how the code works

You know how to do the math already, but I'll explain how the code works here so you'll understand what you've programmed.

First, the code checks whether the user entered inputs in both text fields (height and base). If so, the code runs the usual method to calculate the area of a triangle on the input and displays the output in the `UILabel`. It does this by multiplying the height and base and then dividing the product by 2.

If the user didn't make valid inputs for these text fields, however, the code checks for user input in the other three text fields (side a, side b, and side c). If it finds input for these three text fields, it runs Heron's formula on the input and displays the output in the `UILabel`. The code achieves all this by performing the following steps:

1 It finds the following four numbers:
   - sp (or semi-perimeter)
   - The difference between sp and side a, as sp - a

  - The difference between sp and side b, as sp - b
  - The difference between sp and side c, as sp - c
2. It multiplies the four numbers you got in step 1.
3. Finally, it finds the square root of the number it got in step 2, and that's the area of the triangle.

NOTE If the user doesn't provide input for either the regular method or Heron's method, the program does nothing. It won't crash.

Appendix E

I'm mixed up; make me improper

In this appendix, you learn how to build an app that can convert mixed numbers to improper fractions, and vice versa.

What does this app do?

Start with a fraction or a proper fraction, in the form shown in figure E.1.

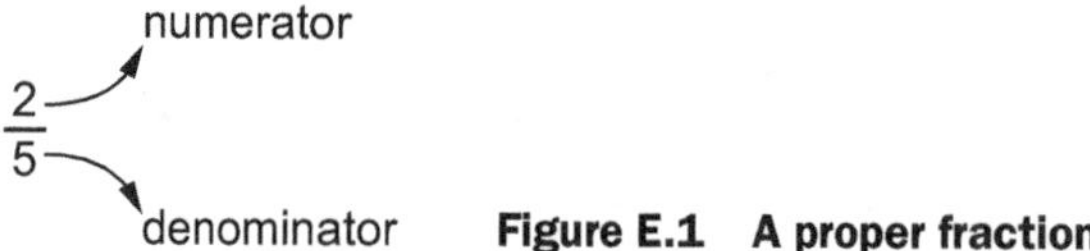

Figure E.1 A proper fraction

Here, 2 and 5 are two integers separated by a horizontal line. The integer part above the line is called a *numerator*, and the bottom part is called a *denominator*. If the numerator is less than the denominator, the fraction is called a *proper fraction*. But if the numerator is greater than the denominator, the fraction is called an *improper fraction*, as shown in figure E.2.

$$\frac{5}{3}$$

Figure E.2 An improper fraction

Such a fraction can be converted to a *mixed number,* which is a combination of a whole number followed by a proper fraction, as shown in figure E.3.

$$1\frac{2}{3}$$

Figure E.3 A mixed number

You're ready to get to the coding now!

NOTE You can find the code for this application in the AppendixE file inside the Hello-Swift-Code-master folder that you downloaded from GitHub. If you haven't downloaded the code from GitHub, go to: https://github.com/tanmayb123/Hello-Swift-Code/archive/master.zip. You should download the code only once for all chapters.

Figure E.4 is a screenshot of the final running app, which is converting an improper fraction to a mixed number.

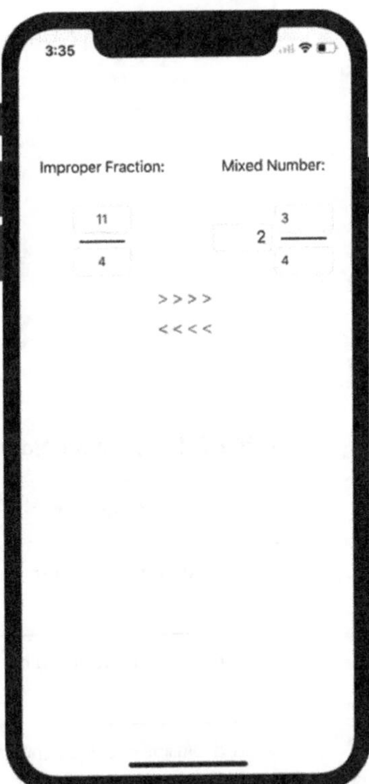

Figure E.4 The final running app

Set up the project, and create the UI

To start, create a user interface (UI) like figure E.5. Details about the elements are in table E.1.

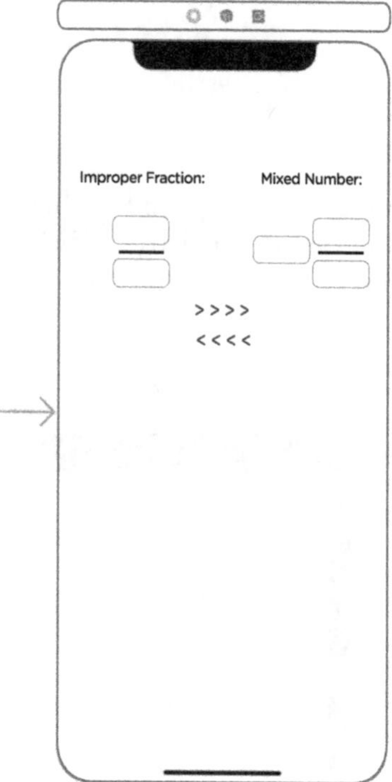

Figure E.5 The UI for the app

Table E.1 UI main elements

Element	Description
`Mixed Number Integer`	This `UITextField` takes the mixed number's integer value as input.
`Mixed Number Numerator`	This `UITextField` takes the mixed number's numerator value as input.
`Mixed Number Denominator`	This `UITextField` takes the mixed number's denominator value as input.

Table E.1 UI main elements *(continued)*

Element	Description
`Improper Fraction Numerator`	This `UITextField` takes the improper fraction's numerator value as input.
`Improper Fraction Denominator`	This `UITextField` takes the improper fraction's denominator value as input.
`Convert IF to MN!` `(> > > >)`	This `UIButton` converts the improper fraction to a mixed number.
`Convert MN to IF!` `(< < < <)`	This `UIButton` converts the mixed number to an improper fraction.

When you've made a similar UI in your application, you can start coding.

Learn how this code works

Before you can start, though, you need to understand the math behind this application.

These are the steps to convert an improper fraction to a mixed number, using an example in which the numerator is 11 and the denominator is 4:

1. Run integer division on the improper fraction, which is the integer part of your mixed number.

   You do the integer division of 11 by 4 and get 2, so 2 is your integer part of the mixed number.
2. Find the remainder (using mod) of the improper fraction, which is the numerator of the fraction part of your mixed number.

   You do 11 ÷ 4 and get 3, because you get a remainder of 3 when you divide 11 by 4. This 3 becomes the numerator part of your mixed number.
3. Finally, set the denominator of the fraction part of your mixed number to the denominator of the improper fraction, which is 4.

You're done!

These are the steps to convert a mixed number back to an improper fraction, using the same example:

1 Multiply the integer from the mixed number with the denominator from the mixed number's fraction.

   In this example, you multiply 2 and 4 to get 8.
2 Add the numerator to the number you calculated in step 1.

   You add 3 and 8 to get 11, which becomes the numerator part of the improper fraction.
3 Set the numerator of the improper fraction to the number you calculated in step 2.
4 Set the denominator of the improper fraction to the denominator of the mixed number's fraction.

Code the app

Now that you know how the algorithm works, you're ready to start coding the application itself.

Create the IBOutlets, functions, and IBActions

To start, add the `IBOutlets`:

```
@IBOutlet var mixedInt: UITextField!
@IBOutlet var mixedNum: UITextField!
@IBOutlet var mixedDen: UITextField!

@IBOutlet var improperNum: UITextField!
@IBOutlet var improperDen: UITextField!
```

Next, add the functions:

```
func mixedNumberToImproperFraction(mixedNumberInteger: Int,
➥ mixedNumberNumerator: Int, mixedNumberDenominator: Int) -> [Int] {
    return [mixedNumberInteger * mixedNumberDenominator +
    ➥ mixedNumberNumerator, mixedNumberDenominator]
}

func improperFractionToMixedNumber(improperFractionNumerator: Int,
➥ improperFractionDenominator: Int) -> [Int] {
    return [Int(improperFractionNumerator /
```

```
➥ improperFractionDenominator), Int(improperFractionNumerator %
➥ improperFractionDenominator), improperFractionDenominator]
}

func factors(of: Int) -> [Int] {
    var factors: [Int] = []
    for i in 1...of {
        if of % i == 0 {
            factors.append(i)
        }
    }
    return factors
}

func GCF(arr1: [Int], arr2: [Int]) -> Int? {
    var finalArr1: [Int] = []
    var finalArr2: [Int] = []
    for i in arr1 {
        if arr2.contains(i) {
            finalArr1.append(i)
        }
    }
    for i in arr2 {
        if arr1.contains(i) {
            finalArr2.append(i)
        }
    }
    return finalArr1.last
}
```

Finally, add your `IBActions`:

```
@IBAction func mixedToImproper() {
    improperNum.text = ""
    improperDen.text = ""
    if Int(mixedInt.text!) != nil && Int(mixedNum.text!) != nil &&
    ➥ Int(mixedDen.text!) != nil {
        var result =
        ➥ mixedNumberToImproperFraction(mixedNumberInteger:
        ➥ Int(mixedInt.text!)!, mixedNumberNumerator:
        ➥ Int(mixedNum.text!)!, mixedNumberDenominator:
        ➥ Int(mixedDen.text!)!)
        let gcf = GCF(arr1: factors(of: result[0]), arr2:
        ➥ factors(of: result[1]))
```

```
            if gcf != nil {
                result[0] = result[0] / gcf!
                result[1] = result[1] / gcf!
            }
            improperNum.text = "\(result[0])"
            improperDen.text = "\(result[1])"
        }
    }

    @IBAction func improperToMixed() {
        mixedInt.text = ""
        mixedNum.text = ""
        mixedDen.text = ""
        if Int(improperNum.text!) != nil && Int(improperDen.text!) !=
        ➥ nil {
            var result =
            ➥ improperFractionToMixedNumber(improperFractionNumerator:
            ➥ Int(improperNum.text!)!, improperFractionDenominator:
            ➥ Int(improperDen.text!)!)
            let gcf = GCF(arr1: factors(of: result[1]), arr2: factors(of:
            ➥ result[2]))
            if gcf != nil {
                result[1] = result[1] / gcf!
                result[2] = result[2] / gcf!
            }
            mixedInt.text = "\(result[0])"
            mixedNum.text = "\(result[1])"
            mixedDen.text = "\(result[2])"
        }
    }
```

There you go! You've successfully implemented a mixed-number and improper-fraction interchanger app in Swift! This app will even simplify your fractions to the lowest terms in the results for you. Now connect your `IBActions` and `IBOutlets` to your text fields and buttons, and you should be good to go.

FOR YOU TO EXPLORE—what happens if you make the denominator of a fraction zero?

Appendix F

Installation

Welcome to installation! In this appendix, you learn how to install and set up your iOS development environment, which includes the installation and setup of Xcode and the setup of your developer account.

First, though, I'll talk about the system requirements. Your Mac computer should have at least macOS 10.14 (Mojave) or later; your iDevice should have iOS 12 or later; and you should have an Apple ID.

To start, complete the following steps at https://help.apple.com/xcode/mac/current/#/dev60b6fbbc7:

1. Add your Apple ID to Xcode's Account Preferences so that Xcode: knows which account to link your applications to.
2. Assign your app's target to a team (your Apple ID).

   Xcode links your application to the account you added in step 1.
3. Add capabilities to your app.

   If you need your application to have some special capabilities (such as notifications), you should complete this step. But you don't need to do this for any of the apps in the book, so you don't need to complete this step during installation.
4. Run your app on your device.

   This is the step in which you register your iDevice with your Apple account. If you don't have an iDevice and want to use the simulator, you don't need to complete this step.

5. Export your signing certificates and provisioning profiles.

   This step allows you to save all the certificates and profiles that Apple creates to ensure that your applications are . . . well, yours. You don't need to complete this step, as you can always download the certificates and profiles again from the Apple Developer site.

These steps take you to the point where you can start your journey of learning iOS development.

Index